WINDOWS™

WISDOM

for C and C++ Programmers

D1567676

WINDOWS™

WISDOM

for C and C++ Programmers

Leendert Ammeraal
Hogeschool Utrecht, The Netherlands

JOHN WILEY & SONS
Chichester • New York • Brisbane • Toronto • Singapore

Copyright © 1993 by John Wiley & Sons Ltd.
Baffins Lane, Chichester
West Sussex PO19 1UD, England

All rights reserved.

No part of this book may be reproduced by any means,
or transmitted, or translated into a machine language
without the written permission of the publisher.

Windows is a trademark and Microsoft is a registered trademark of
Microsoft Corporation
Borland is a registered trademark of Borland International, Inc.

Other Wiley Editorial Offices

John Wiley & Sons, Inc., 605 Third Avenue,
New York, NY 10158-0012, USA

Jacaranda Wiley Ltd, G.P.O. Box 859, Brisbane,
Queensland 4001, Australia

John Wiley & Sons (Canada) Ltd, 22 Worcester Road,
Rexdale, Ontario M9W 1L1, Canada

John Wiley & Sons (SEA) Pte Ltd, 37 Jalan Pemimpin #05-04,
Block B, Union Industrial Building, Singapore 2057

Library of Congress Cataloging-in-Publication Data

Ammeraal, L. (Leendert)
    Windows wisdom for C and C^{++} programmers / Leendert Ammeraal.
        p.   cm.
    Includes bibliographical references and index.
    ISBN 0 471 94004 6
    1. Windows (Computer programs)   2. Microsoft Windows (Computer
file)   3. C (Computer program language)   4. C++ (Computer program
language)   I. Title.
QA76.76.W56A46   1993
005.4'3—dc20   93-10287
                                                                        CIP

British Library Cataloguing in Publication Data

A catalogue record for this book is available from the British Library

ISBN 0 471 94004 6

Produced from camera-ready copy supplied by the author
Printed and bound in Great Britain by Bath Press Ltd, Bath, Avon

Contents

Preface

Although Windows applications can be developed in several programming languages, we had better use C or C++ for this purpose if we want to achieve the greatest possible efficiency and to speak the language of a large community of professional software developers. However, Windows programming in these languages is no easy subject. For one thing, it requires some familiarity with an extremely extensive library of routines, known as the Application Programming Interface (API). The reference manuals published by Microsoft and Borland are not suitable for the uninitiated. To overcome this problem, these manufacturers offer 'User's Guides', which are sometimes even worse because of their complicated examples, covering a great many new subjects at the same time. Another problem is the technical terminology associated with Windows programming. For example, if one wants to write a program that reads some input data, say, the real numbers x, y and z, it is not at all obvious that one should be familiar with the notion of an 'edit control'. This book attempts to explain such technical concepts for beginners. It is not complete in any sense. In my opinion, it is better for a book of this size to discuss only a subset of all Windows programming subjects in detail than to touch also more advanced subjects without making these useful by proper explanations.

We will use only simple examples (except for a slightly more complex one in the final chapter). Hopefully, they enable you to find what you are looking for as you develop your own Windows applications. Most well-known Windows programs, such as text processors and spread sheet packages running under Windows, were written in the C language. I have tested all C programs in this book with the C++ compilers from Microsoft (Version 8.0, also known as *Visual C++*) and Borland (Version 3.1). Unlike five years ago, we can now also use C++ class libraries, which come with the compilers. Unfortunately, the two best-known class libraries for Windows programming, those from Microsoft and Borland, do not have much in common. This book deals with both. I realized that discussing these two ways of using C++ classes, in addition to using plain C, would lead to confusion if I did not make the structure of this book very simple and clear. When reading some other books on the same subject I was sometimes confused by programming examples that were defined and solved at the same time in rather lengthy discussions. I therefore decided to separate the problem definitions from their solutions. All chapters have the same structure, and the names of program files indicate which of the three solutions applies. For example, Chapter 9 is about stars that appear and disappear on the screen, and consists of the following sections (with program-file names, excluding extension, between parentheses):

9.1   Problem Definition
       Defines the programming problem to be solved in this chapter.
9.2   General Aspects
       Discusses aspects shared by the solutions in 9.3, 9.4 and 9.5.
9.3   C Solution
       ANSI C solution (STARS); can be compiled with both Microsoft C or Borland C
       and in both C and C++ mode.
9.4   MFC Solution
       Solution (STARSMFC) based on C++ and the Microsoft Foundation Class Library.
9.5   OWL Solution
       Solution (STARSOWL) based on C++ and the Borland ObjectWindows Library.
9.6   Questions
       Some questions about the material of this chapter, with answers in Appendix A.

All other chapters have the same structure. I am aware that this may make the table of contents look strange and monotonous, but I hope it gives you a good idea of what you can expect in each section, and it may save you time when you are looking for information later.

Windows programs have much in common. When you start writing such programs yourself (which I hope you will be doing), you can begin by copying one from this book and modify it as you like. The accompanying disk will save you typing work. You can use it as a basis for your own programs, copying portions of the supplied source files with your editor. I mention this lest you might be appalled by the prospect of frequently having to type long identifiers, such as *GetSystemMetrics* and *hPrevInstance*.

The title of this book was proposed by Gaynor Redvers-Mutton of Wiley. I would never have chosen such a title myself, because it may seem immodest. However, I do not think it really is, since its second word refers to the development of Microsoft Windows and its programming environment. This book is about how to use this environment by solving small programming problems, and it would make no sense to attach the term wisdom to such solutions. Hoping these will not turn out to be unwise either, I would welcome any comments on them.

The support by Microsoft, The Netherlands, was very useful. Their software specialist Geri Wolters gave me some help that was hard to find elsewhere.

February 1993
Leendert Ammeraal

1

Displaying a Window

1.1 Problem Definition

This chapter is devoted to a programming problem that at first might seem trivial. The only thing we want to do is produce a window as shown in Figure 1.1. Initially this is a full-screen window, but we can change its size by dragging any of its corners or its edges. As you will probably know, *dragging* a point means moving the mouse with the mouse cursor initially on that point and the left mouse button kept down. Once we have made the window smaller than the entire screen, we can also *move* it, by dragging any point of its title bar (shown in black and containing some text in Figure 1.1). At the left of this title bar we find the so-called *control-menu box* in the form of a square with a minus sign in it. Clicking this (with the mouse) produces a set of control-menu commands, as shown in Figure 1.2. If you prefer using the keyboard, you can also use the Alt+space key combination instead of clicking the control-menu box.

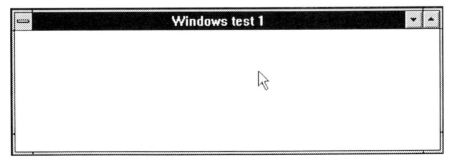

Figure 1.1. Our first window

1

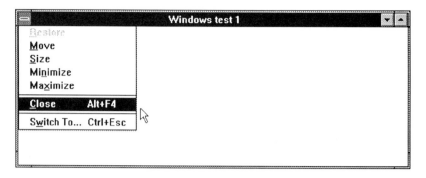

Figure 1.2. Control-menu commands

At the right of the title bar we find the minimize and maximize buttons, displayed as arrow heads pointing downward and upward, respectively. Clicking the minimize button causes the window to become inactive, that is, it turns into an icon (which may be obscured by other windows). We can restore the window by using the Alt+Tab key combination or by double clicking the icon. So much for the minimize button. There is also the maximize button, which enlarges the window so it occupies the entire screen.

We can dispose of the window either by selecting *Close* in the control menu, as shown in Figure 1.2, or by using the Alt+F4 key combination. On the other hand, we can have two or more instances of our window on our screen at the same time. There are two convenient ways to start a Windows application. After using the Alt+Tab key combination to select the Program Manager, we can select the File Manager, display the executable file in question, say, WTEST.EXE, and double click this file name (or just click it and then press the Enter key). Alternatively, we can use the *File* menu of the Program Manager, select *Run* and type the full path name of our program, say, *\test\wtest.exe*. When several instances of our program are active, their corresponding windows may not all be visible. Then we can again use the Alt+Tab key combination to switch between these instances and to make their windows visible. Obviously, a window must be made smaller than the entire screen if we want to display it together with other windows.

If you are an experienced Windows user, you will already be familiar with the actions we have just been discussing. If not, you may want some more information about these elementary user aspects, which you can find in the Microsoft Windows User's Guide and in many other books for Windows users. Windows applications are easy to work with because of their similarities. For example, you can always terminate a windows application by using Alt+F4.

1.2 General Aspects

It will by now be clear that the functionality of the simple window shown in Figure 1.1 is considerable. If we had to write a comparable program for this running under DOS (not using Windows at all), our task would be extremely complex. We must therefore not complain if our first Windows program looks strange and not pretty at all. When we start writing Windows programs we must bear in mind that our program will not have full control over the machine all the time. Instead, it is given control by Windows a great many times. In particular, Windows has control during the time the machine is waiting for a user response. This is different with, for example, a conventional C program, running under DOS, where we have a *main* function that is called once and does not return until program execution terminates. Any functions in such a C program are called directly by our *main* function or by other functions of our own. In a Windows C program, on the other hand, we usually supply a special function, known as a *window procedure*, which is called by Windows, not by our own program. Obviously, the number and types of the parameters of this window procedure are imposed by Windows, and we will need to know the meaning of these parameters and how to use the values that Windows passes through them. This is just an example of many conventions the beginning Windows programmer has to live with. Instead of having complete freedom and designing all aspects of the program ourselves, we must observe a great many rules. We must also know which API functions to use and how to supply these functions with appropriate arguments.

When developing Windows applications in C we can more clearly see what actually happens than when we are using C++ and either the Microsoft Foundation Classes (MFC) or the Borland ObjectWindows Library (OWL). In Section 1.3 we therefore begin with a C program, more or less written in the same style as those presented by Charles Petzold in his well-known book *Programming Windows*. An attractive aspect of this 'traditional' style is that it leads to very small executable files. On the other hand, the newer object-oriented approach, based on C++ class libraries, has the advantages of leading to smaller source code and (possibly) of being less error prone. It is to be expected that this new approach will be the more popular one in the long term. We will use it in Sections 1.4 and 1.5. This division into sections also applies to all other chapters of this book.

A general module-definition file

Besides program files, we will also need a *module-definition file*, which is to be supplied to the linker. We can use the same module-definition file in the Sections 1.3 and 1.4, and in fact for all other programs in this book. It makes sense therefore to discuss this file here, even though it is perhaps unusual to do so at this stage, before having seen any Windows program:

File GEN.DEF:

```
NAME          General
DESCRIPTION   'Written by L. Ammeraal'
EXETYPE       WINDOWS
STUB          'WINSTUB.EXE'
CODE          PRELOAD MOVEABLE DISCARDABLE
DATA          PRELOAD MOVEABLE MULTIPLE
HEAPSIZE      8192
STACKSIZE     8192
```

This file gives the linker some additional information, but it is not very interesting from a programming point of view. Since it will be used for all Windows programs in this book, a brief discussion about it cannot be omitted. The *NAME* line indicates that we are dealing with a *program*, not a dynamic link library. (Dynamic link libraries are not discussed in this book.) The module name on the first line is often the name of the resulting .EXE file, but writing a different name, such as *General* in the above file, does not make any difference for the user. Some text, such as a copyright notice, can be inserted in the .EXE file by means of the description on the second line. The *EXETYPE* line indicates that the program is a Windows program (not an OS/2 program).

The fourth line, *STUB 'WINSTUB.EXE'* causes the following message to appear if the program is started as a command at the DOS prompt:

```
This program requires Microsoft Windows.
```

Remember, the command to execute a Windows program should be given from Windows, for example, by using the *Run* command in the *File* menu.

The *CODE* and *DATA* lines indicate that Windows is to 'preload' both the code and the data; in other words, code and data will immediately be loaded into memory. The word *MOVEABLE* means that Windows can move the code and the data to other locations if it needs to consolidate free blocks of memory. By specifying *DISCARDABLE*, we enable Windows to discard the code segment from memory and later reload it from the .EXE file. The *MULTIPLE* keyword indicates that each instance of the program gets its own separate data segment. By contrast, the code segment is shared by all instances of the program.

The *HEAPSIZE* and the *STACKSIZE* lines specify how much memory will be available for the heap and the stack, respectively. The heap is used for dynamic memory allocation, while the stack accommodates local variables.

Memory models

We will use the *medium* memory model, which means that there is only one data segment but each source module can become a different code segment. We could have used the small memory model for all programs of this book. However, realistic Windows programs are much larger and normally consist of many source code modules. For such programs the medium memory model is recommended. Then, with all these code segments movable and discardable, the amount of space required to fit the code into memory is the size of the largest code segment. The small memory model may seem a more logical choice for beginners, but apart from slightly smaller and faster executable files it has no advantages over the medium model. The Visual C++ Setup program automatically installs prebuilt class libraries for the *medium model*, not for the small model. If we want class libraries (required with MFC and OWL) for the small model, we have to build them ourselves.

Curiously enough, it is the other way round with Borland C++ 3.1. After installation there is no file TCLASSM.LIB (where M stands for Medium) in the directory *\borlandc\classlib\lib*, even if we have specified that we want the medium memory model included in the installation. Fortunately, we can build that file ourselves, using the make file (named MAKEFILE) in the directory *borlandc\classlib*. All we need to do is to enter the following two command lines:

```
cd \borlandc\classlib
make -DMDL=m
```

1.3 C Solution

File WTEST.C shows a C program that solves the problem defined in Section 1.1. As with all other C programs in this book, it runs with both Microsoft Visual C++ and Borland C++ (Version 3.1). Note that each of these two packages includes both a C and a C++ compiler. The C compiler is used by default if the files to be compiled have .C as their file name extension. Instead, we can use .CPP instead of .C if we want to use the C++ compiler, as we will do in Section 1.4. However, we can also override such defaults. Actually, we will use compiler options (-*Tp* for Microsoft and -*P* for Borland) to force compiling in C++ mode. This is possible because our C programs (with .C file-name extensions) will at the same time be valid C++ programs. Throughout this book, that is, even in C programs, we take the liberty of using the new and very convenient C++ comment style, starting with // and ending at the end of the line. Both C compilers mentioned above accept this comment style.

Although the following file is almost as simple a Windows program as is possible, it is more complicated than a conventional small C program and it requires some familiarity with quite a few functions of the Applications Programmer's Interface (API):

File WTEST.C:

```
// WTEST.C: Test windows programming using C.
#include <windows.h>

long FAR PASCAL _export WndProc(HWND hWnd, UINT message,
        WPARAM wParam, LPARAM lParam);

int PASCAL WinMain(HANDLE hInstance, HANDLE hPrevInstance,
    LPSTR lpCmdLine, int nCmdShow)
{   char szAppName[]="wtest";
    WNDCLASS wndclass;
    HWND hWnd;
    MSG msg;
    int xScreen = GetSystemMetrics(SM_CXSCREEN),
        yScreen = GetSystemMetrics(SM_CYSCREEN);
    if (!hPrevInstance)
    {   wndclass.style = CS_HREDRAW | CS_VREDRAW;
        wndclass.lpfnWndProc = WndProc;
        wndclass.cbClsExtra = 0;
        wndclass.cbWndExtra = 0;
```

```
             wndclass.hInstance = hInstance;
             wndclass.hIcon = LoadIcon(NULL, IDI_APPLICATION);
             wndclass.hCursor = LoadCursor(NULL, IDC_ARROW);
             wndclass.hbrBackground = GetStockObject(WHITE_BRUSH);
             wndclass.lpszMenuName =  NULL;
             wndclass.lpszClassName = szAppName;
                       // Name used in call to CreateWindow.
             if (!RegisterClass(&wndclass)) return FALSE;
       }
     hWnd = CreateWindow(
         szAppName,
         "Windows test 1",        // Text for window title bar.
         WS_OVERLAPPEDWINDOW,     // Window style.
         0,                       // Initial x position
         0,                       // Initial y position.
         xScreen,                 // Width.
         yScreen,                 // Height.
         NULL,                    // Parent window handle.
         NULL,                    // Window menu handle.
         hInstance,               // Program instance handle.
         NULL                     // Create parameters.
     );
     ShowWindow(hWnd, nCmdShow);
     UpdateWindow(hWnd);
     while (GetMessage(&msg, NULL, 0, 0))
     {  TranslateMessage(&msg);  // Translates virtual key codes
        DispatchMessage(&msg);   // Dispatches message to window
     }
     return msg.wParam; // Returns the value from PostQuitMessage
 }


long FAR PASCAL _export WndProc(HWND hWnd, UINT message,
         WPARAM wParam, LPARAM lParam)
{  switch (message)
   {  case WM_DESTROY:
          PostQuitMessage(0); break;
      default:
          return DefWindowProc(hWnd, message, wParam, lParam);
   }
   return 0L;
}
```

There are some words in capital letters in this program. They are all defined in the header file WINDOWS.H. For example, *FAR* and *PASCAL* are defined as *far* and *pascal*. These two keywords influence the form of the generated code in a rather technical way which we will discuss here only very briefly. The *FAR* keyword causes pointers to consist of 32 instead of only 16 bits. The other special keyword, *PASCAL*, indicates how the stack, containing function arguments, is to be restored at the end of a function call. It causes this to be done in the function that is called instead of in the calling function.

Program WTEST consists of two functions, the main function *WinMain* and the 'window procedure' *WndProc*. Instead of *WndProc* we could have used a different name. By contrast, we must not change the name *WinMain*. Note that the function name *WndProc* occurs in the line

```
wndclass.lpfnWndProc = WndProc;
```

in the first conditional statement of function *WinMain*. Since *WndProc* is defined later, this function is declared before function *WinMain*. The keyword *_export* indicates that it is to be exported, so it can be called by Windows. (We could omit it, provided we insert an *EXPORTS* statement in the module-definition file.)

In a conventional C program, there is a function *main*, which is called by the operating system. Similarly, function *WinMain* is called by Windows. Its main components are

1 A sequence of statements to fill the structure *wndclass*, which is called a 'window class'.

2 The call *RegisterClass(&wndclass)* to 'register' the window class just created.

3 A call to the Windows API function *CreateWindow* to create the window. Although the created window class *wndclass* is not an argument in this call, there is a (rather indirect) connection: the application name assigned to *wndclass.lpszClassName* also occurs as the first argument of *CreateWindow*. The so-called *window handle* returned by *Create-Window* is stored in the variable *hWnd*. We frequently use *handles*, which are 16-bit numbers that refer to objects. Their actual values, obtained by Windows functions, are unimportant to our program.

4 The two calls

```
ShowWindow(hWnd, nCmdShow);
UpdateWindow(hWnd);
```

The argument *nCmdShow* in the first of these two lines is supplied by Windows itself as a parameter of *WinMain*, so we need not bother about its value. This first call specifies *how* the window is to be displayed. For example, *nCmdShow* may specify that the window is to be represented by an icon (which is not what we would like in our example). The call to *UpdateWindow* 'sends a *WM_PAINT* message to the window', that is, it actually causes the window to appear.

5 The so-called *message loop*

```
while (GetMessage(&msg, NULL, 0, 0))
{  TranslateMessage(&msg);
   DispatchMessage(&msg);
}
```

The message loop is the heart of the program. User actions, such as moving the mouse or pressing a key of the keyboard, are accepted by Windows and passed to our program in the form of *messages*. Actually, these messages are placed in a message queue, which is inspected by function *GetMessage*. If there is a message, it is placed in the structure *msg*, possibly translated by *TranslateMessage*, and passed back to Windows by *Dispatch-Message*. Each message applies to a window, and each window belongs to a window class. Also, each window class uniquely corresponds with one window procedure. 'Sending (or dispatching) a message *m* to a window *W*' simply means that Windows calls the window procedure of *W*, supplying *m* as an argument. In our case, the call to *DispatchMessage* will therefore result in a call to our own window procedure *WndProc*. (Recall that the address of *WndProc* has previously been assigned to the *lpfnWndProc* member of *wndclass*, and that there is a connection between the call to *CreateWindow* and the structure *wndclass*, as discussed above.)

When function *WndProc* is called, the message sent to the window is supplied as the second parameter of this function. Normally, there are quite a few different messages to consider, each requiring its own action in response. Distinguishing messages is usually done by means of a switch-statement. Each message has its own numeric code, written as a symbolic constant, defined in the header file WINDOWS.H. An example of a message is *WM_DESTROY*, which, as its name suggests, applies when the window is closed and the application terminates. Many other messages, such as for altering the window size, are dealt with in our first program by the *default* case, in the call to the function *DefWindow-Proc*, the name of which stands for 'default window procedure'.

Other files

After discussing program file WTEST.C, we must also pay attention to two other files to be used in connection with this program. The first is the module-definition file GEN.DEF, discussed in Section 1.2.

Compiling and linking programs can be done by using *make files*. Like program files and module definition files, make files are created in a normal program editor. Here is a make file that we can use for compiling and linking when using Microsoft Visual C++:

File WTEST.MAK:
```
# WTEST.MAK; usage (with Microsoft C++): nmake -f wtest.mak
wtest.exe: wtest.obj gen.def
        link /nod wtest, wtest, nul, libw+mlibcew, gen.def
wtest.obj: wtest.c
        cl -c -AM -G2sw -Ow -W3 -Zp -Tp wtest.c
# File GEN.DEF can be found in Section 1.2
```

As the comment on its first line shows, we can use this make file by entering the following command at the DOS prompt:

```
nmake -f wtest.mak
```

The compiler and the linker will then use the given files WTEST.C and GEN.DEF to produce the desired executable file WTEST.EXE. There are three types of lines in our make files:

1   Comment lines, beginning with #.
2   Lines expressing dependency; they begin with a file name followed by a colon.
3   Command lines, which are indented.

For example, according to the line

```
wtest.exe: wtest.obj gen.def
```

the file WTEST.EXE depends on the files WTEST.OBJ and GEN.DEF. This means that a new file WTEST.EXE is to be made if there is not yet one or if there is one that is older than any of the two other files. Then the indented line that follows specifies *how* this is to be done:

```
link /nod wtest, wtest, nul, libw+mlibcew, gen.def
```

After the command name, *link*, we find, in this order,

/nod	No default libraries are to be searched (also written as */NOD*)
wtest	Short for *wtest.obj*, the object file to be linked
wtest	Short for *wtest.exe*, the executable file to be created
nul	No map file required (also written as *NUL*)
libw+mlibcew	The libraries to be used for the medium memory model
gen.def	The module definition file, discussed in Section 1.2

The line

```
wtest.obj: wtest.c
```

indicates that a new object file is to be created unless there is already a file WTEST.OBJ and this file is more recent than the file WTEST.C. It can be created by the C++ compiler, which we use by means of the *cl* command:

```
cl -c -AM -G2sw -Ow -W3 -Zp -Tp wtest.c
```

Command name *cl* is followed by some options and a file name. Some of these compiler options are too technical to be explained in detail here, so do not worry if the following is not completely clear:

-c	Compile without linking (since there is a separate link command)
-AM	Use the medium memory model (see discussion at the end of Section 1.2)
-G2sw	Combination of *-G2*, *-Gs* and *-Gw*, the meaning of which is as follows:

-G2	Generate code for 80286 or higher (2 can be replaced with 3 for 386 code if you are using the Professional Edition of Visual C++)
-Gs	Disable checks for stack overflow
-Gw	Insert special code required for Windows
-Ow	Avoid some optimizations that might cause problems with Windows
-W3	Warning level, set rather high to avoid sloppy programming
-Zp	Pack structure fields on byte boundaries, as required by Windows
-Tp	Compile the program in C++ mode
wtest.c	The source file to be compiled

The last option, *-Tp*, is very interesting. It specifies that our program, despite its *.C* file-name extension, is to be regarded as a C++ program. This implies that old C style is no longer allowed, and it prepares for possible C++ extensions to our programs later.

So much for the make file to be used with Microsoft C++. If you are using Borland C++ instead, you can replace the above make file with this one:

File WTESTB.MAK:
```
# WTESTB.MAK; usage (with Borland C++): make -f wtestb.mak
wtest.exe: wtest.obj gen.def
tlink /n /Tw /L\borlandc\lib c0wm wtest, wtest, nul,\
    import mathwm cwm, gen.def
wtest.obj: wtest.c
bcc -c -mm -w-par -P -2 -W wtest.c
# File GEN.DEF can be found in Section 1.2
```

As indicated by comment, we can enter the following line at the DOS prompt to invoke this make file:

```
make -f wtestb.mak
```

The options used for *tlink*, the Turbo linker, are as follows:

/n	Do not search default libraries
/Tw	Create a Windows executable file
/L	Specifies a directory for the libraries

The compiler options used in the last line of the above make file are

-c	Compile but do not link
-mm	Use the medium memory model (see discussion at the end of Section 1.2)
-w-par	Disable warning messages about any unused function parameters
-P	Compile in C++ mode
-2	Generate 286 code (2 can be replaced with 3 for 386 code)
-W	Create an object file for Windows

Using an integrated environment

The use of command lines and make files as discussed above is not the only way of compiling and linking. The alternative is the use of an 'integrated environment'. We then compile, link and test the program without leaving the editor. The Microsoft Visual C++ integrated environment is referred to as the *Visual WorkBench*, while Borland uses the term *Integrated Development Environment* (IDE). Figure 1.3 shows a screen of (the Windows based) Microsoft Visual Workbench.

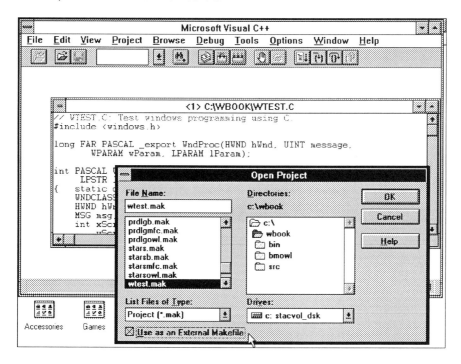

Figure 1.3. *Microsoft Visual C++*

With Visual C++ we can use our make file WTEST.MAK by selecting the checkbox '*Use as an External Makefile*', as shown at the bottom of Figure 1.3. In this way we have the best of both worlds: we use options and files exactly as specified in the make file and at the same time we benefit from the attractive integrated environment.

On the other hand, it is also possible to form a 'project' (that is, a set of files from which one executable module is to be built) without starting with a given make file. In that case we must not check the checkbox just mentioned but enter a new name, such as, for example, *wtest*1.*mak*, in the *File name* box (see Figure 1.3). After pressing OK, we can then enter the names of all source files for the project. In this example, these would be WTEST.C and GEN.DEF.

A similar situation for the Borland C++ 3.1 IDE is shown in Figure 1.4.

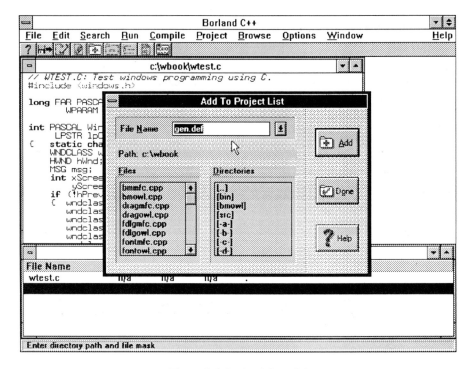

Figure 1.4. Borland C++ 3.1

After selecting *Project*, we must first enter the name (e.g. *wtestb.prj*) of the (new) project file. Then, after pressing the Ins key, we can enter the files belonging to the project.

Integrated environments are very popular, because we normally have to correct and compile our program files several times, alternately using the editor and the compiler. However, they sometimes cause problems because options for compiling and linking are stored internally as settings, hidden somewhere in menus. Complaints about unclear error messages due to some wrong default setting are very common. Command lines (starting with *cl*, *bcc* or *link*), on the other hand, make the compiler and linker options very explicit. If we compare the executable files, produced by two compilers, with regard to size and speed, it would be unfair if code for debugging were included in the EXE file by one compiler and not by the other. Such unfair comparisons are likely to happen when we are using integrated environments because we do not always clearly see the compiler settings. By contrast, *make files* clearly display all options that are used. They enable us to describe these options in a few lines of text, whereas it is more complicated to specify all settings of an integrated environment.

As mentioned above, the notion of 'external make files', available with Visual C++, offers us the best of both worlds. Consequently, the make files for Microsoft C++ in this book are useful even if you are using the Visual C++ integrated environment. Those for Borland C++ can be used either literally, with the DOS prompt, or just to see which files belong to a project for a given program.

1.4 MFC Solution

The programming style used in Section 1.3 is sometimes referred to as 'traditional Windows programming'. Most existing books and Windows applications are based on this style. However, with the advent of C++ people started thinking of how to make Windows programming benefit from the C++ class concept and from the OOP facilities provided by this language. After all, windows are objects consisting of data with associated operations, and dealing with such objects is what object-oriented programming is about.

There are several class libraries available for Windows programming. We will restrict ourselves to two of them, using the Microsoft Foundation Class library (MFC) in this section and the Borland ObjectWindows Library (OWL) in the next.

Before discussing a Windows program based on the MFC, let us first consider the following simple but curious C++ program (which is *not* a Windows application):

```
// DEMO1: Output produced by a global variable definition.
#include <iostream.h>

class test
{ public:
      test(){cout << "Hello\n";}
};

test t;

int main()
{ return 0;
}
```

A very strange aspect of this program is that its *main* contains only a return statement, while the program nevertheless produces the text *Hello* as output. This is because of the *test* constructor, which is called by the definition of the variable *t*. As this program demonstrates, the definition of a variable, such as that of *t*, can have effects that surprise those who are not familiar with the C++ language.

We now turn to another preparatory program, DEMO2, which is more advanced in that it is based on a virtual function, which is overridden.

```
// DEMO2: An application of late binding
#include <iostream.h>

class base
{ public:
      virtual void f(){}
      base();
} *p;

base::base(){p = this;}
```

```
// -------------------------------------
class test: public base
{  public:
       void f(){cout << "Hello\n";}
};

test t;   // Stores the address of t in p
//-------------------------------------

int main()
{  p->f();  // Produces output
   return 0;
}
```

Focusing on the program fragment between the two horizontal lines and realizing that function *f* is not a constructor, it is hard to understand that the line

```
test t;
```

should cause the text *Hello* to appear as output. Actually this does not happen until the *main* function is executed. In contrast to what we have seen in DEMO1, the above line only *prepares* for such an output action. When the *base* constructor is called, it places the address of *t* in the global pointer variable *p*. Later, the *main* function uses this pointer to call the member function *f*. Since *f* is a virtual function, we have *late binding* (also called *dynamic binding*). As a result, the *f* member function of class *test* is executed, even though only pointer *p*, of type *pointer-to-base* (not *pointer-to-test*), is used in the *main* function.

A simple MFC application

Program WTESTMFC.CPP, our first Windows application based on the Microsoft Foundation Classes, is similar to the fragment between the two horizontal lines of program DEMO2, as we will see shortly.

File WTESTMFC.CPP:

```
// WTESTMFC.CPP: Test Windows programming using C++.
#include <afxwin.h>

class CMyWindow: public CFrameWnd
{  public:
   CMyWindow()
   {  int xScreen = GetSystemMetrics(SM_CXSCREEN),
          yScreen = GetSystemMetrics(SM_CYSCREEN);
      RECT rect = {0, 0, xScreen, yScreen};
      Create(NULL,                    // Use default window-class name
      "Windows test 1",               // Text for title bar
      WS_OVERLAPPEDWINDOW,            // Window style
      rect,                           // Size and position of window
```

```
        NULL,                          // No parent window
        NULL);                         // No menu
    }
};

class CApp: public CWinApp
{   public:
    BOOL InitInstance()
    {   m_pMainWnd = new CMyWindow();
        m_pMainWnd->ShowWindow(m_nCmdShow);
        m_pMainWnd->UpdateWindow();
        return TRUE;
    }
};

CApp App;
```

A make file for this program is included here for the sake of completeness:

File WTESTMFC.MAK:

```
# WTESTMFC.MAK; usage (with Microsoft C++): nmake -f wtestmfc.mak
wtestmfc.exe: wtestmfc.obj gen.def
        link /nod wtestmfc, wtestmfc, nul,\
          mafxcw+libw+mlibcew+commdlg+shell, gen.def
wtestmfc.obj: wtestmfc.cpp
        cl -c -AM -G2sw -Ow -W3 -Zp wtestmfc.cpp
# File GEN.DEF can be found in Section 1.2
```

As you can see, file WTESTMFC.CPP is shorter than file WTEST.C in Section 2.1. Since some awkward words, such as *FAR* and *PASCAL*, do not occur in it, it also looks more attractive. In spite of its compactness, however, it is not easy to understand at all. It mainly consists of two class declarations, followed by the definition of the object *App*:

```
class CMyWindow: public CFrameWnd
{ ...
};

class CApp: public CWinApp
{ ...
};

CApp App;
```

Apparently, *CFrameWnd* and *CWinApp* are classes declared in the header file AFX-WIN.H. They are used to derive the classes *CMyWindow* and *CApp* from. This is illustrated by Figure 1.5, which is extracted from the MFC hierarchy shown in Appendix B. Consequently, we may replace the names *CMyWindow* and *CApp* with other names, if we like. At first sight the program does not seem to do very much, since it contains only two class declarations and the definition of an object. Actually, there is also a *WinMain* function, but since this is provided for by the MFC we generally need not bother about it. However, knowing this and recalling the marked portion of program DEMO2 will be helpful in understanding the rather complicated flow of control of our WTESTMFC module.

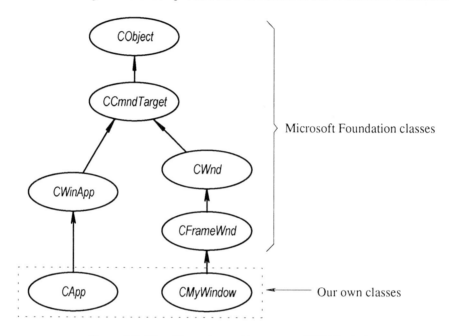

Figure 1.5. Class hierarchy used in program WTEST.MFC

The following five actions take place in this order:

1 The above definition of *App*, of type *CApp*, causes the constructor of *CWinApp*, the base class of *CApp*, to be called. (Note that the derived class *CApp* does not have a constructor.)

2 The following assignment statement is executed by the constructor of base class *CWin-App*:

```
afxCurrentWinApp = this;
```

where *afxCurrentWinApp* is a global pointer variable. Thus the address of our object *App* is stored in this pointer.

3 Function *WinMain*, which is activated after the completion of step 2, now uses this global pointer to call the member function *InitInstance*. Since this member function is declared virtual in class *CWinApp* and pointer *afxCurrentWinApp* points to object *App* of the derived class *CApp*, the call *afxCurrentWinApp->InitInstance( )* applies to our own version of *InitInstance*, which overrides that of the base class *CWinApp*.

4 In our function *InitInstance* the constructor *CMyWindow* is called to create a *CMyWindow* object. The call to *Create* in this constructor is analogous to the call to *CreateWindow* in our previous program, WTEST. The *Create* function is a member function of class *CFrameWnd*, from which we have derived our class *CMyWindow*.

5 Back in function *InitInstance*, these two statements are now executed:

```
m_pMainWnd->ShowWindow(m_nCmdShow);
m_pMainWnd->UpdateWindow();
```

The two functions *ShowWindow* and *UpdateWindow* are members of class *CWnd*, which is the base class of *CFrameWnd* (which, as we know, is the base class of our own class *CMyWindow*). These two functions are similar to those with the same names used in Section 1.3.

1.5 OWL Solution

The Borland ObjectWindows Library is older than the MFC. It is more closely related to traditional Windows programming in that it is based on *handles* (which are 16-bit numbers) and on a *WinMain* function. On the other hand, there are many functions that have names different from those of the API (see Section 1.3), so the MFC is more closely related to the API with regard to function names.

```
// WTESTOWL.CPP: Test Windows programming using C++/OWL
#define WIN31
#include <owl.h>

class TMyWindow: public TWindow
{  public:
   TMyWindow(PTWindowsObject AParent, LPSTR ATitle)
      : TWindow(AParent, ATitle) {}
};

class TApp: public TApplication
{  public:
   TApp(LPSTR Name, HANDLE hInstance, HANDLE hPrevInstance,
        LPSTR lpCmdLine, int nCmdShow)
      : TApplication(Name, hInstance, hPrevInstance,
                     lpCmdLine, nCmdShow){}
   virtual void InitMainWindow()
   {  TWindow *pWin;
      MainWindow = pWin = new TMyWindow(NULL,"Windows test 1");
      pWin->Attr.X = 0;
      pWin->Attr.Y = 0;
      pWin->Attr.W = GetSystemMetrics(SM_CXSCREEN);
      pWin->Attr.H = GetSystemMetrics(SM_CYSCREEN);
   }
};
```

```
int PASCAL WinMain(HANDLE hInstance, HANDLE hPrevInstance,
   LPSTR lpCmdLine, int nCmdShow)
{  TApp App("Wintest1", hInstance, hPrevInstance,
      lpCmdLine, nCmdShow);
   App.Run();
   return App.Status;
}
```

When Windows calls our *WinMain* function, object *App* of type *TApp* is created. This causes a call to the constructor, *TApp*, of our own class, derived from the ObjectWindows class *TApplication*. Consequently, the constructor of this base class is invoked, which prepares for later actions, in a way similar to that discussed at the beginning of Section 1.4. The OWL class hierarchy, as far as required for program WTESTOWL, is shown in Figure 1.6 (see also Appendix C).

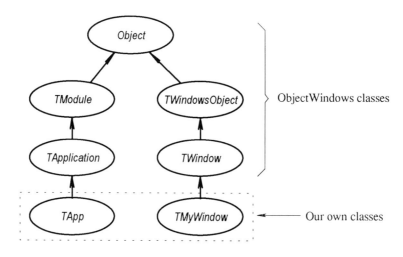

Figure 1.6. OWL class hierarchy for WTESTOWL

Most of the work is done by the call

```
App.Run();
```

This results in a call to the function *InitMainWindow*, supplied by ourselves to override the corresponding virtual member function of *TApplication*. In *InitMainWindow* we use the *new* operator to create an object of class *TMyWindow*, derived from *TWindow*, another important ObjectWindows class. The main window object is then created. Then *Run* starts the main message loop, and returns only when the program terminates. The value of the *Status* data member is then returned by the *WinMain* function. (Writing *virtual* in the declaration of the derived class *TApp* is actually superfluous, for it has to be used only in the base class, *TApplication*. However, the word *virtual* frequently occurs in derived

classes in examples supplied by Borland; it does no harm and it makes it clear that we are
dealing with a virtual function, so we will conform to this usage in this book.)

Note how we can specify the upper-left corner (0, 0), the width and the height of the
window to be displayed. We do this by assigning appropriate values to the X, Y, W and H
members of the *Attr* structure, which is itself a *TWindow* data member. Omitting these
actions would result in a default window size and position; in this book we prefer defining
these characteristics ourselves.

The two pointers *pWin* and *MainWindow* have different types. As you can see, *pWin* is
of type *TWindow*, which is required in statements such as *pWin–>Attr.X* = 0;. The other,
MainWindow, is a pointer member of class *TWindowsObject*, which is a base class of
TWindow.

In this program the declaration of the derived class *TMyWindow* was not really necessary. We could have omitted it, writing *TWindow* instead of *TMyWindow* after the *new*
operator. However, since we normally do use such a derived class in more realistic programs, we might as well get accustomed to it now.

The definition of the constant *WIN*31, at the top of the program, is required by the
compiler. If we omit it, the error message '*OWL application must be built with either
WIN*30 *or WIN*31 *defined*' appears.

This first OWL application is hardly simpler than the corresponding MFC program in
the previous section. In both cases, familiarity with C++ is essential if we want to understand these programs.

Compiling and linking

We can use the following make file to compile and link this program.

File WTESTOWL.MAK:

```
# WTESTOWL.MAK: usage (with Borland C++): make -f wtestowl.mak
wtestowl.exe: wtestowl.obj
      bcc -mm -WE -L\borlandc\owl\lib;\borlandc\classlib\lib \
         wtestowl.obj owlwm.lib tclassm.lib
wtestowl.obj: wtestowl.cpp
      bcc -c -mm -WE \
         -I\borlandc\owl\include;\borlandc\classlib\include \
         wtestowl.cpp
```

Note the backslashes (\) at the very end of two of these lines. Each of these final backslashes indicates continuation. For example, the third line of this file logically replaces the
final backslash of the second line.

As you can see, linking is done here (on the second line) by the *bcc* command. We
could have used the *tlink* command instead, but that would make the command line longer
and more difficult.

A consequence of using *bcc* for linking is that we cannot specify our module-definition
file, GEN.DEF, here. Fortunately, the Borland linker provides a default module-definition
file if we do not supply one ourselves. We then simply ignore a warning from the linker

about this default file. As indicated by comment in the above make file, we can compile and link our first OWL program by entering the following command at the DOS prompt:

```
make -f wtestowl.mak
```

1.6 Questions

1.1   What is meant by the phrase 'sending a message to a window'?
1.2   How do we specify a title to be displayed in the title bar?
1.3   Which of the names *WinMain* and *WndProc* is obligatory?
1.4   How can we terminate program execution (like *exit* in a conventional C program)?
1.5   How do we obtain the width and the height of the screen (in pixels)?
1.6   What is the function *DefWindowProc* for?
1.7   What are the functions *ShowWindow* and *UpdateWindow* for?

About MFC:

1.8   What is the base class of our main window class *CMyWindow*?
1.9   What is the base class of our application class *CApp*?
1.10 When and where is the constructor *CMyWindow* activated?
1.11 When and where is InitInstance (a member function of *CApp*) activated?
1.12 Compare the size of file WTESTMFC.EXE with that of file WTEST.EXE (see Section 1.3).

About OWL:

1.13 Which ObjectWindows classes were discussed in Section 1.5?
1.14 Which classes were derived from them?
1.15 What is the flow of control in program WTESTOWL?
1.16 Generate a .EXE file (a) with the given make file and (b) with Borland's Integrated Development Environment (IDE). Compare the sizes of the generated files. If the size of the file produced with method (b) is large compared with method (a), try to reduce it by altering the IDE settings.
1.17 Compare these file sizes with those of Question 1.12.

2

Text Output

2.1 Problem Definition

Probably the most elementary thing we as programmers need to do is to display text on the screen. We have already seen how to display some text in the title bar of a window, but we will now also use the large area known as the *client rectangle*, which is the blank area below the title bar in Figure 1.1. As discussed in Section 1.1, the user can change the size of the window by dragging its corners or its edges. Then obviously the client rectangle also changes. In this chapter we will display the current width and height of the client rectangle, and we will demonstrate that we can obtain these data in two ways, as the first two lines below the title bar in Figure 2.1 illustrate. These dimensions are expressed in pixels, and when thinking in terms of *x*- and *y*- coordinates, we should bear in mind that the origin of the coordinate system lies in the upper-left corner of the client area, with the *y*-axis pointing downwards. (This applies to *device coordinates*, but not necessarily to *logical coordinates*, to be discussed in Chapter 5.)

On a third line we will display how often the right mouse button has been pressed after starting the program. (Consequently, this chapter is not only about displaying text, as its title suggests, but also about communication with the mouse!)

Finally, pressing the *left* mouse button will produce a smaller window known as a *message box*. This has a title bar and a client rectangle, both displaying text. We will simply display the width *xScreen* and the height *yScreen* of the entire screen in it. Recall that these variables also occurred in our programs of Chapter 1. With standard VGA their values are 640 and 480, as you can see in Figure 2.1. Finally, there is a push-down button with the text OK in the message box. If we click it, or press the Enter key, the message box disappears, and anything that was hidden by it is restored.

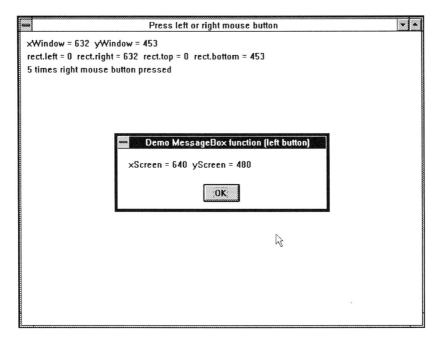

Figure 2.1. Output of program OUTP.C

2.2 General Aspects

It is not necessary to distinguish between text and numeric output, since we can easily convert numbers to character strings and combine these with other text, using the well-known standard function *sprintf*.

A very simple way of displaying text is by using the API function *MessageBox*, which, not surprisingly, produces a message box. Although this function is primarily intended as a means to display error messages, nothing prohibits us from using it for other purposes as well. Remember, however, the message box produced by this function is on the screen only until we click the OK button with the mouse. The message box appears as a window, including a title bar, in which we can place additional text, usually called a *caption*. For example, when using C we can write

```
MessageBox(hWnd, "Hello", "Caption", MB_OK);
```

in our *WndProc* function. The meaning of the four arguments used here is as follows:

hWnd	Window handle, available as the first parameter of the Window function.
"Hello"	Text to appear in the middle of the message box.
"Caption"	Text to appear as a caption in the title bar of the message box.
MB_OK	Causes an OK button to appear.

When using MFC, we can also write the above call to the function *MessageBox*, except for the first argument, *hWnd*, which we simply omit, because this function is a member of our main window class. We will discuss this in more detail in Section 2.4.

Note that we are using the term *message* with two different meanings. Windows programmers normally use it in phrases such as 'sending a message to a window' and 'message loop', as discussed in Section 1.2. The function name *MessageBox*, however, simply means 'a box that displays a message', where the term *message* is used in its traditional meaning of some piece of text, displayed on the screen.

The three lines in the client rectangle of Figure 2.1 are produced by means of the function *TextOut*, which requires some familiarity with the notion of a *device context*, which is an abstraction of an output device, such as a video display or a printer. In our case, a device context will represent the client rectangle of our window. When programming in C, we use an integer variable, called a *handle*, to represent a device context. A typical name for a device-context handle is *hDC*. Graphics functions expect such a handle as their first argument. The same method is used with OWL. With MFC, on the other hand, we use a class object *dc* to represent a device context, and the graphics functions (with the same names as in C) we use are member functions of this class. For example, compare

TextOut(hDC, ...)	in C and with OWL, and
dc.TextOut(...)	with MFC.

Make files

There will not be any make files in this chapter, because these would be similar to those in Chapter 1. In Sections 2.3, 2.4 and 2.5, we can use the make files of Sections 1.3, 1.4 and 1.5, respectively, provided we replace all occurrences of *wtest* with *outp*. Recall that we have defined a general module-definition file, GEN.DEF, which we use throughout this book.

2.3 C Solution

We will now discuss the C program OUTP, which solves the problem defined and discussed in the preceding sections. Let us first see how to use a device-context handle. As in Section 1.3, we will have a window procedure *WndProc*, but this time there will be some more cases in the switch statement. Let us have a look at the following program fragment:

```
long FAR PASCAL _export WndProc(HWND hWnd, UINT message,
        WPARAM wParam, LPARAM lParam)
{  ...
   HDC hDC;
   PAINTSTRUCT ps;
   switch (message)
   {
   ...
```

```
case WM_PAINT:
   hDC = BeginPaint(hWnd, &ps);
   ...
   TextOut(hDC, 10, 10, buf, strlen(buf));
   ...
   EndPaint(hWnd, &ps);
   break;
...
```

Windows can give a signal to our program to 'repaint' the client rectangle. It does so by sending a *WM_PAINT* message to the window. As we know, this means that our *WndProc* function is called, with its second parameter, *message*, equal to *WM_PAINT*. Since we want to call the *TextOut* function, we need to use a device-context handle *hDC*. This handle is declared as being of type *HDC*, and assigned a value by calling *BeginPaint*, as shown above. This function also requires a second argument, which is the address of *ps*, a *PAINTSTRUCT* object. We need not place any value in *ps*; just declaring it and passing its address to *BeginPaint* is all we have to do. We must delete a device context by a call to *EndPaint* in the same way as it was created by *BeginPaint*, and these two actions must take place during the same call to our window procedure. Any inaccuracy on this point has serious consequences, which we will not discuss here. Although not required for our present problem, there is a similar function pair (*GetDC* and *ReleaseDC*) which should be used for messages other than *WM_PAINT*. So remember, *BeginPaint* and *EndPaint* may be used only if *message* is equal to *WM_PAINT*.

The *TextOut* function, used here between the calls to *BeginPaint* and *EndPaint*, is only one out of many functions that has a device-context handle as its first argument. The second and third arguments are the *x*- and *y*-coordinates of the position where the text is to start. The fourth and fifth arguments are the character string to be displayed and its logical length. Curiously enough, *TextOut* is not based on the normal convention of using a terminating null character, but we have to supply the logical string length ourselves. Fortunately, we can use the standard function *strlen* here, because such a null character is supplied by *sprintf* which we will use to give character array *buf* the desired contents.

Both functions *MessageBox* and *TextOut* are demonstrated by program OUTP. As Figure 2.1 shows, there is a title bar which invites us to press either the left or the right mouse button. If we press the left one, a message box (produced by function *MessageBox*) appears, showing the dimensions *xScreen* and *yScreen* of the entire screen. Pressing the right mouse button produces output by means of *TextOut*. Here this output consists of the values of the variables *xWindow* and *yWindow*, the *left*, *right*, *top*, and *bottom* members of the variable *rect*, and the number of times the right mouse button has been pressed. Variable *rect* contains the boundary values (for *x* and *y*) of the client rectangle. The dimensions of the client rectangle are obtained in two ways. When *message* is equal to *WM_SIZE*, the *x*-dimension *xWindow* of the client rectangle can be found in the lower 16 bits of the *long* parameter *lParam*, and the *y*-dimension *yWindow* in the higher 16 bits. We also demonstrate function *GetClientRect*, which assigns values to the *left*, *right*, *top* and *bottom* members of a structure *rect* of type RECT. Both methods are used in program OUTP. Figure 2.1 shows the situation that occurs after having pressed the right mouse button five times, without altering the window size. Using standard VGA, we then have

```
rect.left = 0
rect.right = xWindow = 632
rect.top = 0
rect.bottom = yWindow = 453
```

As usual, we can alter the size of the window by dragging one of its corners, using the left mouse button. When we release that mouse button, 632 and 453 are replaced with other values.

Before discussing some more details of it, let us have a look at the complete program OUTP.C:

File OUTP.C:

```
// OUTP.C: Screen output, programmed in C.
#include <windows.h>
#include <stdio.h>
#include <string.h>

long FAR PASCAL _export WndProc(HWND hWnd, UINT message,
      WPARAM wParam, LPARAM lParam);
int xScreen, yScreen;

int PASCAL WinMain(HANDLE hInstance, HANDLE hPrevInstance,
    LPSTR lpCmdLine, int nCmdShow)
{   char szAppName[]="Outputtest";
    WNDCLASS wndclass;
    HWND hWnd;
    MSG msg;
    xScreen = GetSystemMetrics(SM_CXSCREEN);
    yScreen = GetSystemMetrics(SM_CYSCREEN);
    if (!hPrevInstance)
    {  wndclass.style = CS_HREDRAW | CS_VREDRAW;
       wndclass.lpfnWndProc = WndProc;
       wndclass.cbClsExtra = 0;
       wndclass.cbWndExtra = 0;
       wndclass.hInstance = hInstance;
       wndclass.hIcon = LoadIcon(NULL, IDI_APPLICATION);
       wndclass.hCursor = LoadCursor(NULL, IDC_ARROW);
       wndclass.hbrBackground = GetStockObject(WHITE_BRUSH);
       wndclass.lpszMenuName = NULL;
       wndclass.lpszClassName = szAppName;
       // Name used in call to CreateWindow.
       if (!RegisterClass(&wndclass)) return FALSE;
    }
    hWnd = CreateWindow(
        szAppName,
        "Press left or right mouse button",
                                    // Text for window title bar.
        WS_OVERLAPPEDWINDOW,        // Window style.
```

```
            0,                              // Initial x position
            0,                              // Initial y position.
            xScreen,                        // Width.
            yScreen,                        // Height.
            NULL,                           // Parent window handle.
            NULL,                           // Window menu handle.
            hInstance,                      // Program instance handle.
            NULL                            // Create parameters.
        );
        ShowWindow(hWnd, nCmdShow);
        UpdateWindow(hWnd);
        while (GetMessage(&msg, NULL, 0, 0))
        {   TranslateMessage(&msg);      // Translates virtual key codes
            DispatchMessage(&msg);       // Dispatches message to window
        }
        return msg.wParam;       // Returns the value from PostQuitMessage
}

long FAR PASCAL _export WndProc(HWND hWnd, UINT message,
        WPARAM wParam, LPARAM lParam)
{   char buf[80];
    static int xWindow, yWindow, nRightButtonDown;
    HDC hDC;
    RECT rect;
    PAINTSTRUCT ps;
    switch (message)
    {
    case WM_DESTROY:
        PostQuitMessage(0); break;
    case WM_SIZE:
        xWindow = LOWORD(lParam); yWindow = HIWORD(lParam);
        break;
    case WM_PAINT:
        hDC = BeginPaint(hWnd, &ps);
        sprintf(buf, "xWindow = %d   yWindow = %d", xWindow, yWindow);
        TextOut(hDC, 10, 10, buf, strlen(buf));

        GetClientRect(hWnd, &rect);
        sprintf(buf, "rect.left = %d   rect.right = %d   "
        "rect.top = %d   rect.bottom = %d", rect.left, rect.right,
        rect.top, rect.bottom);
        TextOut(hDC, 10, 30, buf, strlen(buf));

        sprintf(buf, "%d times right mouse button pressed",
            nRightButtonDown);
        TextOut(hDC, 10, 50, buf, strlen(buf));

        EndPaint(hWnd, &ps);
        break;
```

```
      case WM_LBUTTONDOWN:
        sprintf(buf, "xScreen = %d  yScreen = %d", xScreen, yScreen);
        MessageBox(hWnd, buf,
        "Demo MessageBox function (left button)", MB_OK);
        break;
      case WM_RBUTTONDOWN:
        nRightButtonDown++;
        InvalidateRect(hWnd, NULL, TRUE);
        break;
      default:
        return DefWindowProc(hWnd, message, wParam, lParam);
    }
    return 0L;
}
```

The switch-statement in the window procedure *WndProc* contains several cases that need some explanation about when the message in question is sent to the window:

```
  case WM_SIZE:
```

This case applies both at the beginning and each time the user gives the window a new size (by dragging an edge or a corner)

```
  case WM_PAINT:
```

This applies when the window is to be repainted. Such repainting can also be activated by a call to *InvalidateRect* (see *WM_RBUTTONDOWN* below).

```
  case WM_LBUTTONDOWN:
```

This applies when the left mouse button has been pressed.

```
  case WM_RBUTTONDOWN:
```

Similarly for the right mouse button.

Looking at the program code following this line, we find the following call, which causes the window to be repainted:

```
InvalidateRect(hWnd, NULL, TRUE);
```

Actually, it marks the entire client rectangle as 'invalid', which causes a *WM_PAINT* message to be sent to the window.

Notice the keyword *static* for the declaration of the variables *xWindow*, *yWindow* and *nRightButtonDown*, at the beginning of function *WndProc*. This is essential here because these variables are assigned values in one call of this function and used in another. For example, the variable *nRightButtonDown* is increased by one when the right mouse button is pressed down, after which control is passed back to Windows. After this, function

WndProc is called once again with *message* = *WM_PAINT*. It is then essential that *nRight-ButtonDown* still has the value just assigned to it. This will be the case only if this variable has a permanent memory location, so it must be *static*.

Instead of using the solution shown above, we could omit the *WM_PAINT* case, provided we replace the *WM_RBUTTONDOWN* case with the following fragment at the same time:

```
case WM_RBUTTONDOWN:
   nRightButtonDown++;
   hDC = GetDC(hWnd);
   sprintf(buf, "xWindow = %d  yWindow = %d", xWindow, yWindow);
   TextOut(hDC, 10, 10, buf, strlen(buf));

   GetClientRect(hWnd, &rect);
   sprintf(buf, "rect.left = %d  rect.right = %d  "
   "rect.top = %d  rect.bottom = %d", rect.left, rect.right,
   rect.top, rect.bottom);
   TextOut(hDC, 10, 30, buf, strlen(buf));
   sprintf(buf, "%d times right mouse button pressed",
           nRightButtonDown);
   TextOut(hDC, 10, 50, buf, strlen(buf));

   ReleaseDC(hWnd, hDC);
   break;
```

Note the way the functions *GetDC* and *ReleaseDC* are used here instead of *BeginPaint* and *EndPaint* in the original program.

However, after this modification the program behaves slightly differently. The three lines at the top of the client rectangle will now not appear until the right mouse button is pressed down. With the original version we initially read

```
0 times right mouse button pressed
```

at the third line. This line (starting with **0**) will never appear in the modified version because a similar line (with **0** replaced by **1**) appears only when the right mouse button has been pressed.

With this new version, these three lines also disappear when the user changes the screen size, and they are not restored until the right button is pressed again. This is obvious, because with this modification the calls to *TextOut* are not automatically executed each time the window is repainted.

This modification has a more serious drawback, however. If the user makes the window smaller, then presses the right and the left mouse buttons, in that order, the message box may overlap the three lines. This in itself is not serious, for the three lines are restored when the user clicks the OK button. However, if the user first drags the title bar of the message box to move it while it is overlapping part of the three lines, these lines are not restored: the portions that were obscured by the message box remain invisible, regardless of how we move the message box. There is no such problem with the original version of the program.

The lesson to be learned from all this is that in case of doubt we had better display output in response to the *WM_PAINT* message.

As mentioned above, the *WM_PAINT* case is omitted in the modified version. Then the *default* case applies, resulting in a call to the default window function *DefWindowProc*. This has the same effect as if we had written:

```
case WM_PAINT:
   hDC = BeginPaint(hWnd, &ps);
EndPaint(hWnd, &ps);
break;
```

However, it would not be correct if we wrote only

```
case WM_PAINT:
   break;        /* This is incorrect */
```

This is a serious error because in this way the *WM_PAINT* message is not removed from the internal message queue. The window function will therefore again be called with *message = WM_PAINT*, and so on. Apparently, it is required that a *WM_PAINT* message results in calls to *BeginPaint* and *EndPaint*. If we do not write these calls in our program, we should omit the *WM_PAINT* case altogether; function *DefWindowProc* will then have the opportunity to deal with the *WM_PAINT* message in the correct way.

The parameters *wParam* and *lParam*

The parameters *wParam* and *lParam* of the window procedure supply us with additional information about the message in question. Earlier in this section, we have used *lParam* in connection with the *WM_SIZE* message to find the dimensions of the client rectangle. The same principle applies to the *WM_RBUTTONDOWN* message. In this case we can use *lParam* to find the position of the mouse cursor at the moment the right mouse button is pressed down: the *x*-coordinate is in the low-order word and the *y*-coordinate in the high-order word. We will demonstrate this in Chapter 8.

2.4 MFC Solution

We will now see how program OUTP can be rewritten as an MFC version, OUTPMFC. Cases in a switch-statement are replaced with *CMyWindow* member functions known as *message-response functions*. For example, instead of

```
case WM_RBUTTONDOWN:
   nRightButtonDown++;
   InvalidateRect(hWnd, NULL, TRUE);
   break;
```

in function *WndProc*, we now write

```
void CMyWindow::OnRButtonDown(UINT nFlags, CPoint point)
{  nRightButtonDown++;
   InvalidateRect(NULL, TRUE);
}
```

Notice the way Windows supplies us with message-dependent details. In a C program this is done by means of two parameters (*wParam* and *lParam*) of the window function. With MFC, this is instead done by means of special parameters, the number and types of which depend on the message in question. For example, the coordinates of the mouse cursor at the moment the right mouse button is pressed down are given in parameter *point*, a class object of type *CPoint*, with public members *x* and *y*.

As required in C++, we must declare message functions, such as *OnRButtonDown*, in the class of which they are members. The MFC requires that we use the prefix *afx_msg* for each of these function declarations. There must also be a *DECLARE_MESSAGE_MAP( )* macro call. We therefore insert the following five lines in the declaration of class *CMyWindow*, after the *public* keyword:

```
afx_msg void OnPaint();
afx_msg void OnSize(UINT nType, int cx, int cy);
afx_msg void OnLButtonDown(UINT nFlags, CPoint point);
afx_msg void OnRButtonDown(UINT nFlags, CPoint point);
DECLARE_MESSAGE_MAP()
```

Outside this class declaration there is another curious set of macro calls:

```
BEGIN_MESSAGE_MAP(CMyWindow, CFrameWnd)
   ON_WM_PAINT()
   ON_WM_SIZE()
   ON_WM_LBUTTONDOWN()
   ON_WM_RBUTTONDOWN()
END_MESSAGE_MAP()
```

We need these to indicate that our function *OnSize*, for example, corresponds to the Windows message *WM_SIZE*. Note that they are really macro calls, not extensions to the C++ language.

There is no need to use global or static variables in this C++ program: although we need to use *xScreen*, *yScreen*, *xWindow*, *yWindow* and *nRightButtondown* in several functions, these are all member functions of class *CMyWindow*. We can therefore declare these variables as private members of this class:

File OUTPMFC.CPP:

```
// OUTPMFC.CPP: Test Windows screen output, using the MFC.
#include <afxwin.h>
#include <stdio.h>
```

```
class CMyWindow: public CFrameWnd
{  private:  // private keyword may as well be omitted
   int xScreen, yScreen, xWindow, yWindow, nRightButtonDown;
public:
   CMyWindow()
   {  xScreen = GetSystemMetrics(SM_CXSCREEN),
      yScreen = GetSystemMetrics(SM_CYSCREEN);
      RECT rect = {0, 0, xScreen, yScreen};
      Create(NULL, "Press left or right mouse button",
         WS_OVERLAPPEDWINDOW, rect, NULL, NULL);
   }
   afx_msg void OnPaint();
   afx_msg void OnSize(UINT nType, int cx, int cy);
   afx_msg void OnLButtonDown(UINT nFlags, CPoint point);
   afx_msg void OnRButtonDown(UINT nFlags, CPoint point);
   DECLARE_MESSAGE_MAP()
};

class CApp: public CWinApp
{  public:
   BOOL InitInstance()
   {  m_pMainWnd = new CMyWindow();
      m_pMainWnd->ShowWindow(m_nCmdShow);
      m_pMainWnd->UpdateWindow();
      return TRUE;
   }
};

CApp App;

BEGIN_MESSAGE_MAP(CMyWindow, CFrameWnd)
   ON_WM_SIZE()
   ON_WM_PAINT()
   ON_WM_LBUTTONDOWN()
   ON_WM_RBUTTONDOWN()
END_MESSAGE_MAP()

void CMyWindow::OnPaint()
{  char buf[80];
   CPaintDC dc(this);
   RECT rect;
   GetClientRect(&rect);
   sprintf(buf, "xWindow = %d  yWindow = %d", xWindow, yWindow);
   dc.TextOut(10, 10, buf);

   sprintf(buf, "rect.left = %d  rect.right = %d  "
   "rect.top = %d  rect.bottom = %d",
   rect.left, rect.right, rect.top, rect.bottom);
   dc.TextOut(10, 30, buf);
```

```
    sprintf(buf, "%d times right mouse button pressed",
        nRightButtonDown);
    dc.TextOut(10, 50, buf);
}

void CMyWindow::OnSize(UINT nType, int cx, int cy)
{   xWindow = cx; yWindow = cy;
}

void CMyWindow::OnLButtonDown(UINT nFlags, CPoint point)
{   char buf[80];
    sprintf(buf, "xScreen = %d  yScreen = %d", xScreen, yScreen);
    MessageBox(buf, "Demo MessageBox function (left button)", MB_OK);
}

void CMyWindow::OnRButtonDown(UINT nFlags, CPoint point)
{   nRightButtonDown++;
    InvalidateRect(NULL, TRUE);
}
```

As you can see, there are some functions in this C++ program (OUTPMFC) that have the same names as similar functions in our C program (OUTP). These functions used in C++/MFC are class member functions, sometimes called *wrappings* of their API counterparts. Since it is implicitly known to which class object they belong, they do not have a window handle as a parameter. For example, instead of the API call

```
InvalidateRect(hWnd, NULL, TRUE);
```

we write

```
InvalidateRect(NULL, TRUE);
```

when using the MFC. Actually, this line is an abbreviated form of

```
this->InvalidateRect(NULL, TRUE);
```

In other words, a pointer to a window is used instead of a window handler (*hWnd*). We usually omit *this->* in class member functions.
    There is also an interesting difference between

```
TextOut(hDC, 10, 10, buf, strlen(buf));
```

which we used in OUTP.C, and the following call, used in OUTPMFC.CPP:

```
dc.TextOut(10, 10, buf);
```

Here the number of arguments is even reduced by two. First, the prefix *dc.* is used instead of the argument *hDC*. Second, we benefit here from the C++ concept of function over-loading. According to Microsoft's Class Libraries Reference, there are two *TextOut* member functions, namely one with four and the other with three parameters. The latter, which computes the string length itself, is used here.

It is essential for function *CMyWindow::OnPaint* to contain the following line (that is, the application may crash if we omit it):

```
CPaintDC dc(this);
```

This is because the constructor and destructor of *CPaintDC* call the *BeginPaint* and *End-Paint* functions, respectively. As we have seen near the end of Section 2.3, such calls are required when a *WM_PAINT* message is sent.

An alternative version

We have seen that an alternative version of the C program OUTP, without a *WM_PAINT* case, was possible. Here we can do the same. To obtain that version, we have to omit the function *CMyWindow::OnPaint* as well as the two program lines

```
afx_msg void OnPaint();
```

and

```
ON_WM_PAINT()
```

which refer to this function. At the same time, we have to replace function *CMyWin-dow::OnRButtonDown* with the following version:

```
void CMyWindow::OnRButtonDown(UINT nFlags, CPoint point)
{   char buf[80];
    CClientDC dc(this);
    RECT rect;
    nRightButtonDown++;
        sprintf(buf, "xWindow = %d  yWindow = %d", xWindow, yWindow);
    dc.TextOut(10, 10, buf, strlen(buf));

    GetClientRect(&rect);
    sprintf(buf, "rect.left = %d  rect.right = %d  \
    rect.top = %d  rect.bottom = %d",
    rect.left, rect.right, rect.top, rect.bottom);
    dc.TextOut(10, 30, buf);

    sprintf(buf, "%d times right mouse button pressed",
        nRightButtonDown);
    dc.TextOut(10, 50, buf);
}
```

Since a device context is created here in a function other than *OnPaint*, we declare a *CClientDC*, rather than *CPaintDC* object. The *CClientDC* constructor calls *GetDC*, used in program OUTP. Similarly, the destructor of this class calls *ReleaseDC*. This is very convenient, and, more importantly, it is also very safe: since destructors are invoked automatically there is no danger of forgetting about cleaning up.

As with program OUTP, the modified version of OUTPMFC is not completely equivalent to its original. When the program starts it does not display three lines of text but it does so only after we have pressed down the right mouse button. Also, there are no such lines immediately after changing the window size.

2.5 OWL Solution

Using the Borland ObjectWindows Library, we can write program OUTPOWL, listed below, as another solution to the problem defined in Section 2.1.

```
// OUTPOWL.CPP: Screen output, programmed with C++/OWL.
#define WIN31
#include <stdio.h>
#include <string.h>
#include <owl.h>

class TMyWindow: public TWindow
{   int xScreen, yScreen, xWindow, yWindow, nRightButtonDown;
public:
    TMyWindow(PTWindowsObject AParent, LPSTR ATitle);
    virtual void Paint(HDC hDC, PAINTSTRUCT&);
    virtual void WMSize(RTMessage Msg)
        = [WM_FIRST + WM_SIZE];
    virtual void WMLButtonDown(RTMessage Msg)
        = [WM_FIRST + WM_LBUTTONDOWN];
    virtual void WMRButtonDown(RTMessage Msg)
        = [WM_FIRST + WM_RBUTTONDOWN];
};

TMyWindow::TMyWindow(PTWindowsObject AParent, LPSTR ATitle)
    : TWindow(AParent, ATitle)
{   xScreen = GetSystemMetrics(SM_CXSCREEN);
    yScreen = GetSystemMetrics(SM_CYSCREEN);
    nRightButtonDown = 0;
};

void TMyWindow::Paint(HDC hDC, PAINTSTRUCT&)
{   char buf[80];
    RECT rect;
    sprintf(buf, "xWindow = %d  yWindow = %d", xWindow, yWindow);
    TextOut(hDC, 10, 10, buf, strlen(buf));
```

```
      GetClientRect(HWindow, &rect);
      sprintf(buf, "rect.left = %d   rect.right = %d   "
      "rect.top = %d   rect.bottom = %d", rect.left, rect.right,
      rect.top, rect.bottom);
      TextOut(hDC, 10, 30, buf, strlen(buf));
      sprintf(buf, "%d times right mouse button pressed",
        nRightButtonDown);
      TextOut(hDC, 10, 50, buf, strlen(buf));
}

void TMyWindow::WMSize(RTMessage Msg)
{   xWindow = Msg.LP.Lo; yWindow = Msg.LP.Hi;
}

void TMyWindow::WMLButtonDown(RTMessage)
{   char buf[80];
    sprintf(buf, "xScreen = %d   yScreen = %d", xScreen, yScreen);
    MessageBox(HWindow, buf,
    "Demo MessageBox function (left button)", MB_OK);
}

void TMyWindow::WMRButtonDown(RTMessage)
{   nRightButtonDown++;
    InvalidateRect(HWindow, NULL, TRUE);
}

class TMyApp: public TApplication
{   public:
    TMyApp(LPSTR Name, HANDLE hInstance, HANDLE hPrevInstance,
           LPSTR lpCmdLine, int nCmdShow)
      : TApplication(Name, hInstance, hPrevInstance, lpCmdLine,
                     nCmdShow){}
    virtual void InitMainWindow();
};

void TMyApp::InitMainWindow()
{   TWindow *pWin;
    MainWindow = pWin = new TMyWindow(NULL, Name);
    pWin->Attr.X = 0; pWin->Attr.Y = 0;
    pWin->Attr.W = GetSystemMetrics(SM_CXSCREEN);
    pWin->Attr.H = GetSystemMetrics(SM_CYSCREEN);
}

int PASCAL WinMain(HANDLE hInstance, HANDLE hPrevInstance,
   LPSTR lpCmdLine, int nCmdShow)
{   TMyApp App("Press left or right mouse button",
    hInstance, hPrevInstance, lpCmdLine, nCmdShow);
    App.Run();
    return App.Status;
}
```

In contrast to Section 1.5, the constructor of class *TMyWindow* is now only *declared* inside that class and *defined* outside it. There are several other member functions of this class, which are *message-response functions*. To deal with the Windows messages *WM_PAINT*, *WM_SIZE*, *WM_LBUTTONDOWN* and *WM_RBUTTONDOWN*, we use the functions *Paint*, *WMSize*, *WMRButtonDown* and *WMLButtonDown*, respectively. We need not indicate that the *Paint* function corresponds with the *WM_PAINT* message; choosing the name *Paint* is sufficient. Curiously enough, this is different for the other three message-handling functions in this program. Unlike Microsoft, which solved the problem by message-map macros, Borland has resorted to a language extension to specify which function belongs to which message. (It will be clear that the Microsoft solution, which conforms to the C++ language, is the better one with regard to portability.) For example, we specify that the *WMSize* function belongs to the *WM_SIZE* message as follows:

```
virtual void WMSize(RTMessage Msg) = [WM_FIRST + WM_SIZE];
```

The keyword *virtual* may be omitted here: it is required for a virtual function itself, that is, for its original version, declared in the base class, but not for any overriding function in a derived class. It is used here only to conform to the Borland ObjectWindows User's Guide.

The equal sign in this function declaration is followed by an integer expression between brackets. Remember, Windows message identifiers, such as *WM_SIZE*, are defined as integer values in the header file WINDOWS.H. These values must all be increased by a constant value, written here symbolically as *WM_FIRST*, to obtain the value that is actually needed.

As we have seen in Section 1.5, the types known to ObjectWindows normally begin with a capital *T*. If this is preceded by *R*, this means *reference to*. In other words, we might omit this *R*, provided we write an ampersand after the type name. We could therefore also have declared

```
virtual void WMSize(TMessage &Msg) = [WM_FIRST + WM_SIZE];
```

with the same meaning.

As you can see in program OUTPOWL, the *Paint* function receives a device-context handler, *hDC*, in the form of a parameter from its caller, and we can use this straightaway. The required calls to *BeginPaint* and *EndPaint* (see Section 2.3) are then taken care of by ObjectWindows, so we do not write these calls ourselves in this function. The handle *hDC* is used in calls to the API function *TextOut*, in the same way as in Section 2.3.

We also use the normal API function *GetClientRect* to obtain information about the client rectangle. The window handle required as the first argument for this function is immediately available as the data member *HWindow*. Actually, this is a member of class *TWindowsObject*, which is a base class of *TWindow* (which is a base class of *TMyWindow*). The second parameter, of type *PAINTSTRUCT&*, is not used here. In such cases we can omit a parameter name (such as *ps*), to prevent the Borland C++ compiler from displaying a warning about our not using this parameter. We apply the same practice in many other cases, such as in function *WMLButtonDown*. Here too the *HWindow* data member is used, this time in a call to the *MessageBox* function.

Function *WMSize* shows how to use the *Msg* parameter if this denotes *x*- and *y*-values. These are available as *Msg.LP.Lo* and *Msg.LP.Hi*, respectively. Note that this is similar to using the *LOWORD* and *HIWORD* macros, as we did in Section 2.3. Although not required for our present problem, we could have obtained *x*- and *y*-coordinates in the functions *WMLButtonDown* and *WMRButtonDown* in a similar way. They would then have been the coordinates of the mouse cursor at the moment the button in question is pressed down, as we will see in Chapter 8.

An alternative version

With program OUTPOWL, the *WMRButtonDown* function only *prepares* for text being displayed on the screen. The action of updating the window is done by the *Paint* function, in response to a *WM_PAINT* message. As in Sections 2.3 and 2.4, we will also consider the possibility of ignoring *WM_PAINT* messages, and of calling the *TextOut* function immediately in *WMRButtonDown*. As we have seen, this leads to a program that is not completely equivalent to the current version. Remember, if we do not react to *WM_PAINT* messages, but instead to pressing the right mouse button, the output function *TextOut* is invoked neither when the window is created nor when its size changes. The modified version therefore displays three lines of text, such as those at the top of the client rectangle in Figure 2.1, only after the right mouse button is pressed.

This modification is instructive because it shows that in functions other than *Paint* we need to call *GetDC* to obtain a device-context handler, in the same way as we did in Section 2.3. After using this device-context handler, we must not forget to dispose of it by a call to *ReleaseDC*. The modified program is obtained by omitting both the declaration of the *Paint* function in the declaration of class *TMyWindow* and the definition of this function (that is, the function itself). Also, the definition of *WMRButtonDown* is to be replaced with the following modified version, consisting mostly of statements copied from the deleted *Paint* function:

```
void TMyWindow::WMRButtonDown(RTMessage)
{   char buf[80];
    RECT rect;
    nRightButtonDown++;
    HDC hDC = GetDC(HWindow);
    sprintf(buf, "xWindow = %d  yWindow = %d", xWindow, yWindow);
    TextOut(hDC, 10, 10, buf, strlen(buf));
    GetClientRect(HWindow, &rect);
    sprintf(buf, "rect.left = %d  rect.right = %d  "
      "rect.top = %d  rect.bottom = %d", rect.left, rect.right,
      rect.top, rect.bottom);
    TextOut(hDC, 10, 30, buf, strlen(buf));
    sprintf(buf, "%d times right mouse button pressed",
      nRightButtonDown);
    TextOut(hDC, 10, 50, buf, strlen(buf));
    ReleaseDC(HWindow, hDC);
}
```

2.6 Questions

2.1   What is a client rectangle?

2.2   How many arguments has the API function *MessageBox*? What is their meaning?

2.3   What is a device context, and how is it used in calls to the function *TextOut*? Answer this question for C, for MFC, and for OWL.

2.4   When do we use the functions *BeginPaint* and *EndPaint*, and when *GetDC* and *ReleaseDC*?

2.5   What is the function *InvalidateRect* for?

2.6   When do we use type *CPaintDC* and when *CClientDC* with MFC?

2.7   Why is the keyword *static* used for some variables in function *WndProc* of program OUTP.C?

2.8   What about such variables in the programs OUTPMFC.CPP and OUTPOWL.CPP?

2.9   How do we specify the correspondence between Window messages and message-response functions, both with MFC and with OWL?

3

Dialog Boxes for Input

3.1 Problem Definition

Now that we know how to produce output on the screen, we also want to provide our
Windows applications with facilities for input. The example dealt with in this chapter will
be a program that reads a real number x from the keyboard each time the left mouse button
is pressed. Since it would look silly if we did not really use this number after having read it,
we will display both x itself and its square x^2 in the title bar of the main window. This is
shown in Figure 3.1. Actually, this screen was produced by entering the value 0.02 for x
twice: entering it the first time and pressing the OK button caused the dialog box to disappear, leaving the title bar as this is shown in the figure, but without the dialog box. To
show both this title bar and the dialog box, the left button was pressed once again and 0.02
was entered the second time.

3.2 General Aspects

Although the problem defined in the previous section seems very simple, its solution is
more complicated than you might expect. However, what we will learn in this chapter will
apply to almost every Windows program, so the time to be devoted to it will be well spent.

Using header files of our own

In more realistic programs than those of Chapters 1 and 2, there are at least two more
source files involved. A large program usually consists of several modules, in some of
which we use the same types, symbolic constants, macros and functions. It is then wise to

declare these in a header file of our own. The advantage of this is that consistency is guaranteed. From now on, we will use this principle. For example, associated with the program file INP.C will be the header file INP.H. We use double quotes in *#include* lines for these files, so the compiler will (first) look for them in the current directory.

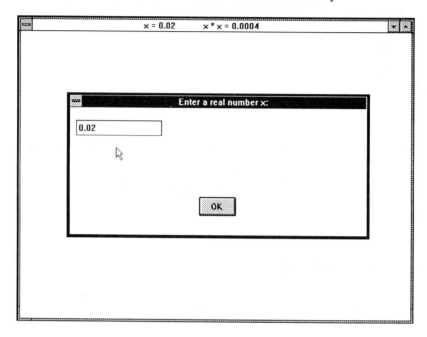

Figure 3.1. Sample screen produced by INP

Dialog boxes and resource script files

We could have used header files also in the program of Chapters 1 and 2, but the usefulness of such files would have been very limited because of the simplicity of these programs. However, header files will now be useful because we will be dealing with another new file type, a so-called *resource script file*, say, INP.RC. The header file INP.H will then be included in both INP.C and INP.RC. We will use this resource script file to specify details about a *dialog box*, an example of which is shown in Figure 3.1. In general, a dialog box is a window containing some smaller rectangles, called *controls*. Here is the resource script file for our program INP:

File INP.RC:

```
// INP.RC
#include <windows.h>
#include "inp.h"
X_INPUT DIALOG 40, 60, 240, 100
STYLE DS_MODALFRAME | WS_SYSMENU | WS_CAPTION
```

```
CAPTION "Enter a real number x:"
BEGIN
   EDITTEXT ID_INPUT, 5, 10, 70, 12
   DEFPUSHBUTTON "OK", ID_OK, 105, 70, 30, 15
END
```

Resource script files are not processed by the C-compiler but by the *resource compiler*. As this example shows, we can use *#include* lines in such files in the same way as in C or C++ programs. The line that follows the #include lines in this file has the form

```
name  DIALOG  x, y, width, height
```

where only *DIALOG* is used literally. The constants *x* and *y* denote the coordinates of the left-upper corner of the dialog box, and, obviously, *width* and *height* denote its width and its height.

These coordinates and dimensions are expressed in special units, not in pixels. The unit for *x* and *width* (measured horizontally) is 1/4 of the average width of one character of the system font (including the small white space between two successive characters). For example, using *width* = 240 in our DIALOG statement means that the width of the dialog box corresponds to the width of a string of about 240/4 = 60 characters. As you may have noticed in Figure 3.1 and elsewhere, the default system font is proportional; for example, most capital letters are wider than the lower-case letter *l*. The number of characters just mentioned may therefore actually be more than 60 or less. The unit for *y* and *height* (measured vertically) is 1/8 of the height of a character (including the space between two lines). For example, *height* = 100 corresponds to the height of 100/8 = 12.5 lines of text.

Not surprisingly, the line that begins with *STYLE* specifies the *style* of the dialog box. There are too many styles available to discuss them all here, so let us restrict ourselves to those used in the above resource script file INP.RC:

DS_MODALFRAME   This identifier provides for a *modal dialog-box frame*. A modal dialog box is one that requires an answer before anything else can be done. This is similar to the well-known input function *scanf* in standard I/O. (By contrast, we can use *modeless* dialog boxes, which allow the user to perform actions not related to the dialog box. We will restrict ourselves to modal dialog boxes, which are more common.)

WS_SYSMENU   The dialog box will have a control menu box, that is, it will have *system menu* in the form of a minus sign at the left end of the title bar; clicking this will create a drop-down menu with the commands *Move* and *Close*.

WS_CAPTION   The dialog box will have a title bar, to be used for a caption.

We use the *CAPTION* line to specify the caption that is to appear in the title bar.

This is followed by so-called *dialog control statements*, written between the delimiters *BEGIN* and *END*, or, alternatively, between the braces { and }. Between *BEGIN* and *END*,

we see here an *EDITTEXT* and a *DEFPUSHBUTTON* statement. They produce what is
called an *edit control* and a *push-button control*, collectively known as *controls*. The button
will display the text *OK* because of the string *"OK"* in the above *DEFPUSHBUTTON*
statement. The three letters *DEF* at the beginning of *DEFPUSHBUTTON* stand for
'default'. This means that this button is considered to be pressed if, after entering a number, we press the Enter key. If we had omitted these three letters, writing simply *PUSH-
BUTTON*, it would have been necessary either to click the OK button or to select this
button by means of the Tab key before pressing the Enter key.

The identifiers *ID_INPUT* and *ID_OK* are our own symbolic constants; we will define
them in the header file INP.H and use them also in our program to refer to these controls.
If we had not used this header file, it would have been necessary either to use numerical
constants, say, 1 and 2, or use *#define* lines for these symbolic constants both in the
resource script and in the program. Obviously, using a common header file is a better
solution. Then, in both statements used here, we specify the position and the dimensions of
the 'controls' in question, in this order:

x, y, width, height

They are expressed in the same units as those discussed above for the *DIALOG* statement.

3.3 C Solution

Besides the file INP.RC, we can use the following files for our C solution to the problem
of the previous section:

File INP.H:

```
// INP.H
#define ID_INPUT 1
#define ID_OK 2
long FAR PASCAL _export WndProc(HWND hWnd, UINT message,
     WPARAM wParam, LPARAM lParam);
int PASCAL WinMain(HANDLE hInstance, HANDLE hPrevInstance,
    LPSTR lpCmdLine, int nCmdShow);
BOOL FAR PASCAL _export InputProc(HWND hDlg, UINT message,
     WPARAM wParam, LPARAM lParam);
```

File INP.C:

```
// INP.C: Simple program to demonstrate input (using C).
#include <windows.h>
#include <stdio.h>
#include "inp.h"

HANDLE hInstGlobal;
HWND hWndGlobal;
```

```
int PASCAL WinMain(HANDLE hInstance, HANDLE hPrevInstance,
    LPSTR lpCmdLine, int nCmdShow)
{   char szAppName[]="INP";
    int xScreen = GetSystemMetrics(SM_CXSCREEN),
        yScreen = GetSystemMetrics(SM_CYSCREEN);
    WNDCLASS wndclass;
    HWND hWnd;
    MSG msg;
    hInstGlobal = hInstance;
    if (!hPrevInstance)
    {   wndclass.style = CS_HREDRAW | CS_VREDRAW;
        wndclass.lpfnWndProc = WndProc;
        wndclass.cbClsExtra = 0;
        wndclass.cbWndExtra = 0;
        wndclass.hInstance = hInstance;
        wndclass.hIcon = LoadIcon(NULL, IDI_APPLICATION);
        wndclass.hCursor = LoadCursor(NULL, IDC_ARROW);
        wndclass.hbrBackground = GetStockObject(WHITE_BRUSH);
        wndclass.lpszMenuName = NULL;
        wndclass.lpszClassName = szAppName;
            // Name used in call to CreateWindow.
        if (!RegisterClass(&wndclass)) return FALSE;
    }
    hWnd = CreateWindow(
        szAppName,
        "Press left mouse button.", // Text for window title bar.
        WS_OVERLAPPEDWINDOW,        // Window style.
        0,                          // Horizontal position.
        0,                          // Vertical position.
        xScreen,                    // Width.
        yScreen,                    // Height.
        NULL,                       // No parent.
        NULL,                       // Use the window class menu.
        hInstance,                  // This instance owns this window.
        NULL                        // Pointer not needed.
    );

    if (!hWnd) return FALSE;
    hWndGlobal = hWnd;

    ShowWindow(hWnd, nCmdShow);
    UpdateWindow(hWnd);

    while (GetMessage(&msg, NULL, 0, 0))
    {   TranslateMessage(&msg);    // Translates virtual key codes
        DispatchMessage(&msg);     // Dispatches message to window
    }
    return msg.wParam;     // Returns the value from PostQuitMessage
}
```

```
long FAR PASCAL _export WndProc(HWND hWnd, UINT message,
      WPARAM wParam, LPARAM lParam)
{  FARPROC lpProcInput;
   switch (message)
   {
   case WM_DESTROY:
      PostQuitMessage(0); break;
   case WM_LBUTTONDOWN:
      lpProcInput =
         MakeProcInstance((FARPROC)InputProc, hInstGlobal);
      DialogBox(hInstGlobal, "X_INPUT", hWnd, lpProcInput);
      FreeProcInstance(lpProcInput);
      break;
   default:
      return DefWindowProc(hWnd, message, wParam, lParam);
   }
   return 0L;
}

BOOL FAR PASCAL _export InputProc(HWND hDlg, UINT message,
      WPARAM wParam, LPARAM lParam)
{  double x;
   char buffer[80];
   switch(message)
   {
   case WM_INITDIALOG:
      SetFocus(GetDlgItem(hDlg, ID_INPUT));
      return TRUE;

   case WM_COMMAND:
      if (wParam == ID_OK)
      {  GetDlgItemText(hDlg, ID_INPUT, buffer, 25);
         EndDialog(hDlg, TRUE);
         if (sscanf(buffer, "%lf", &x) == 1)
         {  sprintf(buffer, "x = %-12g   x * x = %-12g",
                             x, x * x);
            SetWindowText(hWndGlobal, buffer);
         } else SetWindowText(hWndGlobal, "Incorrect input");
         return TRUE;
      }
      break;
   }
   return FALSE;
}
```

As you can see in the call to *CreateWindow*, occurring in function *WinMain*, the text in the title bar of the main window invites the user to press the left mouse button. In function *WndProc* we find the following fragment, which applies to that action:

```
case WM_LBUTTONDOWN:
  lpProcInput =
    MakeProcInstance((FARPROC)InputProc, hInstGlobal);
  DialogBox(hInstGlobal, "X_INPUT", hWnd, lpProcInput);
  FreeProcInstance(lpProcInput);
  break;
```

The call to function *DialogBox*, in the middle of this fragment, causes the dialog box to appear. There are four arguments in this function call:

hInstGlobal	The 'instance handle', passed to function *WinMain* as parameter *hInst*.
"X_INPUT"	A string containing the name *X_INPUT*, which we used in the resource script file INP.RC, at the beginning of the *DIALOG* statement.
hWnd	The first parameter of the *WndProc* function.
lpProcInput	A pointer that gives information about the dialog function to be used.

The fourth argument, *lpProcInput*, is obtained as the value returned by the function *MakeProcInstance*, called on the second line of the above fragment. The expression *(FARPROC)InputProc* is its first argument, *hInstGlobal*, just mentioned, its second. The name *InputProc* is declared in the header file INP.H, so the compiler will regard this name (not followed by parentheses) as a pointer to a function. The cast *(FARPROC)* is required to prevent the C++ compiler from complaining about different pointer types. (We could omit this cast if we did not use compiler options, discussed at the beginning of Section 1.3, to force compiling in C++ mode.) The call to *FreeProcInstance* in the above fragment releases memory that is no longer in use.

Let us now turn to the dialog function *InputProc* itself, listed at the end of file INP.C. Windows calls this function several times, under different circumstances. As usual, these circumstances can be distinguished by means of the *message* parameter, which we use in a switch statement. If *message* is equal to *WM_INITDIALOG*, we have the opportunity to initialize the message box. We make use of this by 'setting the *input focus*' to the edit control, so the user can immediately enter the value of *x* in it. If we did not do this, the user would have to move the mouse cursor to this edit control and press the left mouse button before text can be entered. The statement

```
SetFocus(GetDlgItem(hDlg, ID_INPUT));
```

makes this action superfluous. (Recall that *ID_INPUT* is a symbolic constant of our own, associated with the edit control in our resource script file.) To switch to the other control, the OK button, the user can press the Tab key. Repeatedly pressing this key causes the input focus to switch between the two controls (that is, between the box for *x* and the OK button). We can always tell whether or not a control has input focus. When the edit control has input focus, it shows a vertical bar indicating the position where the next character will be placed. When the button has input focus, there is a dashed rectangle surrounding the text (*OK*, in our case) on it.

When the edit control has input focus, each time the user enters a character, or rather, each time he or she presses or releases a key, the dialog function is called with parameter values *message = WM_COMMAND* and *wParam = ID_INPUT*. If we had wanted to use this, we could have inserted a fragment of the form

```
if (wParam == ID_INPUT)
{   ...
    return TRUE;
}
```

after the line

```
case WM_COMMAND:
```

We have not done so, because we are only interested in the final text in the edit control. More interesting is therefore what happens when the user clicks the OK button. Our use of the constant *ID_OK* on the *DEFPUSHBUTTON* line in the resource script file causes then the following program fragment to be executed:

```
if (wParam == ID_OK)
{   GetDlgItemText(hDlg, ID_INPUT, buffer, 25);
    EndDialog(hDlg, TRUE);
    if (sscanf(buffer, "%lf", &x) == 1)
    {   sprintf(buffer, "x = %-12g   x * x = %-12g", x, x * x);
        SetWindowText(hWndGlobal, buffer);
    } else SetWindowText(hWndGlobal, "Incorrect input");
    return TRUE;
}
```

Function *GetDlgItemText* copies all characters shown in the edit control to the character array *buffer*. We can use the fourth argument of *GetDlgItemText* as a limit to the number of characters to be copied to the area the address of which is given as the third argument. Actually, the fourth argument indicates how many positions, including the terminating null character, may be used in that area. For example, if we had written 3 instead of 25 and the user had entered 9876, then only 98, followed by a trailing null character would have been transferred to *buffer* (even though the edit control would show 9876). We do not need the dialog box any longer after this, hence the call to *EndDialog*. The call to *sscanf* tries to convert the contents of this character array to a value of type *double*. If this attempt succeeds, *sprintf* fills array *buffer* with the text to be displayed. Then the function *SetWindowText* is used to display this text in the title bar of the main window. Instead, the text *Incorrect input* is displayed if the user has entered a nonnumeric character at the beginning. The current version of the program will accept a numeric constant if this is *followed* by a nonnumeric character. For example, we have $x = 123$ if the user enters 123*ABC*.

Considering that program INP does little more than reading a numeric value and computing its square, you may be amazed by its complexity, compared with a conventional C program not running under Windows. However, we should bear in mind that programming a user interface comparable with INP would be very complicated in such a conventional C program. Note also that we had only one edit control, used for the variable x, in our example. It would be very simple to add some more, say, for y and for z. If we did, the user would be able to use Tab or Shift+Tab to switch between x, y, z and the button. In this way the data for the dialog box can be entered in any order. Before 'pressing' the OK button, the user can also change any data just entered. These are very convenient facilities, which do not require any additional programming effort.

We must add information about the resource script file in the make file. Such files, for both Microsoft C++ and Borland C++, are listed below:

File INP.MAK:

```
# INP.MAK; usage (with Microsoft C++): nmake -f inp.mak
inp.exe: inp.obj gen.def inp.res
        link /nod inp, inp, nul, libw+mlibcew, gen.def
        rc inp.res
inp.res: inp.rc inp.h
        rc -r inp.rc
inp.obj: inp.c inp.h
        cl -c -AM -G2sw -Ow -W3 -Zp -Tp inp.c
# File GEN.DEF can be found in Section 1.2
```

Our resource script file INP.RC is translated into the binary file INP.RES by means of

```
rc -r inp.rc
```

This has to be done only if either there is no INP.RES file or there is one that is older than at least one of the files INP.RC and INP.H, hence the line that immediately precedes this command. We can then add the resources to the linked file (INP.EXE) by executing the command

```
rc inp.res
```

which you can also find in the above make file.

File INPB.MAK:

```
# INPB.MAK: usage (with Borland C++): make -f inpb.mak
inp.exe: inp.obj gen.def inp.res
        tlink /n /Tw /L\borlandc\lib cOwm inp, inp, nul,\
           import mathwm cwm, gen.def
        rc inp.res
inp.res: inp.rc inp.h
        rc -r inp.rc
inp.obj: inp.c inp.h
        bcc -c -mm -w-par -P -2 -W inp.c
# File GEN.DEF can be found in Section 1.2
```

3.4 MFC Solution

Program INPMFC, based on C++ and the MFC, is equivalent to program INP, discussed in the previous section. It is much shorter, but it is not exactly a simple program. A rather tricky point is that we must use the symbolic constant *IDOK*, defined as 1 in the header file WINDOWS.H. Consequently, we must not also define *ID_INPUT* as 1. (If we do, clicking the OK button seems to have no effect, and it may take much time to find the cause of the trouble, as I experienced myself.) Although it may seem strange to use the value of *ID_INPUT* shown in the file INPMFC.H below, this value is at least different from *IDOK*.

File INPMFC.RC:

```
// INPMFC.RC:
#include <windows.h>
#include "inpmfc.h"

X_INPUT DIALOG 20, 20, 200, 60
STYLE DS_MODALFRAME | WS_SYSMENU
CAPTION "Enter a real number x:"
{   EDITTEXT ID_INPUT, 5, 10, 50, 12
    DEFPUSHBUTTON "OK", IDOK, 95, 30, 30, 15, WS_GROUP
}
```

File INPMFC.H:

```
// INPMFC.H:
#define ID_INPUT 1234

class CApp: public CWinApp
{   public:
    BOOL InitInstance();
};

class CMyWindow: public CFrameWnd
{   public:
    CMyWindow();
    afx_msg void OnLButtonDown(UINT nFlags, CPoint point);
    DECLARE_MESSAGE_MAP()
};

class CInput: public CDialog
{   public:
    char buffer[80];
    CInput(CWnd *pParentWnd): CDialog("X_INPUT", pParentWnd){}
    afx_msg void OnOK();
};
```

File INPMFC.CPP:

```cpp
// INPMFC.CPP: When the left mouse button is pressed, the user
//             is asked to enter a real number x.
//             The value of x * x is then displayed.

#include <afxwin.h>
#include <stdio.h>
#include "inpmfc.h"

BOOL CApp::InitInstance()
{   m_pMainWnd = new CMyWindow();
    m_pMainWnd->ShowWindow(m_nCmdShow);
    m_pMainWnd->UpdateWindow();
    return TRUE;
}

CApp App;

CMyWindow::CMyWindow()
{   int xScreen = GetSystemMetrics(SM_CXSCREEN),
        yScreen = GetSystemMetrics(SM_CYSCREEN);
    RECT rect = {0, 0, xScreen, yScreen};
    Create(NULL, "Press left mouse button",
    WS_OVERLAPPEDWINDOW, rect, NULL);
}

BEGIN_MESSAGE_MAP(CMyWindow, CFrameWnd)
    ON_WM_LBUTTONDOWN()
END_MESSAGE_MAP()

void CMyWindow::OnLButtonDown(UINT nFlags, CPoint point)
{   double x;
    CInput input(this);
    input.DoModal();

    if (sscanf(input.buffer, "%lf", &x) == 1)
    {   sprintf(input.buffer,
            "x = %-12g    x * x = %-12g",
            x, x * x);
        SetWindowText(input.buffer);
    } else SetWindowText("Incorrect input");
}

void CInput::OnOK()
{   GetDlgItemText(ID_INPUT, buffer, 25);
    EndDialog(IDOK);
}
```

File INPMFC.MAK:

```
# INPMFC.MAK; usage (with Microsoft C++): nmake -f inpmfc.mak
inpmfc.exe: inpmfc.obj gen.def inpmfc.res
        link /nod inpmfc, inpmfc, nul,\
           mafxcw+libw+mlibcew+commdlg+shell, gen.def
        rc inpmfc.res
inpmfc.res: inpmfc.rc inpmfc.h
        rc -r inpmfc.rc
inpmfc.obj: inpmfc.cpp inpmfc.h
        cl -c -AM -G2sw -Ow -W3 -Zp inpmfc.cpp
# File GEN.DEF can be found in Section 1.2
```

Note the use of *IDOK* (defined in WINDOWS.H) in the file INPMFC.RC. This identifier is associated with the function *OnOK*. Since there is a virtual function *OnOK* of the Foundation class *CDialog*, *OnOK* is another name which we must not replace by a name of our own. You can find *CDialog* in Figure B2 (in Appendix B). We use it as a base class for our own class *CInput*, as shown both by file INPMFC.H and in Figure 3.2.

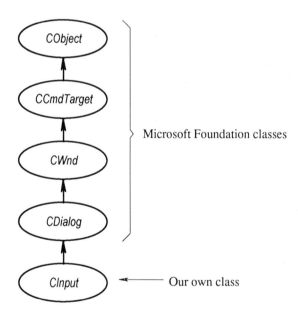

Figure 3.2. Derivation of CInput

Any *CInput* object is also a *CDialog* object; any *CDialog* object is also a *CWnd* object, and so on. Incidentally, you may also find class *CModalDialog* in older MFC programs. This class name is still accepted, but it no longer occurs in the class hierarchy of the new Foundation classes that come with Visual C++. If we like, we can simply replace *CModalDialog* with *CDialog* in our programs.

We override the default function *OnOK* (which is a member of class *CDialog*) to copy the contents of the edit control to character array *buffer*. This could have been a global array, but we prefer to include this object in the class *CInput*.

Most of the work is done by the two lines

```
CInput input(this);
input.DoModal();
```

in function *CMyWindow::OnLButtonDown*. First object *input* of type *CInput* is created. The actual creation of the dialog box is then done by function *DoModal*, which is also a member function of the base class *CDialog*. This function handles all interaction with the user while the dialog box is active. When the user clicks the OK button, function *OnOK* is called. The default function *OnOK* simply closes the dialog box by calling *EndDialog*, while our own version also calls *GetDlgItemText* to fill array *input.buffer* with the data entered by the user. Back in function *OnLButtonDown*, we use this array to convert its contents to the numeric variable *x*, and to display the values of both *x* and *x * x* in the title bar of the main window.

The functions *GetDlgItemText* and *EndDialog* are members of the base classes *CWnd* and *CDialog*, respectively. The Microsoft Foundation classes and their member functions are listed in the *Class Libraries Reference* in alphabetical order of the classes. If we do not know to which class a given function (such as *GetDlgItemText*) belongs, the only reasonable way to find it in this reference manual (consisting of more than 1000 pages) is by consulting its Index.

3.5 OWL Solution

ObjectWindows offers a special facility to solve our problem with less work than we have seen so far. This is based on a given resource script file, stored in a standard include directory. If we want to use this in the simplest possible way, we must not be very particular about the form of the dialog box. After all, this form is defined in the given resource script file.

Let us first have a look at all the files we need. Again, we use a header file for class declarations and symbolic constants.

File INPOWL.RC:

```
// INPOWL.RC:

#include <windows.h>
#include <owlrc.h>

#include "inputdia.dlg"
```

File INPOWL.H:

```
// INPOWL.H:
class TMyWindow : public TWindow
{ public:
   TMyWindow(PTWindowsObject AParent, LPSTR ATitle)
      : TWindow(AParent, ATitle){}
   virtual void WMLButtonDown(RTMessage Msg)
      = [WM_FIRST + WM_LBUTTONDOWN];
};

class TApp : public TApplication
{ public:
   TApp(LPSTR AName, HINSTANCE hInstance, HINSTANCE hPrevInstance,
      LPSTR lpCmdLine, int nCmdShow)
      : TApplication(AName, hInstance, hPrevInstance,
                     lpCmdLine, nCmdShow) {}
   virtual void InitMainWindow();
};
```

File INPOWL.CPP:

```
// INPOWL.CPP: When the left mouse button is pressed, the user
//             is asked to enter a real number x.
//             The value of x * x is then displayed.
#define WIN31
#include <stdio.h>
#include <stdlib.h>
#include <owl.h>
#include <inputdia.h>
#include "inpowl.h"
void TMyWindow::WMLButtonDown(RTMessage)
{  double x;
   char buffer[80]="";
   TInputDialog *p=
      new TInputDialog(this, "Enter a real number x:",
         "(to compute x * x)", buffer, sizeof(buffer));
   if (GetApplication()->ExecDialog(p) == IDOK)
   {  if (sscanf(buffer, "%lf", &x) == 1)
      {  sprintf(buffer, "x = %-12g   x * x = %-12g", x, x * x);
         SetWindowText(HWindow, buffer);
      } else SetWindowText(HWindow, "Incorrect input");
   }
}

void TApp::InitMainWindow()
{  TWindow *pWin;
   MainWindow = pWin = new TMyWindow(NULL, Name);
   pWin->Attr.X = 0;
```

```
    pWin->Attr.Y = 0;
    pWin->Attr.W = GetSystemMetrics(SM_CXSCREEN);
    pWin->Attr.H = GetSystemMetrics(SM_CYSCREEN);
}


int PASCAL WinMain(HINSTANCE hInstance, HINSTANCE hPrevInstance,
    LPSTR lpCmdLine, int nCmdShow)
{  TApp App("Press left mouse button", hInstance, hPrevInstance,
                lpCmdLine, nCmdShow);
    App.Run();
    return App.Status;
}
```

File INPOWL.MAK:

```
# INPOWL.MAK; usage (with Borland C++): make -f inpowl.mak
inpowl.exe: inpowl.obj inpowl.res
     bcc -mm -WE -L\borlandc\owl\lib;\borlandc\classlib\lib \
        inpowl.obj owlwm.lib tclassm.lib
     rc inpowl.res
inpowl.res: inpowl.rc
     rc -r -i\borlandc\owl\include inpowl.rc
inpowl.obj: inpowl.cpp inpowl.h
     bcc -c -mm -WE \
        -I\borlandc\owl\include;\borlandc\classlib\include \
        inpowl.cpp
```

The following program fragment, occurring in function *WMLButtonDown*, deserves our attention:

```
TInputDialog *p=
    new TInputDialog(this, "Enter a real number x:",
        "(to compute x * x)", buffer, sizeof(buffer));
if (GetApplication()->ExecDialog(p) == IDOK)
```

Apart from class *TInputDialog*, occurring both in the above program fragment and in Figure 3.3, this fragment is also based on some classes whose names do not occur in it. Function *GetApplication* is a (public) member of class *TWindowsObject* and therefore also a member of our windows class *TMyWindow*, so it is possible to call this function in a *TMyWindows* member function, as we are doing here. *GetApplication* returns a pointer to a *TApplication* object, and *ExecDialog* is a member of *TModule* (from which *TApplication* is derived). This partly explains the function call *GetApplication( )–>ExecDialog(p)*, where *p* supplies this function with the *TInputDialog* object we have just created by using the *new* operator followed by a call to a constructor.

Besides text for the title bar, we can also supply this constructor with some text to be displayed in the client rectangle of the dialog box, just above the 'edit control' in which the value of *x* is to be entered.

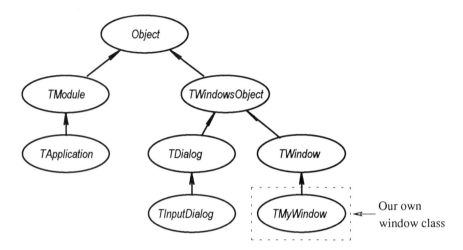

*Figure 3.3. Class **TMyWindow** and OWL classes*

The resulting dialog box is shown in Figure 3.4. If we do not want this additional text, such as

```
(to compute x * x)
```

in our example, we can simply replace the string containing this text with the empty string "".

After creating the dialog box, we have to examine whether the user has 'pressed' the OK button. We therefore test whether the *ExecDialog* function returns *IDOK* in the last line of the above program fragment.

The resource script file INPOWL.RC at the beginning of this section does not directly show the structure of the dialog box. Note, however, the following line in this file:

```
#include "inputdia.dlg"
```

As we know, this means that the contents file INPUTDIA.DLG logically replaces this *#include* line. With normal installation of Borland C++ 3.1, the full path name of this file is:

```
\borlandc\owl\include\inputdia.dlg
```

You can look at this file to see why the dialog box of Figure 3.4 differs from the one shown in Figure 3.1. If we want it changed, we should copy this file to our current directory and modify this copy rather than the original file. This explains why we have written *"inputdia.dlg"* rather than *<inputdia.dlg>* in the above *#include* line. Remember, using double quotes here means that the current directory is searched first for this include file. If it cannot be found there, the standard include directories are searched. On the other hand, if we do not want the current directory to be searched because there is no such include file in it, we might as well use the < > brackets in the above include line.

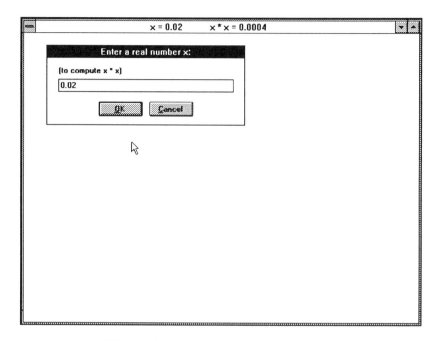

Figure 3.4. Demonstration of program INPOWL

3.6 Questions

3.1   Give two examples of 'controls'.

3.2   Which units are used for x and y in resource script files?

3.3   What are the *EDITTEXT* and *DEFPUSHBUTTON* statements for in resource script files?

3.4   What is function *MakeProcInstance* for, and which function should be used in connection with it?

3.5   How do we refer to the OK button in our program?

3.6   In the resource script files shown in Sections 3.3 and 3.4, we used the name *X_INPUT* in the *DIALOG* statements. Where does this name occur in our programs?

4

Menus

4.1 Problem Definition

In this chapter we will see how our program can interact with the user by means of menus. There will be a horizontal menu bar just below the title bar at the top of our main window. This menu bar displays the main menu, consisting of several submenus. The word *menu* is used both for the main menu and for each of its submenus. For example, the main menu of a typical Windows application shows the submenus *File*, *Edit* and *Help*. It is not unusual to speak in this case of a File menu, an Edit menu and a Help menu (although it might be argued that these are actually submenus). It is normally clear from the context whether the term *menu* refers to the main menu or to one of its submenus.

To keep the problem of this chapter very simple, we will instead use two (sub)menus, *Animals* and *Plants*. Selecting one of these menus, either by clicking on its name using the mouse or by entering the first letter of its name while holding the Alt-key down, causes the menu in question to be opened, that is, the menu itself appears; it consists of *menu items*, also called *commands*. Selecting one of these menu items then initiates some action. In the program we will be discussing, each menu will consist of two menu items, as listed below:

Menus	*Menu items*	*Examples*
Animals	Mammals	Elephant, horse, dog
	Birds	Sparrow, pigeon, swallow
Plants	Trees	Oak, maple, pine
	Flowers	Rose, sunflower, daisy

Each menu item, when selected, will produce a message box that shows the examples mentioned above. For example, after selecting the *Plants* menu, we will be able to choose *Trees* or *Flowers*, as Figure 4.1 illustrates. (The size of this window was reduced by dragging one of its corners.) When we select *Trees*, a message box with the text *oak, maple, pine* appears, as shown in Figure 4.2.

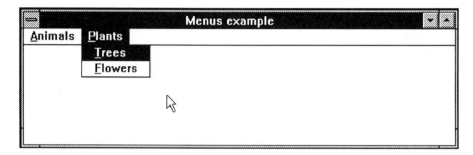

Figure 4.1.The Plants menu

Figure 4.2. Message box appearing after selecting Trees

4.2 General Aspects

Menus are normally not specified in C or in C++ programs themselves but in resource script files. Here is a resource script file that we can use for our example:

File MENUS.RC:

```
// MENUS.RC:

#include <windows.h>
#include "menus.h"
```

```
SampleMenu MENU
BEGIN
   POPUP "&Animals"
   BEGIN
      MENUITEM "&Mammals", IDM_MAMMALS
      MENUITEM "&Birds", IDM_BIRDS
   END
   POPUP "&Plants"
   BEGIN
      MENUITEM "&Trees", IDM_TREES
      MENUITEM "&Flowers", IDM_FLOWERS
   END
END
```

Each ampersand causes the letter that follows it to be underlined when it is displayed on the screen. Note that there are only symbolic constants (of the form *IDM_...*) for the menu items (*Mammals*, *Birds*, *Trees* and *Flowers*), not for the menus (*Animals* and *Plants*) themselves.

Make files

If you want to use make files in this chapter, you can use the corresponding make files of Chapter 3, after replacing all occurrences of *inp* with *menus*.

More dynamic methods

We will restrict ourselves to one main menu, which is available from the start of the program until its end. It is also possible to generate or change menus while the program is running, by using the API functions *LoadMenu*, *LoadMenuIndirect*, *SetMenu* and *DrawMenuBar*.

4.3 C Solution

A menu selected by the user automatically pops up according to what we specify in the resource script file. Thanks to the statement

```
TranslateMessage(&msg);
```

in the message loop in function *WinMain*, the user can select a menu not only by using the mouse but also by pressing the Alt-key in combination with the underlined character. For example, the user can enter Alt+P to select *Plants* because we specified

```
POPUP "&Plants"
```

in the resource script file.

The Alt-key is not used for the menu items, which are selected either by using the mouse or by simply typing the indicated letter. For example, when the *Animals* menu shows we can type *B* (or *b*) to select *Birds* because the *B* is preceded by & in the resource script file. The menu items are processed in the window procedure. Selecting a menu item, say, *Trees*, causes function *WndProc* to be called with parameter values *message* = *WM_COMMAND* and *wParam* = *IDM_TREES*. Recall that we have used the line

```
MENUITEM "&Birds", IDM_BIRDS
```

in the resource script file to indicate that *IDM_BIRDS* is the symbolic constant that corresponds to menu item *Birds*. This makes menu items easy to deal with. There is one other thing we must not forget: we use the statement

```
wndclass.lpszMenuName = "SampleMenu";
```

in the *WinMain* function, where *SampleMenu* is the menu name used in the resource script file. This file, MENUS.RC, was listed in Section 4.2 so that we could discuss it there, but it actually belongs to the following set of files:

File MENUS.H:

```
// MENUS.H:

#define IDM_MAMMALS 1001
#define IDM_BIRDS 1002
#define IDM_TREES 1003
#define IDM_FLOWERS 1004

long FAR PASCAL _export WndProc(HWND hWnd, UINT message,
     WPARAM wParam, LPARAM lParam);
int PASCAL WinMain(HANDLE hInstance, HANDLE hPrevInstance,
    LPSTR lpCmdLine, int nCmdShow);
```

File MENUS.C:

```
// MENUS.C: Demonstrates a menu

#include <windows.h>
#include "menus.h"

int PASCAL WinMain(HANDLE hInstance, HANDLE hPrevInstance,
    LPSTR lpCmdLine, int nCmdShow)
{   char szAppName[]="menus";
    WNDCLASS wndclass;
    HWND hWnd;
    MSG msg;
    int xScreen = GetSystemMetrics(SM_CXSCREEN),
        yScreen = GetSystemMetrics(SM_CYSCREEN);
```

```
    if (!hPrevInstance)
    {   wndclass.style = CS_HREDRAW | CS_VREDRAW;
        wndclass.lpfnWndProc = WndProc;
        wndclass.cbClsExtra = 0;
        wndclass.cbWndExtra = 0;
        wndclass.hInstance = hInstance;
        wndclass.hIcon = LoadIcon(NULL, IDI_APPLICATION);
        wndclass.hCursor = LoadCursor(NULL, IDC_ARROW);
        wndclass.hbrBackground = GetStockObject(WHITE_BRUSH);
        wndclass.lpszMenuName = "SampleMenu";
            // Reference to menu name in file MENU.RC
        wndclass.lpszClassName = szAppName;
            // Name used in call to CreateWindow.
        if (!RegisterClass(&wndclass)) return FALSE;
    }
    hWnd = CreateWindow(
        szAppName,
        "Menus example",               // Text for window title bar.
        WS_OVERLAPPEDWINDOW,           // Window style.
        0,                             // Initial x position
        0,                             // Initial y position.
        xScreen,                       // Width.
        yScreen,                       // Height.
        NULL,                          // Parent window handle.
        NULL,                          // Window menu handle.
        hInstance,                     // Program instance handle.
        NULL                           // Create parameters.
    );
    ShowWindow(hWnd, nCmdShow);
    UpdateWindow(hWnd);
    while (GetMessage(&msg, NULL, 0, 0))
    {   TranslateMessage(&msg);     // Translates virtual key codes
        DispatchMessage(&msg);      // Dispatches message to window
    }
    return msg.wParam;      // Returns the value from PostQuitMessage
}

long FAR PASCAL _export WndProc(HWND hWnd, UINT message,
        WPARAM wParam, LPARAM lParam)
{   switch (message)
    {
    case WM_COMMAND:
        if (wParam == IDM_MAMMALS)
            MessageBox(hWnd, "elephant, horse, dog", "Examples:", MB_OK);
        else if (wParam == IDM_BIRDS)
            MessageBox(hWnd, "sparrow, pigeon, swallow", "Examples:",
                MB_OK);
        else if (wParam == IDM_TREES)
            MessageBox(hWnd, "oak, maple, pine", "Examples:", MB_OK);
```

```
            else if (wParam == IDM_FLOWERS)
               MessageBox(hWnd, "rose, sunflower, daisy", "Examples:",
                   MB_OK);
            break;
        case WM_DESTROY:
               PostQuitMessage(0); break;
        default:
               return DefWindowProc(hWnd, message, wParam, lParam);
        }
        return 0L;
    }
```

It is curious that, as far as programming is concerned, providing the user with a menu is considerably simpler than reading a number, as discussed in the previous chapter.

4.4 MFC Solution

Dealing with menus in a C++ program using the MFC is also fairly easy. Here the menu name *SampleMenu* is specified, again in the form of a string, as the sixth argument of function *Create* in the *CMyWindow* constructor. For each of the four menu items, we supply a member function of the *CMyWindow* class. There must also be a message map, to specify, for example, that identifier *IDM_BIRDS* is associated with function *OnBirds*. We express this correspondence in the message map as

```
  ON_COMMAND(IDM_BIRDS, OnBirds)
```

As usual, we also have to include the line

```
  DECLARE_MESSAGE_MAP()
```

in the declaration of class *CMyWindow*. Except for the name of our header file, the resource script file is identical with the one shown in Section 4.2:

File MENUSMFC.RC:

```
  // MENUSMFC.RC:
  #include <windows.h>
  #include "menusmfc.h"

  SampleMenu MENU
  BEGIN
     POPUP "&Animals"
     BEGIN
        MENUITEM "&Mammals", IDM_MAMMALS
        MENUITEM "&Birds", IDM_BIRDS
     END
```

```
    POPUP "&Plants"
    BEGIN
        MENUITEM "&Trees", IDM_TREES
        MENUITEM "&Flowers", IDM_FLOWERS
    END
END
```

File MENUSMFC.H:

```
// MENUSMFC.H

#define IDM_MAMMALS 1001
#define IDM_BIRDS 1002
#define IDM_TREES 1003
#define IDM_FLOWERS 1004

class CApp: public CWinApp
{ public:
    BOOL InitInstance();
};

class CMyWindow: public CFrameWnd
{ public:
    CMyWindow();
    afx_msg void OnMammals();
    afx_msg void OnBirds();
    afx_msg void OnTrees();
    afx_msg void OnFlowers();
    DECLARE_MESSAGE_MAP()
};
```

File MENUSMFC.CPP:

```
// MENUSMFC.CPP: Demonstrates a menu.

#include <afxwin.h>
#include <stdio.h>
#include "menusmfc.h"

BOOL CApp::InitInstance()
{   m_pMainWnd = new CMyWindow();
    m_pMainWnd->ShowWindow(m_nCmdShow);
    m_pMainWnd->UpdateWindow();
    return TRUE;
}

CApp App;
```

```
CMyWindow::CMyWindow()
{  int xScreen = GetSystemMetrics(SM_CXSCREEN),
       yScreen = GetSystemMetrics(SM_CYSCREEN);
   RECT rect = {0, 0, xScreen, yScreen};
   Create(NULL, "Menus example", WS_OVERLAPPEDWINDOW,
      rect, NULL, "SampleMenu");
}

BEGIN_MESSAGE_MAP(CMyWindow, CFrameWnd)
   ON_COMMAND(IDM_MAMMALS, OnMammals)
   ON_COMMAND(IDM_BIRDS, OnBirds)
   ON_COMMAND(IDM_TREES, OnTrees)
   ON_COMMAND(IDM_FLOWERS, OnFlowers)
END_MESSAGE_MAP()

void CMyWindow::OnMammals()
{  MessageBox("elephant, horse, dog", "Examples:", MB_OK);
}

void CMyWindow::OnBirds()
{  MessageBox("sparrow, pigeon, swallow", "Examples:", MB_OK);
}

void CMyWindow::OnTrees()
{  MessageBox("oak, maple, pine", "Examples:", MB_OK);
}

void CMyWindow::OnFlowers()
{  MessageBox("rose, sunflower, daisy", "Examples:", MB_OK);
}
```

4.5 OWL Solution

We can use the following files to solve our problem using the Borland ObjectWindows library:

File MENUSOWL.RC:

```
// MENUSOWL.RC:
#include <windows.h>
#include "menusowl.h"
SampleMenu MENU
BEGIN
   POPUP "&Animals"
   BEGIN
      MENUITEM "&Mammals", IDM_MAMMALS
      MENUITEM "&Birds", IDM_BIRDS
   END
```

```
      POPUP "&Plants"
      BEGIN
         MENUITEM "&Trees", IDM_TREES
         MENUITEM "&Flowers", IDM_FLOWERS
      END
END
```

File MENUSOWL.H:

```
// MENUSOWL.H:
#define IDM_MAMMALS 1001
#define IDM_BIRDS 1002
#define IDM_TREES 1003
#define IDM_FLOWERS 1004

class TApp: public TApplication
{  public:
   TApp(LPSTR Name, HANDLE hInstance, HANDLE hPrevInstance,
        LPSTR lpCmdLine, int nCmdShow)
      : TApplication(Name, hInstance, hPrevInstance, lpCmdLine,
                     nCmdShow){}
   virtual void InitMainWindow();
};

class TMyWindow: public TWindow
{  public:
   TMyWindow(PTWindowsObject AParent, LPSTR ATitle);
   void OnMammals(RTMessage Msg) = [CM_FIRST + IDM_MAMMALS];
   void OnBirds(RTMessage Msg) = [CM_FIRST + IDM_BIRDS];
   void OnTrees(RTMessage Msg) = [CM_FIRST + IDM_TREES];
   void OnFlowers(RTMessage Msg) = [CM_FIRST + IDM_FLOWERS];
};
```

File MENUSOWL.CPP:

```
// MENUSOWL.CPP: Menus, programmed with C++/OWL.
#define WIN31
#include <owl.h>
#include "menusowl.h"

void TApp::InitMainWindow()
{  TWindow *pWin;
   MainWindow = pWin = new TMyWindow(NULL, Name);
   pWin->Attr.X = 0;
   pWin->Attr.Y = 0;
   pWin->Attr.W = GetSystemMetrics(SM_CXSCREEN);
   pWin->Attr.H = GetSystemMetrics(SM_CYSCREEN);
}
```

```
TMyWindow::TMyWindow(PTWindowsObject AParent, LPSTR ATitle)
    : TWindow(AParent, ATitle)
{  AssignMenu("SampleMenu");
}

void TMyWindow::OnMammals(RTMessage)
{  MessageBox(HWindow, "elephant, horse, dog", "Examples:", MB_OK);
}

void TMyWindow::OnBirds(RTMessage)
{  MessageBox(HWindow, "sparrow, pigeon, swallow", "Examples:",
      MB_OK);
}

void TMyWindow::OnTrees(RTMessage)
{  MessageBox(HWindow, "oak, maple, pine", "Examples:", MB_OK);
}

void TMyWindow::OnFlowers(RTMessage)
{  MessageBox(HWindow, "rose, sunflower, daisy", "Examples:", MB_OK);
}

int PASCAL WinMain(HANDLE hInstance, HANDLE hPrevInstance,
    LPSTR lpCmdLine, int nCmdShow)
{  TApp App("Menus example",
    hInstance, hPrevInstance, lpCmdLine, nCmdShow);
    App.Run();
    return App.Status;
}
```

Note that we use the constant *CM_FIRST* in lines such as

```
void OnFlowers(RTMessage Msg) = [CM_FIRST + IDM_FLOWERS];
```

occurring in the header file MENUSOWL.H, while we wrote (and discussed) *WM_FIRST* in Section 3.5. This latter constant applies to normal Windows messages, but we replace it with *CM_FIRST* for menu commands.

As discussed in Section 2.5, the syntax of the above line is non-standard C++, specific to Borland.

4.6 Questions

4.1   Where in our programs do we use the identifiers, such as *IDM_BIRDS*, that correspond with menu items?

4.2   Where in our programs do we refer to the whole menu?

4.3   When programming with OWL, where do we use *CM_FIRST* and where *WM_FIRST*?

5

Elementary Graphics

5.1 Problem Definition

This chapter is about producing pictures by means of line drawing and area filling. We will draw a red right-angled triangle ABC, with the right angle A at the bottom left. To the right of triangle ABC, we will display triangle DEF, congruent with triangle ABC but different in appearance: the whole triangle DEF, including its interior, will be blue. Thus, triangle DEF will not be *drawn* in blue but rather be *filled* with that color. The horizontal and the vertical sides of the triangles will have equal lengths; in other words, we will have two isosceles, right-angled triangles. Besides a red triangle, we will also draw a red *rectangle* that is almost as large as the client rectangle of the window we are using. Although not in colors, Figure 5.1 shows the two triangles and the large rectangle.

5.2 General Aspects

Most new functions to be used in this chapter are based on the notion of a *device context*, and they are said to belong to the *Graphics Device Interface* (GDI). As in conventional art work, the terms *pen* and *brush* are used for drawing and filling, respectively. We need a *red pen* to draw both triangle ABC and the large rectangle, and a *blue brush* to fill triangle DEF. Since a triangle is a special case of a polygon, we will use the function *Polygon* for both triangles. When drawing triangle ABC, we will use what is called a 'null brush' to prevent the interior of the triangle being filled. Analogously, we will use a 'null pen' for triangle DEF, to prevent the triangle sides being drawn. (Alternatively, we could use a blue pen in this case.) This special pen and brush are obtained by using the identifiers *NULL_PEN* and *NULL_BRUSH* as arguments in calls to the function *GetStockObject*. As far as pens and brushes are concerned, there are the following other possible arguments for this function:

BLACK_PEN, WHITE_PEN, BLACK_BRUSH, WHITE_BRUSH,
GRAY_BRUSH, DKGRAY_BRUSH, LTGRAY_BRUSH, HOLLOW_BRUSH

Recall that we have already used the identifier *WHITE_BRUSH* several times to specify the background color in *WinMain* functions.

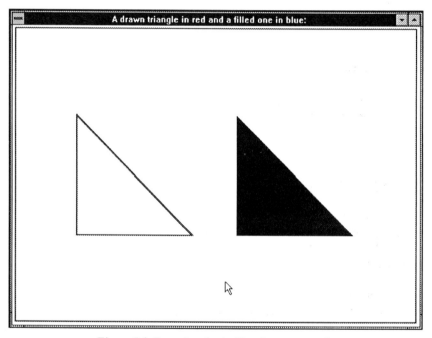

Figure 5.1. *Two triangles inside a large rectangle*

Coordinate systems

So far, we have used a coordinate system with the origin in the top left corner of the client rectangle, with a positive *y*-axis pointing downward. Our coordinates were expressed in so-called *device units*, that is, in pixels. The coordinates of this system are referred to as *device coordinates*. It depends on the graphics device whether or not one such unit on the *x*-axis is equal to one on the *y*-axis. In graphics programming it is normally more convenient to use a *logical* coordinate system, with a *y*-axis pointing upward. Windows has facilities for using such logical coordinates. We will not discuss all possible coordinate systems, each based on a *mapping mode*, but rather restrict ourselves to one that in many applications is very pleasant to work with. The default mapping mode, used so far, is identified by the constant *MM_TEXT*. With this mapping mode, logical coordinates and device coordinates are identical. Other possible mapping modes are *MM_ISOTROPIC* (to be used here), *MM_ANISOTROPIC* (to be used in Chapter 13), *MM_HIMETRIC*, *MM_LOMETRIC*, *MM_HIENGLISH*, *MM_LOENGLISH*, *MM_TWIPS*.

To define a logical coordinate system, we will take four steps, and base our discussion on traditional C Windows programming. Replacing the program text discussed here with that required for the MFC or the OWL will be straightforward, as we will see in Sections 5.4 and 5.5.

Step 1: Select the mapping mode

To use logical coordinates, we begin by selecting a mapping mode. For a given device context with handle *hDC*, we select the *isotropic* mapping mode by means of the following function call:

```
SetMapMode(hDC, MM_ISOTROPIC);
```

The word *isotropic* indicates that a unit of length measured horizontally will be equal to one measured vertically. In other words, a square remains a square if the user changes the window size. (If, instead, we want horizontal and vertical dimensions of rectangles to change independently, in the same ratio as those of the client rectangle of the window, the second argument in the above call should be *MM_ANISOTROPIC*. We will see in Chapter 13 that this can also be useful.)

Step 2: Define the origin of the logical coordinate system

For example, we will choose the center of the client rectangle as the origin (0, 0) of the logical coordinate system. Suppose we have obtained the width w and height h of the client area as follows:

```
GetClientRect(hWnd, &rect);
w = rect.right;
h = rect.bottom;
```

This width and height are in fact numbers of pixels. Expressed in device coordinates, (0, 0) is the upper-left and (w, h) the lower-right corner of the client rectangle. Point ($w/2$, $h/2$) is therefore the center of the screen. We write

```
SetViewportOrg(hDC, w/2, h/2);
```

to specify that this center is to be the origin of the logical coordinate system. The terms *viewport* and *window* are used in connection with device coordinates and logical coordinates, respectively. Apparently, function *SetViewportOrg* defines the origin of the window in terms of viewport coordinates. If we had wanted the origin ($x = y = 0$) of the window to be in the left-bottom corner, that is, corresponding with viewport coordinates $x = 0$ and $y = h$, we would instead have written

```
SetViewportOrg(hDC, 0, h);
```

Step 3: Specify the ratio of the extents for the window and the viewport

To compute device coordinates from logical coordinates, Windows must also be told how much a device x-coordinate is to increase when the corresponding logical x-coordinate increases by 1, and the same must be done for the y-coordinates. Actually, this is done by using two large integers, rather than by a floating-point ratio. For example, we can use the following two function calls:

```
SetWindowExt(hDC, 2000, 2000);
SetViewportExt(hDC, w, -h);
```

The second arguments in these function calls indicate that, in principle, the logical x-coordinate is to increase by 2000 when the device x-coordinate increases by w.

The final arguments in these calls refer to the vertical axes: in principle, the logical y-coordinate is to increase by 2000 when the device y-coordinate increases by $-h$. This minus sign indicates that the device and the logical y-axes have opposite directions.

The above requirements about a ratio both for x and for y may be in contradiction with the isotropic character of the mapping mode. For example, VGA has square pixels, which implies that equal x- and y- device extents of 2000 would be possible only if the logical x-extent w were equal to the logical y-extent h. In our example, the smaller of the values $w/2000$ and $h/2000$ will therefore be used as a scale factor when device coordinates are computed from the corresponding logical coordinates. Since we have chosen the logical origin in the center, it will be possible for the logical coordinates x and y to range from -1000 to $+1000$. In the case of a 'landscape' client rectangle (with $w > h$), the value of x may exceed that range; analogously, y may be less than -1000 or greater than $+1000$ in the case of a 'portrait' client rectangle (with $w < h$). The main thing to remember, however, is that, with the above function calls, we can always use the interval from -1000 to $+1000$, regardless of the current dimensions of the client rectangle. Remember that this interval is only an example, so we can use values other than -1000 and $+1000$ if we like. Being also device independent, logical coordinates are clearly more convenient than device coordinates.

Step 4 (Optional): Find the largest possible logical ranges for both x and y

The above three steps provide us with enough information to produce the two triangles in our example. However, we also want to draw a very large rectangle, for which we must know the largest possible ranges for the logical coordinates x and y. For example, if we have a 'landscape' client rectangle, we are interested in the logical x range (with a lower limit less than -1000 and an upper limit greater than $+1000$ in our example). Using *rect* obtained by the above call to *GetClientRect* (see Step 2), that is, with *rect.left* = 0, *rect.right* = w, *rect.top* = 0, *rect.bottom* = h, we can replace these device coordinates in *rect* with the corresponding logical coordinates by means of the following call

```
DPtoLP(hDC, (LPPOINT) &rect, 2);
```

Type name *LPPOINT* is used for 'long pointers' to objects of type *POINT*. Such an object is a structure with integer *x* and *y* members. Both *POINT* and *LPPOINT* are declared in WINDOWS.H. Function *DPtoLP* converts the device coordinates of an array of *POINT* objects to the corresponding logical coordinates. Its third argument indicates how many array elements are to be converted in this way. Since the second argument is not an array here, the above call is rather tricky. It is based on the fact that the members *left*, *top*, *right*, and *bottom* of a *rect* structure are stored in that order. We can verify the correctness of this call by replacing it with the following, longer but equivalent program text, in which the second argument of *DPtoLP* is an array:

```
{   POINT point[2];
    point[0].x = rect.left; point[0].y = rect.top;
    point[1].x = rect.right; point[1].y = rect.bottom;
    DPtoLP(hDC, point, 2);
    rect.left = point[0].x; rect.top = point[0].y;
    rect.right = point[1].x; rect.bottom = point[1].y;
}
```

After the execution of either program fragment, the logical *x*-range can be found in *rect.left* and *rect.right*, and the logical *y*-range in *rect.bottom* and *rect.top* (where *rect.bottom* is less than *rect.top*).

5.3 C Solution

The complete set of files to accomplish our task using C and API functions is shown below:

File GR.H:

```
// GR.H:
long FAR PASCAL _export WndProc(HWND hWnd, UINT message,
       WPARAM wParam, LPARAM lParam);
int PASCAL WinMain(HANDLE hInstance, HANDLE hPrevInstance,
     LPSTR lpCmdLine, int nCmdShow);
```

File GR.C:

```
// GR.C: Simple graphics, programmed in C.
#include <windows.h>
#include "gr.h"

int PASCAL WinMain(HANDLE hInstance, HANDLE hPrevInstance,
     LPSTR lpCmdLine, int nCmdShow)
{   char szAppName[]="gr";
    int xScreen, yScreen;
    WNDCLASS wndclass;
```

```
      HWND hWnd;
      MSG msg;
      xScreen = GetSystemMetrics(SM_CXSCREEN);
      yScreen = GetSystemMetrics(SM_CYSCREEN);
      if (!hPrevInstance)
      {  wndclass.style = CS_HREDRAW | CS_VREDRAW;
         wndclass.lpfnWndProc = WndProc;
         wndclass.cbClsExtra = 0;
         wndclass.cbWndExtra = 0;
         wndclass.hInstance = hInstance;
         wndclass.hIcon = LoadIcon(NULL, IDI_APPLICATION);
         wndclass.hCursor = LoadCursor(NULL, IDC_ARROW);
         wndclass.hbrBackground = GetStockObject(WHITE_BRUSH);
         wndclass.lpszMenuName =  NULL;
         wndclass.lpszClassName = szAppName;
            // Name used in call to CreateWindow.
         if (!RegisterClass(&wndclass)) return FALSE;
      }
      hWnd = CreateWindow(
         szAppName,
         "A drawn triangle in red and a filled one in blue:",
                                          // Text for window title bar.
         WS_OVERLAPPEDWINDOW,             // Window style.
         0,                               // Initial x position
         0,                               // Initial y position.
         xScreen,                         // Width.
         yScreen,                         // Height.
         NULL,                            // Parent window handle.
         NULL,                            // Window menu handle.
         hInstance,                       // Program instance handle.
         NULL                             // Create parameters.
      );
      ShowWindow(hWnd, nCmdShow);
      UpdateWindow(hWnd);
      while (GetMessage(&msg, NULL, 0, 0))
      {  TranslateMessage(&msg);     // Translates virtual key codes
         DispatchMessage(&msg);      // Dispatches message to window
      }
      return msg.wParam;      // Returns the value from PostQuitMessage
}


long FAR PASCAL _export WndProc(HWND hWnd, UINT message,
        WPARAM wParam, LPARAM lParam)
{  HDC hDC;
   RECT rect;
   int w, h;
   POINT A, B, C, D, E, F, ABC[3], DEF[3];
   PAINTSTRUCT ps;
   HPEN hRedPen, hOldPen;
   HBRUSH hBlueBrush, hOldBrush;
```

```
switch (message)
{
case WM_PAINT:
   hDC = BeginPaint(hWnd, &ps);
   GetClientRect(hWnd, &rect);
   w = rect.right;
   h = rect.bottom;
   SetMapMode(hDC, MM_ISOTROPIC);
         // Horizontal and vertical units are equal

   SetViewportOrg(hDC, w/2, h/2);
   // The point with device coordinates (w/2, h/2)
   // lying in the center of the window,
   // will have logical coordinates (0, 0).

   SetWindowExt(hDC, 2000, 2000);
   SetViewportExt(hDC, w, -h);
   // Increasing device coordinate x by w means
   // increasing logical coordinate x by 2000.
   // Increasing device coordinate y by -h means
   // increasing logical coordinate y by 2000.

   /* ABC is a right-angled triangle.
      AB is a horizontal side at the bottom and AC is a
      vertical side at the left.
      Triangle DEF is congruent with triangle ABC and is
      obtained by translating ABC
      to the right.
      We will draw ABC with a red pen and fill DEF with
      a blue brush.
      All horizontal and vertical sides will have length 800.
   */
   A.x = C.x = -950; B.x = -150;
   D.x = F.x = 150; E.x = 950;
   A.y = B.y = D.y = E.y = -400;
   C.y = F.y = 400;
   ABC[0] = A; ABC[1] = B; ABC[2] = C;
   DEF[0] = D; DEF[1] = E; DEF[2] = F;

    // Red pen, pen width 10:
   hRedPen = CreatePen(PS_SOLID, 10, RGB(255, 0, 0));
   hBlueBrush = CreateSolidBrush(RGB(0, 0, 255));
   // Draw red triangle ABC:
   hOldPen = SelectObject(hDC, hRedPen);
   // Null brush to prevent triangle ABC from being filled:
   hOldBrush = SelectObject(hDC, GetStockObject(NULL_BRUSH));
   Polygon(hDC, ABC, 3);
   // Null pen prevents drawing the sides of triangle DEF:
   SelectObject(hDC, GetStockObject(NULL_PEN));
```

```
          // Fill blue triangle DEF:
          SelectObject(hDC, hBlueBrush);
          Polygon(hDC, DEF, 3);

          DPtoLP(hDC, (LPPOINT) &rect, 2);
          SelectObject(hDC, hRedPen);
          // Null brush to prevent rectangle from being filled:
          SelectObject(hDC, GetStockObject(NULL_BRUSH));
          // Draw large rectangle:
          Rectangle(hDC, rect.left + 20, rect.top - 20,
             rect.right - 20, rect.bottom + 20);
          SelectObject(hDC, hOldPen);
          SelectObject(hDC, hOldBrush);
          DeleteObject(hRedPen);
          DeleteObject(hBlueBrush);
          EndPaint(hWnd, &ps);
          break;
      case WM_DESTROY:
          PostQuitMessage(0); break;
      default:
          return DefWindowProc(hWnd, message, wParam, lParam);
      }
      return 0L;
   }
```

File GR.MAK:

```
# GR.MAK; usage (with Microsoft C++): nmake -f gr.mak
gr.exe: gr.obj gen.def
        link /nod gr, gr, nul, libw+mlibcew, gen.def
gr.obj: gr.c gr.h
        cl -c -AM -G2sw -Ow -W3 -Zp -Tp gr.c
# File GEN.DEF can be found in Section 1.2
```

File GRB.MAK:

```
# GRB.MAK; usage (with Borland C++): make -f grb.mak
gr.exe: gr.obj gen.def
        tlink /n /Tw /L\borlandc\lib cOwm gr, gr, nul,\
           import mathwm cwm, gen.def
gr.obj: gr.c gr.h
        bcc -c -mm -w-par -P -2 -W gr.c
# File GEN.DEF can be found in Section 1.2
```

Most of the work is done when Windows calls function *WndProc* with parameter value *message = WM_PAINT*. As in program OUTP.C (see Section 2.3), we use a device-context handler *hDC*, a rectangle *rect*, and a paint structure *ps*. The values placed in *rect* by *GetClientRect* form the basis to compute the coordinates of the triangle vertices A, B, C, D, E and F.

Instead of *unsigned int*, we write *HPEN* and *HBRUSH* as the types of the handles that identify two pens and two brushes:

```
HPEN hRedPen, hOldPen;
HBRUSH hBlueBrush, hOldBrush;
```

We obtain handles for a red pen and for a blue brush by calling the functions *CreatePen* and *CreateSolidBrush*, respectively:

```
hRedPen = CreatePen(PS_SOLID, 10, RGB(255, 0, 0));
hBlueBrush = CreateSolidBrush(RGB(0, 0, 255));
```

Once we have pens and brushes available, we must indicate that we want to use them. This is done by calling the function *SelectObject*, and such a call is technically referred to as

selecting an object into the device context.

Remember, we may have several pens, but at any time only one can be selected into the device context. It follows that selecting a new pen into the device context implies replacing an old one. The old pen is then said to be *deselected*, or alternatively, to be *selected out of* the device context. It is this old pen (or rather, a handle to it) that is returned by *Select-Object*. It is good practice to restore this old pen (which we did not select ourselves into the device context) when we do not use our own pens any longer. We should carefully pay attention to the following, simplified program fragment, in which indentation is used in the same way as matching delimiters are in programming languages. This fragment is also reminiscent of corresponding push and pop operations on a stack:

```
hDC = BeginPaint(hWnd, &ps);              // Obtain device-context handle
   hRedPen = CreatePen(...);                  // Create red pen
      hOldPen = SelectObject(hDC, hRedPen);   // Select red pen
      ...                                      // Use red pen
      SelectObject(hDC, hOldPen);             // Restore old pen
   DeleteObject(hRedPen);                     // Delete red pen
EndPaint(hWnd, &ps);                      // Release device context
```

For each call to *BeginPaint* there must also be a call to *EndPaint*. Also, each pen created with *CreatePen* must be deleted with *DeleteObject*. However, we must not do this while the pen is still selected into the device context. We prevent such a serious error here by selecting the red pen out of the device context, restoring the old pen at the same time. As indicated here by indentation, *BeginPaint* corresponds with *EndPaint*, *CreatePen* with *DeleteObject*, and the first call to *SelectObject* with the second.

Actually, things are slightly more complicated. Besides a red pen, we also want to use a blue brush. As you can see in program GR.C, brushes are selected into and out of the device context in the same way as pens are. We normally have several pens and brushes, of which at any time only one pen and one brush are selected into the device context. We then store the old pen handler returned by *SelectObject* only the first time a pen is selected.

Similarly, we store the old brush handler only the first time a brush is selected. Because of the complicating factors just mentioned, the above way of indenting is normally not used. However, we should have this program structure in mind whenever we are dealing with device contexts and with GDI objects, such as pens and brushes.

Besides *CreatePen* and *CreateSolidBrush*, there is also the function *GetStockObject*, which we can use to obtain a handle to a stock pen or a stock brush. This function is used in our program for a *null pen* and *null brush*, as we will see shortly. We must never apply the *DeleteObject* function to stock objects. Recall that we have also discussed function *GetStockObject* at the beginning of Section 5.2.

A color can be conveniently specified by using the *RGB* macro. This macro has three integer arguments, ranging from 0 to 255 and specifying the intensities of red, green and blue, in that order. The first argument, *PS_SOLID*, of function *CreatePen* is the pen style; other possible pen styles, not used here, are *PS_DASH*, *PS_DOT*, *PS_DASHDOT*, *PS_DASHDOTDOT*, *PS_NULL* and *PS_INSIDEFRAME*. The second argument, 10, indicates the pen width. If we want the lines to be very thin, we should use 1.

After selecting a red pen into the device context, we draw a red triangle by a call to *Polygon*, as shown by the following fragment, copied from GR.C:

```
// Red pen, pen width 10:
hRedPen = CreatePen(PS_SOLID, 10, RGB(255, 0, 0));
hBlueBrush = CreateSolidBrush(RGB(0, 0, 255));
// Draw red triangle ABC:
hOldPen = SelectObject(hDC, hRedPen);
// Null brush to prevent triangle ABC from being filled:
hOldBrush = SelectObject(hDC, GetStockObject(NULL_BRUSH));
Polygon(hDC, ABC, 3);
// Null pen prevents drawing the sides of triangle DEF:
SelectObject(hDC, GetStockObject(NULL_PEN));
// Fill blue triangle DEF:
SelectObject(hDC, hBlueBrush);
Polygon(hDC, DEF, 3);
```

Once we have several pens or brushes available, we can easily switch between them by calls to function *SelectObject*. For example, after selecting a red pen into the device context, we draw a red triangle by a call to *Polygon*. Alternatively, we could have drawn the sides of the triangle in a more elementary way as follows:

```
MoveTo(hDC, A.x, A.y); LineTo(hDC, B.x, B.y);
LineTo(hDC, C.x, C.y); LineTo(hDC, A.x, A.y);
```

In this way it would not have been necessary to select a (null) brush for triangle ABC, because the functions *MoveTo* and *LineTo* do not use a brush: if the lines formed by several calls to these functions happen to produce a polygon, that polygon is not filled. Function *Polygon*, on the other hand, both draws and fills a polygon, so that it uses both a pen and a brush. By selecting a null brush into the device context, the polygon is only drawn, not filled. Similarly, a null pen prevents the outline of a polygon to be drawn when we want to use only a brush. The polygon is given as an array of *POINT* objects, where each such object is a structure with integer *x* and *y* components. The third argument of *Polygon* denotes the number of vertices. Since a triangle is a polygon with three vertices, this argument is 3.

5.4 MFC Solution

We will now use C++ and the MFC to solve the same problem as in the previous section. Here are the files to be used:

File GRMFC.H:

```
// GRMFC.H: Test Windows programming using C++.
class CApp: public CWinApp
{  public:
     BOOL InitInstance();
};

class CMyWindow: public CFrameWnd
{  public:
     CMyWindow();
     afx_msg void OnPaint();
     DECLARE_MESSAGE_MAP()
};
```

File GRMFC.CPP:

```
// GRMFC.CPP: Simple graphics, programmed in C++.
#include <afxwin.h>
#include "grmfc.h"

BOOL CApp::InitInstance()
{  m_pMainWnd = new CMyWindow();
   m_pMainWnd->ShowWindow(m_nCmdShow);
   m_pMainWnd->UpdateWindow();
   return TRUE;
}

CApp App;

CMyWindow::CMyWindow()
{  int xScreen = GetSystemMetrics(SM_CXSCREEN),
       yScreen = GetSystemMetrics(SM_CYSCREEN);
   RECT rect = {0, 0, xScreen, yScreen};
   Create(NULL, "A drawn triangle in red and a filled one in blue:",
   WS_OVERLAPPEDWINDOW, rect, NULL, NULL);
}
```

```
BEGIN_MESSAGE_MAP(CMyWindow, CFrameWnd)
    ON_WM_PAINT()
END_MESSAGE_MAP()

void CMyWindow::OnPaint()
{   CPaintDC dc(this);
    RECT rect;
    int w, h;
    POINT A, B, C, D, E, F, ABC[3], DEF[3];
    GetClientRect(&rect);
    CPen RedPen, NullPen, *pOldPen;
    CBrush BlueBrush, NullBrush, *pOldBrush;
    w = rect.right;
    h = rect.bottom;
    dc.SetMapMode(MM_ISOTROPIC);
        // Horizontal and vertical units are equal

    dc.SetViewportOrg(w/2, h/2);
    // The point with physical coordinates (w/2, h/2),
    // lying in the center of the window,
    // will have logical coordinates (0, 0).

    dc.SetWindowExt(2000, 2000);
    dc.SetViewportExt(w, -h);
    // Increasing physical x by w means increasing logical x by 2000
    // Increasing physical y by -h will correspond to increasing
    // logical y by 2000.

    /* ABC is a right-angled triangle.
       AB is a horizontal side at the bottom and AC is a vertical
       side at the left.
       Triangle DEF is congruent with triangle ABC and is obtained
       by translating ABC
       to the right.
       We will draw ABC with a red pen and fill DEF with a blue brush.
       All horizontal and vertical sides will have length 800.
    */
    A.x = C.x = -950; B.x = -150;
    D.x = F.x = 150; E.x = 950;
    A.y = B.y = D.y = E.y = -400;
    C.y = F.y = 400;
    ABC[0] = A; ABC[1] = B; ABC[2] = C;
    DEF[0] = D; DEF[1] = E; DEF[2] = F;
    RedPen.CreatePen(PS_SOLID, 10, RGB(255, 0, 0)); // Pen width 10
    NullPen.CreateStockObject(NULL_PEN);
    BlueBrush.CreateSolidBrush(RGB(0, 0, 255));
    NullBrush.CreateStockObject(NULL_BRUSH);
    // Draw red triangle ABC:
    pOldPen = dc.SelectObject(&RedPen);
    pOldBrush = dc.SelectObject(&NullBrush); // Don't fill triangle ABC
```

```
        dc.Polygon(ABC, 3);
        // Fill blue triangle DEF:
        dc.SelectObject(&NullPen); // Do not draw the sides of triangle DEF
        dc.SelectObject(&BlueBrush);
        dc.Polygon(DEF, 3);
        dc.DPtoLP((LPPOINT) &rect, 2);
        dc.SelectObject(&RedPen);
        dc.SelectObject(&NullBrush); // Do not fill rectangle
        dc.Rectangle(rect.left + 20, rect.top - 20, rect.right - 20,
                     rect.bottom + 20); // Very large rectangle
        dc.SelectObject(pOldPen);
        dc.SelectObject(pOldBrush);
}
```

File GRMFC.MAK:

```
# GRMFC.MAK; usage (with Microsoft C++): nmake -f grmfc.mak
grmfc.exe: grmfc.obj gen.def
        link /nod grmfc, grmfc, nul,\
          mafxcw+libw+mlibcew+commdlg+shell, gen.def
grmfc.obj: grmfc.cpp grmfc.h
        cl -c -AM -G2sw -Ow -W3 -Zp grmfc.cpp
# File GEN.DEF can be found in Section 1.2
```

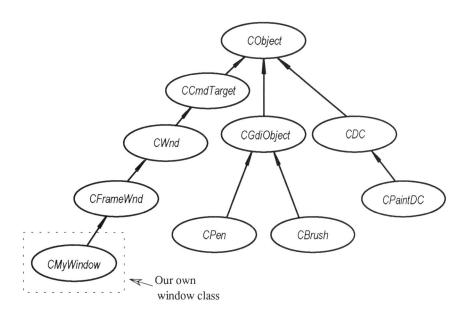

Figure 5.2. *Some Microsoft Foundation classes*

Instead of a device-context *handler* (which is an integer), we use the *CPaintDC* object *dc*, as we did in program OUTPMFC in Section 2.4. Recall that creating this object in the *OnPaint* function is essential because the constructor and destructor of *CPaintDC* call the functions *BeginPaint* and *EndPaint*, respectively. The version of *GetClientRect* used here is a member function of the window class, so we might have written *this–>* in front of *GetClientRect(&rect)*. Actually, *GetClientRect* it is a member function of class *CWnd*, which is the base class of *CFrameWnd*, which is the base class of *CMyWindow*. The relationship between these classes is more clearly indicated in Figure 5.2, which has been extracted from Appendix B.

By contrast, the GDI functions *SelectObject*, *MoveTo*, *LineTo* and *Polygon* are member functions of class *CDC*, the base class of *CPaintDC*. We must therefore not forget to write the prefix *dc.* in calls to these functions. Apart from this, the C++ version is very similar to the C version of the previous section. Figure 5.2 also shows the names of some other classes used in this chapter: *CPaintDC* is derived from *CDC*, while *CPen* and *CBrush* have *CGdiObject* as their base class.

5.5 OWL Solution

The files that solve our problem by using the ObjectWindows Library are listed below. Program GROWL.CPP is similar to program GR.C in that it is based on handles for a device context, pens and brushes. However, we do not use *BeginPaint* and *EndPaint* here, and the device-context handler that we need is supplied by Windows as a parameter of our *Paint* function. Recall that we have discussed this also in Section 2.5.

```
// GROWL.H:

class TApp: public TApplication
{  public:
   TApp(LPSTR Name, HANDLE hInstance, HANDLE hPrevInstance,
         LPSTR lpCmdLine, int nCmdShow)
      : TApplication(Name, hInstance, hPrevInstance, lpCmdLine,
                     nCmdShow){}
   virtual void InitMainWindow();
};


class TMyWindow: public TWindow
{  public:
   TMyWindow(PTWindowsObject AParent, LPSTR ATitle)
      : TWindow(AParent, ATitle){}
   virtual void Paint(HDC hDC, PAINTSTRUCT &ps);
};
```

File GROWL.CPP:

```
// GROWL.CPP: Screen output, programmed with C++/OWL.

#define WIN31
#include <owl.h>
#include "growl.h"

void TApp::InitMainWindow()
{  TWindow *pWin;
   MainWindow = pWin = new TMyWindow(NULL, Name);
   pWin->Attr.X = 0;
   pWin->Attr.Y = 0;
   pWin->Attr.W = GetSystemMetrics(SM_CXSCREEN);
   pWin->Attr.H = GetSystemMetrics(SM_CYSCREEN);
}

void TMyWindow::Paint(HDC hDC, PAINTSTRUCT&)
{  int w, h;
   RECT rect;
   POINT A, B, C, D, E, F, ABC[3], DEF[3];
   GetClientRect(HWindow, &rect);
   HPEN hRedPen, hNullPen, hOldPen;
   HBRUSH hBlueBrush, hNullBrush, hOldBrush;
   w = rect.right;
   h = rect.bottom;
   SetMapMode(hDC, MM_ISOTROPIC);
        // Horizontal and vertical units are equal
   SetViewportOrg(hDC, w/2, h/2);
   // The point with physical coordinates (w/2, h/2),
   // lying in the center of the window,
   // will have logical coordinates (0, 0).

   SetWindowExt(hDC, 2000, 2000);
   SetViewportExt(hDC, w, -h);
   // Increasing physical x by w means increasing
   // logical x by 2000.
   // Increasing physical y by -h will correspond
   // to increasing logical y by 2000.

   /* ABC is a right-angled triangle.
      AB is a horizontal side at the bottom and AC is a
      vertical side at the left.
      Triangle DEF is congruent with triangle ABC and is
      obtained by translating ABC to the right.
      We will draw ABC with a red pen and fill DEF with
      a blue brush.
      All horizontal and vertical sides will have length 800.
   */
```

```
   A.x = C.x = -950; B.x = -150;
   D.x = F.x = 150; E.x = 950;
   A.y = B.y = D.y = E.y = -400;
   C.y = F.y = 400;
   ABC[0] = A; ABC[1] = B; ABC[2] = C;
   DEF[0] = D; DEF[1] = E; DEF[2] = F;

   hRedPen = CreatePen(PS_SOLID, 10, RGB(255, 0, 0)); // Pen width 10
   hNullPen = GetStockObject(NULL_PEN);
   hBlueBrush = CreateSolidBrush(RGB(0, 0, 255));
   hNullBrush = GetStockObject(NULL_BRUSH);
   // Draw red triangle ABC:
   hOldPen = SelectObject(hDC, hRedPen);
   hOldBrush = SelectObject(hDC, hNullBrush);
                               // Do not fill triangle ABC
   Polygon(hDC, ABC, 3);
   // Fill blue triangle DEF:
   SelectObject(hDC, hNullPen);
      // Do not draw the sides of triangle DEF
   SelectObject(hDC, hBlueBrush);
   Polygon(hDC, DEF, 3);
   DPtoLP(hDC, (LPPOINT) &rect, 2);
   SelectObject(hDC, hRedPen);
   SelectObject(hDC, hNullBrush); // Do not fill rectangle
   Rectangle(hDC, rect.left + 20, rect.top - 20, rect.right - 20,
               rect.bottom + 20); // Very large rectangle
   SelectObject(hDC, hOldPen);
   SelectObject(hDC, hOldBrush);
}


int PASCAL WinMain(HANDLE hInstance, HANDLE hPrevInstance,
   LPSTR lpCmdLine, int nCmdShow)
{  TApp App("A drawn triangle in red and a filled one in blue",
   hInstance, hPrevInstance, lpCmdLine, nCmdShow);
   App.Run();
   return App.Status;
}
```

File GROWL.MAK:

```
# GROWL.MAK: usage (with Borland C++): make -f growl.mak
growl.exe: growl.obj
        bcc -mm -WE -L\borlandc\owl\lib;\borlandc\classlib\lib \
        growl.obj owlwm.lib tclassm.lib
growl.obj: growl.cpp growl.h
        bcc -c -mm -WE \
          -I\borlandc\owl\include;\borlandc\classlib\include \
          growl.cpp
```

5.6 Questions

5.1   What is the difference between a viewport and a window? What are the coordinates used for each called?

5.2   What is a mapping mode, and what is the meaning of the word *isotropic*?

5.3   What is the meaning of *x* and *y* in the call *SetViewportOrg(hDC, x, y)*?

5.4   After creating a pen, we cannot use it until it is selected into the device context. Why is this necessary?

5.5   Which function is used to create a pen? Which to create a brush?

5.6   When responding to a *WM_PAINT* message, how do we obtain a device context and how do we dispose of it?

5.7   Which errors, related to pens and brushes, must we avoid?

5.8   It is possible to write a correct version of GR.C without ever using the value returned by *SelectObject*. How? Remember that we may call *EndPaint* when our pens and brushes are still selected into the device context. They are no longer after this call, so that we can then delete them.

6

Colors and Palettes

6.1 Problem Definition

Windows enables us to select colors in a device-independent way. If we try to use more colors than those that are available as pure colors, Windows uses a technique called *dithering* to approximate the desired colors by means of dot patterns. We will illustrate this by writing a program that displays a yellow rectangle with a blue background. This rectangle will be very dark yellow at the left and very light at the right: as we move from left to right the color gradually becomes brighter. Since the illustrations in this book are only in black and white, you should use your imagination when looking at Figure 6.1.

This choice of colors, with a blue background and many shades of yellow as foreground colors, can also be found in *Programming Principles in Computer Graphics, 2nd Edition*, listed in the Bibliography. These colors are used there to display realistic images of three-dimensional objects. Actually, only 16 colors (available at the same time with standard VGA, resolution 640 × 480) were used in that book. Here we want to be device independent. In other words, we want to use as many colors as we like, expecting that Windows will approximate these colors in the best possible way. Fortunately, this is possible. In our example, we will use as many as 150 different colors, that is, one blue background color and 149 shades of yellow in the rectangle.

6.2 General Aspects

The problem we are defining can be understood only if we are familiar with the way the basic colors red, green and blue can be combined to form other colors. For each of these basic colors we have to supply an integer, ranging from 0 to some maximum value, which is 255 with Windows. These three integer values, R, G and B, indicate how much of each color is present. They are stored together in a *long int*, technically referred to as type *COLORREF*. A value of this type is returned by the macro *RGB*, which we have already used in Chapter 5. This macro enables us to form colors simply by writing $RGB(R, G, B)$, without bothering about how R, G and B are stored in the resulting *COLORREF* value.

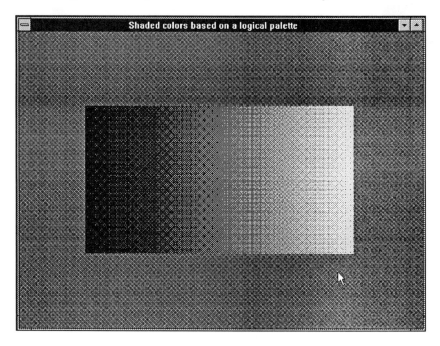

Figure 6.1. Rectangle consisting of 149 very narrow rectangles

Since they represent quantities of light, the resulting color will be black if $R = G = B = 0$. With as much light as possible, that is, with $R = G = B = 255$, the color is white. These and some other important special cases are shown in the following table, where x is some positive value not greater than 255:

R	G	B	
0	0	0	Black
0	0	x	Blue
0	x	0	Green
0	x	x	Cyan
x	0	0	Red
x	0	x	Magenta
x	x	0	Yellow
x	x	x	Gray (or white if $x = 255$)

We obtain dark colors by taking small values for x. For example, $RGB(0, 0, 128)$ gives a rather dark blue. The brightest 'pure' blue is $RGB(0, 0, 255)$. If we find this still too dark, we can mix it with white, using $RGB(128, 128, 255)$, for example.

If we know in advance which colors we want, we can specify them by means of a *logical palette*. In our example, we will use a light shade of blue, $RGB(128, 128, 255)$, as the background color, and $n - 1$ shades of yellow, $RGB(i * c, i * c, 0)$, where

$n = 150$ (chosen rather arbitrarily)
$c = 255/(n - 1)$
$i = 1, ..., n - 1$

Thus, altogether we have n colors 0, 1, 2, ..., $n - 1$, where color 0 is the blue background color, color 1 a very dark shade of yellow, color 2 a slightly less dark shade of yellow, and so on, color $n - 1$ being bright yellow. Program PAL produces these colors, as represented by shades of grey in Figure 6.1. The large rectangle shown here consists of $n - 1$ very narrow rectangles beside each other (where $n = 150$).

In Section 6.3 we will discuss some program code that (with very few changes) also applies to the MFC and OWL solutions, given in Sections 6.4 and 6.5. Reading the next section is therefore recommended, even if you are an MFC or OWL user.

Make files

If you want to use make files in this chapter, take those of Chapter 5 and replace all occurrences of *gr* with *pal*.

6.3 C Solution

Let us first have a look at the program files, and then discuss some aspects of them:

File PAL.H:

```
// PAL.H:

long FAR PASCAL _export WndProc(HWND hWnd, UINT message,
        WPARAM wParam, LPARAM lParam);

int PASCAL WinMain(HANDLE hInstance, HANDLE hPrevInstance,
        LPSTR lpCmdLine, int nCmdShow);
```

File PAL.C:

```
// PAL.C: Using a logical palette.

#include <windows.h>
#include "pal.h"
```

```
int PASCAL WinMain(HANDLE hInstance, HANDLE hPrevInstance,
    LPSTR lpCmdLine, int nCmdShow)
{ char szAppName[]="Palette";
  int xScreen, yScreen;
  WNDCLASS wndclass;
  HWND hWnd;
  MSG msg;
  xScreen = GetSystemMetrics(SM_CXSCREEN);
  yScreen = GetSystemMetrics(SM_CYSCREEN);

  if (!hPrevInstance)
  { wndclass.style = CS_HREDRAW | CS_VREDRAW;
    wndclass.lpfnWndProc = WndProc;
    wndclass.cbClsExtra = 0;
    wndclass.cbWndExtra = 0;
    wndclass.hInstance = hInstance;
    wndclass.hIcon = LoadIcon(NULL, IDI_APPLICATION);
    wndclass.hCursor = LoadCursor(NULL, IDC_ARROW);
    wndclass.hbrBackground = GetStockObject(WHITE_BRUSH);
    wndclass.lpszMenuName =  NULL;
    wndclass.lpszClassName = szAppName;
        // Name used in call to CreateWindow.
    if (!RegisterClass(&wndclass)) return FALSE;
  }

  hWnd = CreateWindow(
    szAppName,
    "Shaded colors based on a logical palette",
                                    // Text for window title bar.
    WS_OVERLAPPEDWINDOW,            // Window style.
    0,                              // Initial x position
    0,                              // Initial y position.
    xScreen,                        // Width.
    yScreen,                        // Height.
    NULL,                           // Parent window handle.
    NULL,                           // Window menu handle.
    hInstance,                      // Program instance handle.
    NULL                            // Create parameters.
  );

  ShowWindow(hWnd, nCmdShow);
  UpdateWindow(hWnd);

  while (GetMessage(&msg, NULL, 0, 0))
  { TranslateMessage(&msg);    // Translates virtual key codes
    DispatchMessage(&msg);     // Dispatches message to window
  }
  return msg.wParam;     // Returns the value from PostQuitMessage
}
```

```
long FAR PASCAL _export WndProc(HWND hWnd, UINT message,
      WPARAM wParam, LPARAM lParam)
{ HDC hDC;
  PAINTSTRUCT ps;
  RECT rect;
  LOGPALETTE *pPal;
  HPALETTE hOldPalette;
  static HPALETTE hLogPal;
  static LOCALHANDLE hLocMem;
  int i, n=150, left, right;
  long w;
  HBRUSH hBrush;
  switch (message)
  {
  case WM_CREATE:
     SetClassWord(hWnd, GCW_HBRBACKGROUND,
        CreateSolidBrush(RGB(128, 128, 255)));
     hLocMem = LocalAlloc(LPTR,
        sizeof(LOGPALETTE) + (n-1) * sizeof(PALETTEENTRY));
     pPal = (LOGPALETTE *) LocalLock(hLocMem);
     pPal->palVersion = 0x300;
     pPal->palNumEntries = n;
     pPal->palPalEntry[0].peRed = 128;
     pPal->palPalEntry[0].peGreen = 128;
     pPal->palPalEntry[0].peBlue = 255;
     for (i=1; i<n; i++)
     { pPal->palPalEntry[i].peRed =
       pPal->palPalEntry[i].peGreen = (int)(i * 255L / (n - 1));
       pPal->palPalEntry[i].peBlue = 0;
     }
     hLogPal = CreatePalette(pPal);
     break;
  case WM_DESTROY:
     DeleteObject(hLogPal);
     DeleteObject(SetClassWord(hWnd, GCW_HBRBACKGROUND,
        GetStockObject(WHITE_BRUSH)));
     LocalUnlock(hLocMem);
     LocalFree(hLocMem);
     PostQuitMessage(0); break;
  case WM_PAINT:
     hDC = BeginPaint(hWnd, &ps);
     hOldPalette = SelectPalette(hDC, hLogPal, 0);
     RealizePalette(hDC);
     GetClientRect(hWnd, &rect);
     rect.top = rect.bottom / 4;
     rect.bottom = 3 * rect.top;
     left = rect.right/6;
     right = 5 * left;
     w = right - left;
```

```
        rect.right = left;
        for (i=1; i<n; i++)
        {   rect.left = rect.right;
            rect.right = left + (int)(i * w / (n - 1));
            hBrush = CreateSolidBrush(PALETTEINDEX(i));
            FillRect(hDC, &rect, hBrush);
            DeleteObject(hBrush);
        }
        SelectPalette(hDC, hOldPalette, 0);
        EndPaint(hWnd, &ps);
        break;
    default:
        return DefWindowProc(hWnd, message, wParam, lParam);
    }
    return 0L;
}
```

When the *WM_CREATE* message is sent to the window, we set the background color to *RGB*(128, 128, 255), which is light blue. This is done in the following, rather complicated way:

```
SetClassWord(hWnd, GCW_HBRBACKGROUND,
    CreateSolidBrush(RGB(128, 128, 255)));
```

This is the way to assign a new value to the *hbrBackground* member of the window class structure (see the *WinMain* function). Although *GetStockObject(WHITE_BRUSH)* was already assigned to this member in *WinMain*, the window is immediately displayed with a blue background when we start the program. The second argument in the above call indicates that we are dealing with the background brush. Other possible values for this argument include *GCW_HCURSOR* for a cursor and *GCW_HICON* for an icon.

As we have seen in the previous chapter, a brush created by *CreateSolidBrush* must be deleted by *DeleteObject*. We do this when a *WM_DESTROY* message is sent to the window by means of an even more complicated statement:

```
DeleteObject(SetClassWord(hWnd, GCW_HBRBACKGROUND,
    GetStockObject(WHITE_BRUSH)));
```

Actually, this statement performs two actions. The call to *SetClassWord* restores the white background brush, which was also used in the *WinMain* function. This function returns the previous value (in the same way as *SelectObject* does), which is our light blue brush, which we want to delete. This explains why this call to *SetClassWord* occurs as an argument of *DeleteObject*. So much for the light blue background.

We now turn to the palette that we will be using. Let us first have a look at the declarations of the types *PALETTEENTRY* and *LOGPALETTE*, as these occur in the header file WINDOWS.H:

```
typedef struct tagPALETTEENTRY
{
    BYTE    peRed;
    BYTE    peGreen;
    BYTE    peBlue;
    BYTE    peFlags;
} PALETTEENTRY;

typedef struct tagLOGPALETTE
{
    WORD    palVersion;
    WORD    palNumEntries;
    PALETTEENTRY palPalEntry[1];
} LOGPALETTE;
```

Since the number of palette entries is unknown here, array *palPalEntry* is given length 1 in this declaration, which is based on the assumption that memory space for $n - 1$ more array elements will be made available if we want the array length to be n. This explains why we use the value $n - 1$ in the following statement, which allocates memory for a *LOG-PALETTE* object:

```
hLocMem = LocalAlloc(LPTR,
    sizeof(LOGPALETTE) + (n-1) * sizeof(PALETTEENTRY));
```

The first argument, *LPTR*, of *LocalAlloc* means 'local pointer' and specifies how to allocate memory; we will not discuss this in detail. Unlike the well-known standard function *malloc*, which returns an address, *LocalAlloc* returns a handle (that is, an integer). We can nevertheless obtain the corresponding address by supplying the handle just obtained:

```
pPal = (LOGPALETTE *) LocalLock(hLocMem);
```

This *LocalLock* function also locks the memory in question, so it cannot be moved or discarded. Before discussing the way *pPal* is used, let us see how this memory will be unlocked and released later. When a *WM_DESTROY* message is sent to the window, we do this as follows:

```
LocalUnlock(hLocMem);
LocalFree(hLocMem);
```

Note that it is essential that *hLocMem* is *static* because its value used in response to a *WM_DESTROY* message was assigned to this variable in response to a *WM_CREATE* message, that is, during a different call to the *WndProc* function. It is therefore necessary for *hLocMem* to have a permanent memory location, which is achieved by means of the *static* keyword.

The functions *LocalAlloc*, *LocalFree*, *LocalLock* and *LocalUnlock* are used for the allocation (and deallocation) of *local* memory. The amount of this is limited to 64 KB less the combined size of the static variables and the stack. This limitation does not apply to *global* memory, for which we can use the functions *GlobalAlloc*, *GlobalFree*, *GlobalLock* and *GlobalUnlock*. The amount of memory available by means of these functions can be almost 16 MB with an 80386 (and almost 1 MB with an 80286). If the limitation mentioned is not a problem, the use of local memory is preferred for reasons of efficiency. It is also possible to use the standard memory allocation functions *malloc* and *free*, but then the linker actually uses equivalent Windows functions. The same applies to the C++ operators *new* and *delete*.

The pointer *pPal*, pointing to the *LOGPALETTE* object obtained by *LocalAlloc*, is now used to assign values to the members of this object, and to 'create' the palette:

```
pPal->palVersion = 0x300;
pPal->palNumEntries = n;
pPal->palPalEntry[0].peRed = 128;
pPal->palPalEntry[0].peGreen = 128;
pPal->palPalEntry[0].peBlue = 255;
for (i=1; i<n; i++)
{  pPal->palPalEntry[i].peRed =
   pPal->palPalEntry[i].peGreen = (int)(i * 255L / (n - 1));
   pPal->palPalEntry[i].peBlue = 0;
}
hLogPal = CreatePalette(pPal);
```

Some of the selected color intensities are shown here:

i	R	G	B	
0	128	128	255	(light blue)
1	1	1	0	(very dark yellow)
2	3	3	0	
3	5	5	0	
4	6	6	0	
5	8	8	0	
⋮	⋮	⋮	⋮	
149	255	255	0	(very bright yellow)

The above call to the *CreatePalette* function indicates that the *LOGPALETTE* object under discussion is really to be used as a palette. This function returns a handle, *hLogPal*, to a logical palette. Since this handle is to be used during several calls to *WndProc*, it must also be declared *static*.

The palette just created is actually used in response to *WM_CREATE* messages. After calling *BeginPaint* to obtain a device-context handle, we must select the palette into the device context, which is similar to what we do with pens and brushes, as discussed in Chapter 5. However, this time we use the *SelectPalette* rather than the *SelectObject* function. We then also have to call the *RealizePalette* function before we can use the palette:

```
hOldPalette = SelectPalette(hDC, hLogPal, 0);
RealizePalette(hDC);
```

We restore the old palette later, deselecting our own palette before we call *EndPaint*:

```
SelectPalette(hDC, hOldPalette, 0);
EndPaint(hWnd, &ps);
```

Between selecting and deselecting our palette, the large rectangle is produced by filling $n - 1$ very narrow rectangles, all of the same height, which is half the height of the client rectangle. Together, these narrow rectangles form a large yellow rectangle, with width w equal to 2/3 of the client rectangle's width and lying in the center of the client rectangle. This is implemented by means of a structure *rect* (of type *RECT*) which has the members *top*, *bottom*, *left* and *right*. Note that *rect.left* and *rect.right* change for each narrow rectangle. These structure members should not be confused with the variables *left* and *right*, denoting the left and right boundaries of the large rectangle:

```
GetClientRect(hWnd, &rect);
rect.top = rect.bottom / 4; rect.bottom = 3 * rect.top;
left = rect.right/6; right = 5 * left; w = right - left;
rect.right = left;
for (i=1; i<n; i++)
{  rect.left = rect.right;
   rect.right = left + (int)(i * w / (n - 1));
   hBrush = CreateSolidBrush(PALETTEINDEX(i));
   FillRect(hDC, &rect, hBrush);
   DeleteObject(hBrush);
}
```

We refer to the color of the *i*th palette entry as

```
PALETTEINDEX(i)
```

This color is used as an argument for *CreateSolidBrush*, which returns a brush handle *hBrush*. We use this handle in the call to *FillRect*. Unlike the *Polygon* function, used in Chapter 5, *FillRect* takes a brush handle as an argument, which means that we need not select this brush into the device context here. Since the brush is used only once, we can immediately delete it by calling *DeleteObject*. Note that we are allowed to do this here only because the brush is not selected into the device context. The tricky point here is that omitting this call to *DeleteObject* would not immediately show up as an error. Instead, the filling process would be increasingly slower when the user changes the size of the window several times or starts new instances of this program while the old ones are still active. There are no such problems with the current version, thanks to these calls to *DeleteObject*.

You may have noticed that *PALETTEINDEX*(0), denoting the background color, is never used in this program. Recall that, instead, we have defined the background color by using the function *SetClassWord*. A palette entry was nevertheless reserved for the background color because this might be useful in other programs, based on PAL.C. For example, we could make a rectangular hole in the large yellow rectangle simply by calling *Fill-Rect* to fill a small rectangle inside the large one, using the background color.

6.4 MFC Solution

Except for the way of specifying the background color (to be discussed at the end of this section), our C++/MFC solution to the problem of this chapter can be derived rather straightforwardly from that of the previous section. Function calls with a handle as their first argument are simply replaced with member functions with the same name. For example, we replace

```
DeleteObject(hBrush)
```

with

```
Brush.DeleteObject();
```

The same principle applies to the following call:

```
FillRect(hDC, &rect, hBrush);
```

Instead of *hDC* as the first argument, we use the prefix *dc* in

```
dc.FillRect(&rect, &Brush)
```

However, there is another difference here: instead of the handle *hBrush* we use the address of object *Brush* as the final argument.

Sometimes there is no such prefix in the MFC version. For example, instead of

```
GetClientRect(hWnd, &rect);
```

we simply write

```
GetClientRect(&rect);
```

This call occurs in the function *OnPaint*, which is member of class *CMyWindow*, derived from class *CWnd*. This explains that we are actually using member function *CWnd::GetClientRect* here, and we could write *this–>* in front of this last call. The files of our MFC solution are listed below:

File PALMFC.H:

```
// PALMFC.H:
class CApp: public CWinApp
{  public:
   BOOL InitInstance();
};

class CMyWindow: public CFrameWnd
{  CPalette Pal;
   LOCALHANDLE hLocMem;
   int n;
   CBrush bgBrush;
public:
   CMyWindow();
   afx_msg int OnCreate(LPCREATESTRUCT);
   afx_msg void OnDestroy();
   afx_msg void OnPaint();
   DECLARE_MESSAGE_MAP()
};
```

File PALMFC.CPP:

```
// PALMFC.CPP: Logical palette, programmed with the MFC.
#include <afxwin.h>
#include "palmfc.h"

BOOL CApp::InitInstance()
{  m_pMainWnd = new CMyWindow();
   m_pMainWnd->ShowWindow(m_nCmdShow);
   m_pMainWnd->UpdateWindow();
   return TRUE;
}

CApp App;

CMyWindow::CMyWindow()
{  int xScreen = GetSystemMetrics(SM_CXSCREEN),
       yScreen = GetSystemMetrics(SM_CYSCREEN);
   bgBrush.CreateSolidBrush(RGB(128, 128, 255));
   RECT rect = {0, 0, xScreen, yScreen};
   CString ClassName = AfxRegisterWndClass(
      CS_HREDRAW | CS_VREDRAW,
      NULL,
      HBRUSH(bgBrush.m_hObject),
      NULL);
   Create(ClassName, "Shaded colors based on a logical palette",
          WS_OVERLAPPEDWINDOW, rect, NULL, NULL);
}
```

```
BEGIN_MESSAGE_MAP(CMyWindow, CFrameWnd)
   ON_WM_CREATE()
   ON_WM_DESTROY()
   ON_WM_PAINT()
END_MESSAGE_MAP()

int CMyWindow::OnCreate(LPCREATESTRUCT)
{   n = 150;
    hLocMem = LocalAlloc(LPTR,
        sizeof(LOGPALETTE) + (n-1) * sizeof(PALETTEENTRY));
    LOGPALETTE *pPal = (LOGPALETTE *) LocalLock(hLocMem);
    pPal->palVersion = 0x300;
    pPal->palNumEntries = n;
    pPal->palPalEntry[0].peRed = 128;
    pPal->palPalEntry[0].peGreen = 128;
    pPal->palPalEntry[0].peBlue = 255;
    for (int i=1; i<n; i++)
    {   pPal->palPalEntry[i].peRed = pPal->palPalEntry[i].peGreen =
            (int)(i * 255L / (n - 1));
        pPal->palPalEntry[i].peBlue = 0;
    }
    Pal.CreatePalette(pPal);
    return 0;
}

void CMyWindow::OnDestroy()
{   bgBrush.DeleteObject(); LocalUnlock(hLocMem); LocalFree(hLocMem);
}

void CMyWindow::OnPaint()
{   CPaintDC dc(this);
    RECT rect;
    int i, left, right;
    long w;
    CBrush Brush;
    CPalette *pOldPalette = dc.SelectPalette(&Pal, 0);
    dc.RealizePalette();
    GetClientRect(&rect);
    rect.top = rect.bottom / 4; rect.bottom = 3 * rect.top;
    left = rect.right/6; right = 5 * left; w = right - left;
    rect.right = left;
    for (i=1; i<n; i++)
    {   rect.left = rect.right;
        rect.right = left + (int)(i * w / (n - 1));
        Brush.CreateSolidBrush(PALETTEINDEX(i));
        dc.FillRect(&rect, &Brush);
        Brush.DeleteObject();
    }
    dc.SelectPalette(pOldPalette, 0);
}
```

As we have seen in Figure 5.2 of the previous chapter, the classes *CPen* and *CBrush* have *CGdiObject* as their base class. The same applies to class *CPalette*, as Figure 6.2 shows.

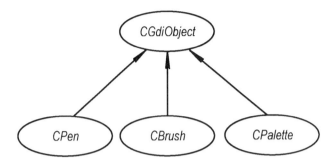

Figure 6.2. *Some classes derived from* **CGdiObject**

Background color

In the *CMyWindow* constructor, we set the background color by supplying the *CString* variable *ClassName* (instead of *NULL*) as the first argument of the *Create* function. Before calling this function, we fill *ClassName* in the following way:

```
bgBrush.CreateSolidBrush(RGB(128, 128, 255));
...
CString ClassName = AfxRegisterWndClass(
    CS_HREDRAW | CS_VREDRAW,
    NULL,
    HBRUSH(bgBrush.m_hObject),
    NULL);
```

The variable *bgBrush*, of type *CBrush*, is a private member of class *CMyWindow*, as you can see in file PALMFC.H. Function *AfxRegisterWndClass* takes the following arguments, in this order:

- Windows class style
- Handle to cursor resource (or *NULL* for the standard cursor), see Sections 7.4 and 8.4
- Background brush (or *NULL*)
- Handle to icon resource (or *NULL*), see Section 7.4

6.5 OWL Solution

In the solution for the ObjectWindows library we provide the window class *TMyWindow* with the private members *n*, *hLogPal* and *hLocMem*. Recall that *hLogPal* and *hLocMem* were *static* variables of function *WndProc* in Section 6.3. In this way we can have access

to these variables in several (member) functions, without using global variables. Here is the
header file that we will use:

File PALOWL.H:

```
// PALOWL.H:
class TApp: public TApplication
{  public:
   TApp(LPSTR Name, HANDLE hInstance, HANDLE hPrevInstance,
        LPSTR lpCmdLine, int nCmdShow)
     : TApplication(Name, hInstance, hPrevInstance, lpCmdLine,
                    nCmdShow){}
   virtual void InitMainWindow();
};

class TMyWindow: public TWindow
{  int n;
   HPALETTE hLogPal;
   LOCALHANDLE hLocMem;
public:
   TMyWindow(PTWindowsObject AParent, LPSTR ATitle)
     : TWindow(AParent, ATitle){}
   virtual void WMCreate(RTMessage) = [WM_FIRST + WM_CREATE];
   virtual void WMDestroy(RTMessage) = [WM_FIRST + WM_DESTROY];
   virtual void Paint(HDC hDC, PAINTSTRUCT &ps);
};
```

Note the way *WM_CREATE* and *WM_DESTROY* messages are dealt with. It may seem
strange that the names of the response functions for these messages begin with *WM*, while
that is not the case with function *Paint*, nor do we use the notation = [...] for the latter
function. Actually, there is also a function *WMPaint*. The above declarations of the three
functions in question would have looked more consistent if we had used that function, but
we prefer the *Paint* function because it is more convenient in that it provides us with a
device-context handle *hDC* as a parameter.

File PALOWL.CPP:

```
// PALOWL.CPP: Screen output, programmed with C++/OWL.
#define WIN31
#include <owl.h>
#include "palowl.h"

void TApp::InitMainWindow()
{  TWindow *pWin;
   MainWindow = pWin = new TMyWindow(NULL, Name);
   pWin->Attr.X = 0; pWin->Attr.Y = 0;
   pWin->Attr.W = GetSystemMetrics(SM_CXSCREEN);
   pWin->Attr.H = GetSystemMetrics(SM_CYSCREEN);
}
```

```
void TMyWindow::WMCreate(RTMessage)
{  n - 150;
   SetClassWord(HWindow, GCW_HBRBACKGROUND,
      CreateSolidBrush(RGB(128, 128, 255)));
   hLocMem = LocalAlloc(LPTR,
      sizeof(LOGPALETTE) + (n-1) * sizeof(PALETTEENTRY));
   LOGPALETTE *pPal = (LOGPALETTE *) LocalLock(hLocMem);
   pPal->palVersion - 0x300;
   pPal->palNumEntries - n;
   pPal->palPalEntry[0].peRed - 128;
   pPal->palPalEntry[0].peGreen = 128;
   pPal->palPalEntry[0].peBlue - 255;
   for (int i=1; i<n; i++)
   {  pPal->palPalEntry[i].peRed =
      pPal->palPalEntry[i].peGreen = (int)(i * 255L / (n - 1));
      pPal->palPalEntry[i].peBlue = 0;
   }
   hLogPal = CreatePalette(pPal);
}

void TMyWindow::WMDestroy(RTMessage)
{  DeleteObject(hLogPal);
   DeleteObject(SetClassWord(HWindow, GCW_HBRBACKGROUND,
      GetStockObject(WHITE_BRUSH)));
   LocalUnlock(hLocMem);
   LocalFree(hLocMem);
   PostQuitMessage(0);
}

void TMyWindow::Paint(HDC hDC, PAINTSTRUCT&)
{  int i, left, right;
   long w;
   HBRUSH hBrush;
   RECT rect;
   HPALETTE hOldPal = SelectPalette(hDC, hLogPal, 0);
   RealizePalette(hDC);
   GetClientRect(HWindow, &rect);
   rect.top = rect.bottom / 4; rect.bottom = 3 * rect.top;
   left - rect.right/6; right = 5 * left; w = right - left;
   rect.right - left;
   for (i=1; i<n; i++)
   {  rect.left - rect.right;
      rect.right - left + (int)(i * w / (n - 1));
      hBrush = CreateSolidBrush(PALETTEINDEX(i));
      FillRect(hDC, &rect, hBrush);
      DeleteObject(hBrush);
   }
   SelectPalette(hDC, hOldPal, 0);
}
```

```
int PASCAL WinMain(HANDLE hInstance, HANDLE hPrevInstance,
   LPSTR lpCmdLine, int nCmdShow)
{  TApp App("Shaded colors based on a logical palette",
   hInstance, hPrevInstance, lpCmdLine, nCmdShow);
   App.Run();
   return App.Status;
}
```

6.6 Questions

6.1   Standard VGA, resolution 640×480, can display only 16 colors at the same time. Which technique is used by Windows to give the impression that we are using many more colors?

6.2   Which RGB values are used for black? Which for white?

6.3   How can we change the background color?

6.4   Which functions are related to memory allocated in C programs running under Windows?

6.5   Mention some useful applications of *SetClassWord*.

6.6   How can we obtain the *i*th color of the currently selected palette?

7

Bitmaps, Cursors and Icons

7.1 Problem Definition

This chapter is about pictures, displayed on the screen by copying blocks of bits. We will draw such bit images 'by hand', using an *image editor*, store the results in a file, and use these as resources in our programs. Such pictures are called *bitmaps*. We will also deal with the subjects of *cursors* and *icons*, which are bitmaps for special purposes. We will design our own cursor and use this instead of the standard arrow cursor, used so far. (Incidentally, there are some other predefined cursors, as we will see in Section 7.2. Furthermore, it is also possible to create bitmaps, cursors and icons dynamically, as will be demonstrated for bitmaps in Chapter 9.) Our own cursor will have the form of a bird, as you can see about in the middle of Figure 7.1. We will also design an icon of our own, shown both at the lower-right corner of the window and below the window. Finally, our program will display the face of a man at the current position of the cursor when we press the left mouse button. Each next man's face produced in this way will be somewhat smaller than the previous one. Similarly, each time we press the right mouse button the face of a woman will appear, also in decreasing sizes. All this is shown in Figure 7.1. When the user changes the size of the window, the client rectangle is cleared, except for the icon at the lower-right corner. Pressing a mouse button then causes the head of a man or a woman to appear with the same size as the very first one, the next one again being slightly smaller, and so on.

Actually, the special icon below the window appears only if we iconize the window of this program and those of all others, including that of the Program Manager. Displaying this program's window as well, as shown in Figure 7.1, is possible by starting the program twice, and iconizing (or 'minimizing') one of the two instances.

Figure 7.1. Bitmaps, a new cursor and a new icon

7.2 General Aspects

We will briefly discuss how to prepare these bit images by using the image editor of *App Studio*, which is part of Microsoft Visual C++, as you can see in Figure 7.2. Like its competitor from Borland, this image editor is pleasant to work with.

The program App Studio is a *resource editor*, which can be used for many purposes. For example, we can also use it to design dialog boxes. After starting App Studio, we click the *New* button and select *Bitmap*. The default width and height are both 48, but we can change them by dragging indicated points in the middle of the edges of the work area. Figure 7.3 shows the situation where the width and the height are 64. Although we could use many colors, only black and white were used here.

Note the cursor in the form of a small pencil, in front of the lady's eye. As just mentioned, there are 64×64 elementary squares, or *pixels*. Pressing the left mouse button causes the pixel indicated by the pencil to turn black. We can also draw a curve by keeping that button pressed as we move the mouse. Analogously, we can press the *right* mouse button to turn pixels white. Incidentally, this way of drawing and painting also applies to Microsoft's PaintBrush, which is very well known because it comes with Windows. The picture produced in this way is saved by selecting *Save* in the *File* menu. We use BMP as a file-name extension for a bitmap. If, instead of *Bitmap*, we had initially selected *Cursor* or *Icon*, we would have used the file-name extension CUR or ICO, respectively.

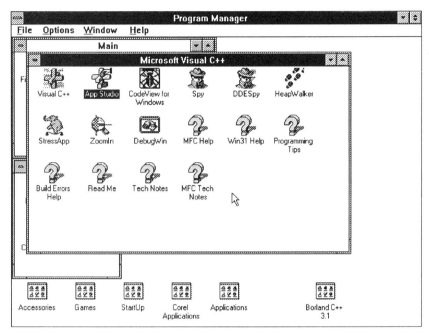

Figure 7.2. App Studio icon in Visual C++ window

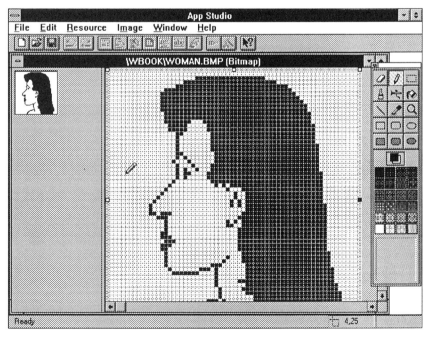

Figure 7.3. Bitmap WOMAN.BMP

Besides the file WOMAN.BMP, I also produced the files MAN.BMP, BIRD.CUR and PEOPLE.ICO. I used 32 as the width and the height for these other three pictures. Only for WOMAN.BMP did I use a 64 × 64 bitmap: I did not dare to deform a woman's face too much by choosing too low a resolution.

Figure 7.1, produced by the program we have to write, shows the four different images just mentioned. There are several occurrences (in different sizes) of the picture stored in the file MAN.BMP, and of the one stored in WOMAN.BMP. The bird in the middle of the window corresponds to the file BIRD.CUR, denoting a rather unusual mouse cursor. Both in the lower-right corner of the client rectangle and in the lower-left corner of the screen, you find our own icon corresponding to file PEOPLE.ICO. If the one left outside the client rectangle is not immediately visible, it may be obscured by other windows, which we can also minimize. To obtain Figure 7.1, the icon was dragged to the bottom, then a second instance of the application was created by starting the program once again, the 2 × 4 heads were generated by pressing the mouse buttons, and, finally, the main window of this was slightly reduced (by dragging its corners), to reveal the icons at the bottom.

Predefined cursors

It is not likely that our bird cursor will be of great practical value. It is only an example of how to design cursors ourselves, which might be useful. However, it would be strange if we completely ignored some useful predefined cursors. Each of these is identified by a symbolic constant, denoting an integer value:

Value	Meaning
IDC_ARROW	Standard arrow cursor.
IDC_CROSS	Crosshair cursor.
IDC_IBEAM	Text I-beam cursor.
IDC_ICON	Empty icon.
IDC_SIZE	A square with a smaller square inside its lower-right corner.
IDC_SIZENESW	Double-pointed cursor with arrows pointing northeast and southwest.
IDC_SIZENS	Double-pointed cursor with arrows pointing north and south.
IDC_SIZENWSE	Double-pointed cursor with arrows pointing northwest and southeast.
IDC_SIZEWE	Double-pointed cursor with arrows pointing west and east.
IDC_UPARROW	Vertical arrow cursor.
IDC_WAIT	Hourglass cursor.

Recall that, when programming in C, we normally assign *IDC_ARROW* to the structure member *wndclass.hCursor* in the *WinMain* function. In the next chapter we will see how to use *IDC_CROSS* instead, not only in C, but also with MFC and OWL. So much for predefined cursors.

Make files

As in Chapters 3 and 4, we will use resource script files. We can therefore borrow the make files from Chapter 3, replacing all occurrences of *inp* with *bm*.

Now that so many files are involved, you may wonder when and where exactly they are used. The main thing to remember is that the resulting executable files contain all information that is required to run the program. The image files BIRD.CUR, PEOPLE.ICO, MAN.BMP and WOMAN.BMP are used by the resource compiler RC. For example, the files BM.RC and BM.H of the next section, together with the four files just mentioned, are input for RC to produce BM.RES, which in turn is supplied to the linker. Consequently, it would be a good idea to replace the dependency rule

```
bm.res: bm.rc bm.h
```

obtained by replacing *inp* with *bm* in the make file BM.MAK of Chapter 3, with the following line:

```
bm.res: bm.rc bm.h bird.cur people.ico man.bmp woman.bmp
```

In this way, any change in the four image files will cause the resource compiler to produce a new file BM.RES. With the former and shorter dependency rule, we would have to delete the old file BM.RES if we changed, for example, file BIRD.CUR and we wanted to use our make file to make this change effective. Note that the names of the four image files do not occur in the RC command. However, their names do occur in file BM.RC so the resource compiler will be able to find them. This is analogous to the way compilers find the header files they need.

With Microsoft C, for example, we will be using as many as eleven files in Section 7.3. We can find their names in Figure 7.4, which also shows how the Microsoft C compiler CL, the resource compiler RC and the linker LINK use or produce these files.

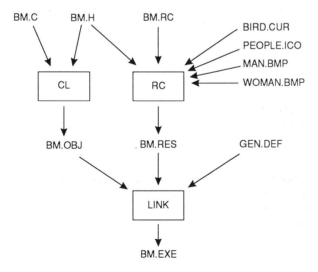

Figure 7.4. *Files related to program BM*

7.3 C Solution

When dealing with dialog boxes and menus, the resource script file contains much information about how things are to be displayed, as we have seen in Chapters 3 and 4. By contrast, the following resource script contains little more than references to the files BIRD.CUR, PEOPLE.ICO, MAN.BMP and WOMAN.BMP. The four identifiers at the left can be chosen arbitrarily. They will used in our program in strings, such as *"IDCURSOR"* etc., as we will see shortly. The keywords *CURSOR*, *ICON* and *BITMAP* denote resource types. They are followed by the names of the files produced by the image editor, discussed in the previous section.

File BM.RC:

```
// BM.RC:
IDCURSOR    CURSOR   bird.cur
IDICON      ICON     people.ico
IDMAN       BITMAP   man.bmp
IDWOMAN     BITMAP   woman.bmp
```

When using the names *IDCURSOR*, *IDICON*, *IDMAN* and *IDWOMAN* in our program, we actually refer to the files BIRD.CUR, PEOPLE.ICO, MAN.BMP and WOMAN.BMP.

File BM.H:

```
// BM.H
long FAR PASCAL _export WndProc(HWND hWnd, UINT message,
        WPARAM wParam, LPARAM lParam);
int PASCAL WinMain(HANDLE hInstance, HANDLE hPrevInstance,
     LPSTR lpCmdLine, int nCmdShow);
```

File BM.C:

```
// BM.C: Bitmap, cursor and icon.

#include <windows.h>
#include "bm.h"

HANDLE hInst;

int PASCAL WinMain(HANDLE hInstance, HANDLE hPrevInstance,
     LPSTR lpCmdLine, int nCmdShow)
{   char szAppName[]="bm";
    int xScreen, yScreen;
    WNDCLASS wndclass;
    HWND hWnd;
    MSG msg;
    xScreen = GetSystemMetrics(SM_CXSCREEN);
    yScreen = GetSystemMetrics(SM_CYSCREEN);
```

```
    if (!hPrevInstance)
    { wndclass.style = CS_HREDRAW | CS_VREDRAW;
        wndclass.lpfnWndProc = WndProc;
        wndclass.cbClsExtra = 0;
        wndclass.cbWndExtra = 0;
        wndclass.hInstance = hInstance;
        wndclass.hIcon = LoadIcon(hInstance, "IDICON");
        wndclass.hCursor = LoadCursor(hInstance, "IDCURSOR");
        wndclass.hbrBackground = GetStockObject(WHITE_BRUSH);
        wndclass.lpszMenuName = NULL;
        wndclass.lpszClassName = szAppName;
            // Name used in call to CreateWindow.
        if (!RegisterClass(&wndclass)) return FALSE;
    }
    hInst = hInstance;

    hWnd = CreateWindow(
        szAppName,
        "Bitmap, cursor and icon",
                                        // Text for window title bar.
        WS_OVERLAPPEDWINDOW,            // Window style.
        0,                              // Initial x position
        0,                              // Initial y position.
        xScreen,                        // Width.
        yScreen,                        // Height.
        NULL,                           // Parent window handle.
        NULL,                           // Window menu handle.
        hInstance,                      // Program instance handle.
        NULL                            // Create parameters.
    );
    ShowWindow(hWnd, nCmdShow);
    UpdateWindow(hWnd);
    while (GetMessage(&msg, NULL, 0, 0))
    { TranslateMessage(&msg);       // Translates virtual key codes
        DispatchMessage(&msg);      // Dispatches message to window
    }
    return msg.wParam;      // Returns the value from PostQuitMessage
}

long FAR PASCAL _export WndProc(HWND hWnd, UINT message,
        WPARAM wParam, LPARAM lParam)
{ int bitmaplen;
    static RECT rect;
    static int xScreen, yScreen, SizeMan, SizeWoman,
        LButtonPressed, RButtonPressed;
    PAINTSTRUCT ps;
    HDC hDC, hdcMem;
    HBITMAP hBm, hOldBm;
    HICON hIcon;
```

```
switch (message)
{
case WM_PAINT:
   hDC = BeginPaint(hWnd, &ps);
   hIcon = LoadIcon(hInst, "IDICON");
   DrawIcon(hDC, xScreen-50, yScreen-50, hIcon);
   if (LButtonPressed)
   { bitmaplen = 32; SizeMan /= 2;
     hBm = LoadBitmap(hInst, "IDMAN");
   } else
   if (RButtonPressed)
   { bitmaplen = 64; SizeWoman /= 2;
     hBm = LoadBitmap(hInst, "IDWOMAN");
   }
   hdcMem = CreateCompatibleDC(hDC);
   hOldBm = SelectObject(hdcMem, hBm);
   StretchBlt(hDC, rect.left, rect.top,
      rect.right - rect.left, rect.bottom - rect.top,
      hdcMem, 0, 0, bitmaplen, bitmaplen,
      SRCCOPY);
   SelectObject(hdcMem, hOldBm);
   DeleteDC(hdcMem);
   EndPaint(hWnd, &ps);
   LButtonPressed = RButtonPressed = 0;
   break;
case WM_SIZE:
   xScreen = LOWORD(lParam);
   yScreen = HIWORD(lParam);
   SizeMan = SizeWoman =
      (xScreen < yScreen ? xScreen : yScreen)/4;
   LButtonPressed = RButtonPressed = 0;
   break;
case WM_LBUTTONDOWN:
   LButtonPressed = 1;
   rect.left = LOWORD(lParam);
   rect.top = HIWORD(lParam);
   rect.right = rect.left + SizeMan;
   rect.bottom = rect.top + SizeMan;
   InvalidateRect(hWnd, &rect, FALSE);
   break;
case WM_RBUTTONDOWN:
   RButtonPressed = 1;
   rect.left = LOWORD(lParam);
   rect.top = HIWORD(lParam);
   rect.right = rect.left + SizeWoman;
   rect.bottom = rect.top + SizeWoman;
   InvalidateRect(hWnd, &rect, FALSE);
   break;
case WM_DESTROY:
```

```
        PostQuitMessage(0); break;
    default:
        return DefWindowProc(hWnd, message, wParam, lParam);
    }
    return 0L;
}
```

The special icon is displayed in the lower-right corner of the window by the following statements, occurring in the *WndProc* function:

```
hIcon = LoadIcon(hInst, "IDICON");
DrawIcon(hDC, xScreen-50, yScreen-50, hIcon);
```

We now turn to the files MAN.BMP and WOMAN.BMP, related to pressing the left and the right mouse buttons, respectively. We therefore consider the *WM_LBUTTONDOWN* and *WM_RBUTTONDOWN* cases in the *WndProc* function. Parameter *lParam* of this function is used to find the coordinates $x = LOWORD(lParam)$ and $y = HIWORD(lParam)$ of the mouse cursor when the mouse button was pressed. Remember, these functions are called by Windows, not by our own program. We can rely on Windows supplying these functions with the coordinates of the cursor's 'hot spot' when the mouse button was pressed. Incidentally, when we are creating our own cursor, such as the bird in Figure 7.1, the Image Editor enables us to define a point in our bitmap to be used as this hot spot. I used the bird's beak for this purpose. In our program these *x* and *y* values are stored in the *left* and *top* members of structure *rect*. It is essential for *rect* to be declared *static*, so we can use it later, when a *WM_PAINT* is sent. Actually, *rect* defines not only a single point but rather the rectangle that the bitmap will cover on the screen. This rectangle is then 'invalidated' by the call

```
InvalidateRect(hWnd, &rect, FALSE);
```

This means that we specify the rectangle to be repainted. This is the first time that we use *InvalidateRect* in this way. We more often use it as

```
InvalidateRect(hWnd, NULL, TRUE)
```

to invalidate the entire client rectangle. If we used this more familiar form here, the user would be able to draw the head of only one man or woman on the screen at a time: any such pictures drawn previously would be erased when a new one appeared.

After a *WM_PAINT* message is sent, we *stretch* a given bitmap, that is, instead of its original dimension *Size*, we use the new, variable dimension *bitmaplen*. This is done by the function *StretchBlt*, which is based on the concept of a *memory device context*, which is a block of memory that represents a display surface. A discussion that completely clarifies why we should need this concept would be very technical and difficult. Let us instead take the cookbook approach, focusing on the essential steps that we have to take:

1 We declare handles of types *HDC* and *HBITMAP*, and we call *BeginPaint* to obtain a
   device context handle:

```
HDC hDC, hdcMem;
HBITMAP hBm, hOldBm;
hDC = BeginPaint(hWnd, &ps);
```

The variable *hdcMem* is a handle to the memory device context, while *hBm* is a handle
to a bitmap. We now specify how the bitmap is to be loaded, writing, for example,

```
hBm = LoadBitmap(hInst, "IDWOMAN");
```

2 We create a memory device context that is compatible with *hDC*:

```
hdcMem = CreateCompatibleDC(hDC);
```

3 We select our bitmap with handle *hBm* into this memory device context, saving the
   handle to the old bitmap:

```
hOldBm = SelectObject(hdcMem, hBm);
```

Apparently a bitmap, like a pen or a brush, is to be selected into a device context.

4 The bitmap is now copied from the source device context (with handle) *hdcMem* to the
   destination device context *hDC*.

```
StretchBlt(hDC, rect.left, rect.top,
   rect.right - rect.left, rect.bottom - rect.top,
   hdcMem, 0, 0, bitmaplen, bitmaplen,
   SRCCOPY);
```

Actually, function *StretchBlt* maps a source rectangle to a destination rectangle that may
have different dimensions, hence the word *Stretch* in its name. Incidentally, *Blt* stands
for *block transfer*. Such a block represents a rectangle, specified by the coordinates of
its upper left corner, its width and its height. This explains why *StretchBlt* has so many
arguments. Altogether, we have
-    the destination (*hDC*, followed by four arguments denoting a rectangle)
-    the source (*hdcMem*, followed by four arguments denoting a rectangle)
- *SRCCOPY*, indicating that the old destination rectangle simply is to be overwritten; a
     different way of copying, based on an *OR* operation between the old destination and
     the source rectangle, is realized by using *SRCPAINT* instead of *SRCCOPY* (see also
     Section 9.2).

5 We restore the old bitmap, using the handle *hOldBm*, obtained in step 3, delete the
   memory device context, and call *EndPaint*:

```
SelectObject(hdcMem, hOldBm);
DeleteDC(hdcMem);
EndPaint(hWnd, &ps);
```

7.4 MFC Solution

The solution shown below is based on the Microsoft Foundation class *CBitmap*, which, like *CPen*, *CBrush* and *CPalette*, is derived from class *CGdiObject* (see Figure B3 in Appendix B).

Except for the comment line, the resource script file to be used is identical with the one of Section 7.3:

File BMMFC.RC:

```
// BMMFC.RC:
IDCURSOR   CURSOR   bird.cur
IDICON     ICON     people.ico
IDMAN      BITMAP   man.bmp
IDWOMAN    BITMAP   woman.bmp
```

The header file for this program is very simple. You can see from it that we will respond to the three messages *WM_LBUTTONDOWN*, *WM_RBUTTONDOWN* and *WM_PAINT*. Note that we have added several (private) data members to our window class *CMyWindow*, which are immediately available in all message response functions because these are also members of *CMyWindow*:

File BMMFC.H:

```
// BMMFC.H: Bitmap, cursor and icon

class CApp: public CWinApp
{  public:
   BOOL InitInstance();
};

class CMyWindow: public CFrameWnd
{  int SizeMan, SizeWoman, xScreen, yScreen,
      LButtonPressed, RButtonPressed;
   CPoint PointSelected;
public:
   CMyWindow();
   afx_msg void OnPaint();
   afx_msg void OnSize(UINT nType, int cx, int cy);
   afx_msg void OnLButtonDown(UINT nFlags, CPoint point);
   afx_msg void OnRButtonDown(UINT nFlags, CPoint point);
   DECLARE_MESSAGE_MAP()
};
```

When using the MFC we have so far written *NULL* as the first argument in calls to *Create*, to indicate that we wanted the default window class to be used. Instead of *NULL*, we now use the object *ClassName*, which is of type *CString* and is obtained by means of a rather

complicated call to the function *AfxRegisterWndClass*. The *CMyWindow* constructor in the
following program file shows this in detail:

File BMMFC.CPP:

```cpp
// BMMFC.CPP: Bitmap, cursor and icon
#include <afxwin.h>
#include "bmmfc.h"

BOOL CApp::InitInstance()
{  m_pMainWnd = new CMyWindow();
   m_pMainWnd->ShowWindow(m_nCmdShow);
   m_pMainWnd->UpdateWindow();
   return TRUE;
}

CApp App;

CMyWindow::CMyWindow()
{  xScreen = GetSystemMetrics(SM_CXSCREEN),
   yScreen = GetSystemMetrics(SM_CYSCREEN);
   SizeMan = SizeWoman = min(xScreen, yScreen)/4;
                         // Initial sizes of bitmaps
   RECT rect = {0, 0, xScreen, yScreen};
   LButtonPressed = RButtonPressed = 0;
   CPoint PointSelected;
   CString ClassName = AfxRegisterWndClass(
      CS_HREDRAW | CS_VREDRAW,              // Class style
      AfxGetApp()->LoadCursor("IDCURSOR"), // Cursor
      HBRUSH(GetStockObject(WHITE_BRUSH)), // Background color
      AfxGetApp()->LoadIcon("IDICON"));    // Icon
   Create(ClassName, "Bitmap, cursor and icon",
          WS_OVERLAPPEDWINDOW, rect, NULL, NULL);
}

BEGIN_MESSAGE_MAP(CMyWindow, CFrameWnd)
   ON_WM_PAINT()
   ON_WM_SIZE()
   ON_WM_LBUTTONDOWN()
   ON_WM_RBUTTONDOWN()
END_MESSAGE_MAP()

void CMyWindow::OnPaint()
{  CPaintDC dc(this);
   int Size;
   HICON hIcon = AfxGetApp()->LoadIcon("IDICON");
   dc.DrawIcon(xScreen-50, yScreen-50, hIcon);
   if (LButtonPressed || RButtonPressed)
   {  int bitmaplen;
      CDC dcCompDC;
```

```
                 CBitmap bm, *pOldBitmap;
                 if (LButtonPressed)
                 {  bitmaplen = 32; Size = SizeMan; SizeMan /= 2;
                    bm.LoadBitmap("IDMAN");
                 } else  // (RButtonPressed)
                 {  bitmaplen = 64; Size = SizeWoman; SizeWoman /= 2;
                    bm.LoadBitmap("IDWOMAN");
                 }
                 dcCompDC.CreateCompatibleDC(&dc);
                 pOldBitmap = dcCompDC.SelectObject(&bm);
                 dc.StretchBlt(PointSelected.x, PointSelected.y, Size, Size,
                    &dcCompDC, 0, 0, bitmaplen, bitmaplen, SRCCOPY);
                 dcCompDC.SelectObject(pOldBitmap);
                 LButtonPressed = RButtonPressed = 0;
              }
         }

      void CMyWindow::OnSize(UINT nType, int cx, int cy)
      {  SizeMan = SizeWoman = min(cx, cy)/4; // Initial sizes of bitmaps
         xScreen = cx; yScreen = cy;
         LButtonPressed = RButtonPressed   = 0;
      }

      void CMyWindow::OnLButtonDown(UINT nFlags, CPoint point)
      {  LButtonPressed = 1; PointSelected = point;
         RECT rect = {point.x, point.y, point.x + SizeMan,
                                       point.y + SizeMan};
         InvalidateRect(&rect);
      }

      void CMyWindow::OnRButtonDown(UINT nFlags, CPoint point)
      {  RButtonPressed = 1; PointSelected = point;
         RECT rect = {point.x, point.y, point.x + SizeWoman,
                                       point.y + SizeWoman};
         InvalidateRect(&rect);
      }
```

With MFC we use *LoadCursor* and *LoadIcon* member functions of class *CWinApp*, so what we need is a pointer to the *CWinApp* object of our application. This pointer is supplied by the call to *AfxGetApp*. The *LoadCursor* and *LoadIcon* functions return handles, which we use as the second and the fourth arguments in a call to function *AfxRegister-WndClass*. We must then also supply this function with a first and a third argument. The first is the class style *CS_HREDRAW | CS_VREDRAW*, which, when the size of the window changes, causes the entire client rectangle to be cleared before it is repainted. The third argument of *AfxRegisterWndClass* is a handle to the background brush, written as *GetStockObject(WHITE_BRUSH)* with a cast to type *HBRUSH*. You can find the latter call also in our C programs (see Section 1.2, for example). This discussion must be extremely difficult to understand for those who want to program only with the MFC; it makes sense only if we are also familiar with traditional Windows programming, as used in the previous section.

We also have to discuss the other bitmaps, based on the files MAN.BMP and WOMAN.BMP, and in our program related to the left and the right mouse buttons, respectively. The functions *OnLButtonDown* and *OnRButtonDown* are very simple but yet instructive. They use the *point* parameter (supplied by Windows) to find out the location that has been clicked. We can rely on Windows supplying these functions with the coordinates of the cursor's 'hot spot', that is, the bird's beak. In our program the point in question is stored in the *CMyWindow* member variable *PointSelected*, so we can use it later in the *OnPaint* function. It is also used to define the rectangle that the bitmap will cover on the screen. This rectangle is then 'invalidated' by the call

```
InvalidateRect(&rect)
```

This means that we specify the rectangle that will be repainted later by *OnPaint*. We use instead the call

```
InvalidateRect(NULL, TRUE)
```

which we have used several times to invalidate the entire client rectangle. It we used this more familiar form here, the user would be able to draw the head of only one man or woman on the screen at a time: any such pictures drawn previously would be erased when a new one appeared.

The *OnPaint* function in our program stretches a given bitmap: instead of its original dimension *Size*, a new, variable dimension *bitmaplen* is used. This is done by the function *StretchBlt*, the name of which indicates 'stretching and block transfer'. This function is based on the concept of a *memory device context*, which is a block of memory that represents a display surface. When using this function, we take the following steps:

1   We declare objects of types *CPaintDC*, *CDC* and *CBitmap*:

```
CPaintDC dc(this);
CDC dcCompDC;
CBitmap bm, *pOldBitmap;
```

Constructing the device context *dc* by its declaration and destroying it when it goes out of scope corresponds to calling the functions *BeginPaint* and *EndPaint* in a C program. The CDC object *dcCompDC* is the memory device context. Finally, we need a *CBitmap* object *bm* and a *CBitmap* pointer. We now specify how the bitmap is to be loaded, writing, for example

```
bm.LoadBitmap("IDWOMAN");
```

2   We create a memory device context that is compatible with *dc*:

```
dcCompDC.CreateCompatibleDC(&dc);
```

3 We select our bitmap *bm* into this memory device context *dcCompDC*, saving the address of the old bitmap in a pointer:

```
pOldBitmap = dcCompDC.SelectObject(&bm);
```

Apparently a *CBitmap* object, like a pen or a brush, is to be selected into a device context.

4 We do the actual stretching and drawing of the bitmap:

```
dc.StretchBlt(Pglobal.x, Pglobal.y, Size, Size,
    &dcCompDC, 0, 0, bitmaplen, bitmaplen, SRCCOPY);
```

The bitmap is now copied from the source device context *dcCompDC* to the destination device context *dc*. Actually, a source rectangle is mapped to a destination rectangle that may have different dimensions. For each rectangle, the coordinates of its upper left corner, its width and its height are given. The first four arguments of *StretchBlt* denote the destination rectangle in *dc*. The address of the source device context is given as the fifth argument, followed by four arguments that specify the dimensions of the source rectangle. The final argument, *SRCCOPY*, specifies that the old destination rectangle is to be simply overwritten. There are several other possibilities, such as *SRCPAINT*, which would perform an *OR* operation between the old destination rectangle and the rectangle obtained from the source (see also Chapter 9).

5 We restore the old bitmap, using the pointer stored in step 3:

```
dcCompDC.SelectObject(pOldBitmap);
```

In this way we prevent any problems arising from destroying *bm* (by its destructor) while it is still selected in the device context *dcCompDC*.

Drawing an icon in the client rectangle

We also draw the icon stored in the file PEOPLE.ICO in the client rectangle. Recall that the name of this file occurs in our resource script file as follows:

```
IDICON ICON PEOPLE.ICON
```

Then we use the statements

```
HICON hIcon = AfxGetApp()->LoadIcon("IDICON");
dc.DrawIcon(xScreen-50, yScreen-50, hIcon);
```

in our *OnPaint* function to draw the icon. We must be careful with regard to the place where we insert these two lines. If we do this in the large if-statement, starting with

```
if (LButtonPressed || RButtonPressed)
```

the icon will not appear. We can understand this by realizing when and how *OnPaint* is activated. First of all, this happens as a result of the call to *UpdateWindow* in function *CApp::InitInstance* and when the window size is changed. Such calls send a *WM_PAINT* message to the window to paint the *entire client rectangle* (which is then said to be invalidated). Since the variables *LButtonPressed* and *RButtonPressed* are then zero, the above *DrawIcon* function is called only if it is placed outside the large if-statement just mentioned. By contrast, function *OnPaint* is also activated after pressing a mouse button. However, only the small rectangle *rect* is then invalidated because of the way we call *InvalidateRect* in the functions *OnLButtonDown* and *OnRButtonDown*. If the rectangle determined by the *x* and *y* arguments of *DrawIcon* lies outside this small rectangle *rect*, which is very likely, the icon will not appear. So remember, the effect of the *OnPaint* function depends on the current invalidated rectangle. Any call of the form *dc.xxx* in our *OnPaint* function, where *dc* is the device context, can paint only the invalidated rectangle. If this happens to be the entire client rectangle, there is no problem.

7.5 OWL Solution

The following files form an ObjectWindows solution to the problem of this chapter. You should compare this program with those of Sections 7.3 and 7.4. Our special cursor and icon are loaded in a peculiar way. We override the two virtual functions *GetClassName*, which simply returns a character string containing the name *TMyWindow* of our derived class, and *GetWindowClass*, in which we load our cursor and our icon. Before we do this, we call the *GetWindowClass* member function of the base class, *TWindow*. This fills its reference argument, a *WNDCLASS* structure, with registration attributes, which we then modify with regard to the cursor and the icon. Note that there is no API function *GetWindowClass*. It is an example of a member-function name specific to the ObjectWindows Library (while MFC member functions usually have the same names as their API counterparts).

File BMOWL.RC:

```
// BMOWL.RC:
IDCURSOR   CURSOR   bird.cur
IDICON     ICON     people.ico
IDMAN      BITMAP   man.bmp
IDWOMAN    BITMAP   woman.bmp
```

File BMOWL.H:

```
// BMOWL.H
class TApp: public TApplication
{ public:
    TApp(LPSTR Name, HANDLE hInstance, HANDLE hPrevInstance,
```

```
                LPSTR lpCmdLine, int nCmdShow)
          : TApplication(Name, hInstance, hPrevInstance, lpCmdLine,
                          nCmdShow){}
     virtual void InitMainWindow();
};

class TMyWindow: public TWindow
{  int xScreen, yScreen, LButtonPressed, RButtonPressed,
       SizeMan, SizeWoman;
   POINT P;
public:
   TMyWindow(PTWindowsObject AParent, LPSTR ATitle)
        : TWindow(AParent, ATitle){}
   virtual void Paint(HDC hDC, PAINTSTRUCT &ps);
   virtual void WMSize(RTMessage Msg);
   virtual void GetWindowClass(WNDCLASS _FAR &AWndClass);
   virtual LPSTR GetClassName();
   virtual void WMLButtonDown(RTMessage Msg)
     = [WM_FIRST + WM_LBUTTONDOWN];
   virtual void WMRButtonDown(RTMessage Msg)
     = [WM_FIRST + WM_RBUTTONDOWN];
};
```

File BMOWL.CPP:

```
// BMOWL.CPP: Bitmap, cursor and icon
#define WIN31
#include <owl.h>
#include "bmowl.h"

HANDLE hInstGlob;

inline int min(int x, int y){return x<y ? x : y;}

void TApp::InitMainWindow()
{  TWindow *pWin;
   MainWindow = pWin = new TMyWindow(NULL, Name);
   pWin->Attr.X = 0;
   pWin->Attr.Y = 0;
   pWin->Attr.W = GetSystemMetrics(SM_CXSCREEN);
   pWin->Attr.H = GetSystemMetrics(SM_CYSCREEN);
}

void TMyWindow::GetWindowClass(WNDCLASS _FAR &AWndClass)
{  TWindow::GetWindowClass(AWndClass);
   AWndClass.hCursor = LoadCursor(hInstGlob, "IDCURSOR");
   AWndClass.hIcon = LoadIcon(hInstGlob, "IDICON");
}
```

```
LPSTR TMyWindow::GetClassName()
{  return "TMyWindow";
}

void TMyWindow::Paint(HDC hDC, PAINTSTRUCT&)
{  HICON hIcon = LoadIcon(hInstGlob, "IDICON");
   DrawIcon(hDC, xScreen-50, yScreen-50, hIcon);
   if (LButtonPressed || RButtonPressed)
   {  int bitmaplen, Size;
      HDC hCompDC;
      BITMAP bm;
      HBITMAP hBm, hOldBm;
      if (LButtonPressed)
      {  bitmaplen = 32; Size = SizeMan; SizeMan /= 2;
         hBm = LoadBitmap(hInstGlob, "IDMAN");
      } else  // (RButtonPressed)
      {  bitmaplen = 64; Size = SizeWoman; SizeWoman /= 2;
         hBm = LoadBitmap(hInstGlob, "IDWOMAN");
      }
      GetObject(hBm, sizeof(BITMAP), &bm);
      hCompDC = CreateCompatibleDC(hDC);
      hOldBm = SelectObject(hCompDC, hBm);
      StretchBlt(hDC, P.x, P.y, Size, Size,
          hCompDC, 0, 0, bitmaplen, bitmaplen, SRCCOPY);
      SelectObject(hCompDC, hOldBm);
      DeleteDC(hCompDC);
      LButtonPressed = RButtonPressed = 0;
   }
}

void TMyWindow::WMSize(RTMessage Msg)
{  xScreen = Msg.LP.Lo;
   yScreen = Msg.LP.Hi;
   SizeMan = SizeWoman =
   min(xScreen, yScreen)/4; // Initial sizes of bitmaps
   LButtonPressed = RButtonPressed  = 0;
}

void TMyWindow::WMLButtonDown(RTMessage Msg)
{  LButtonPressed = 1;
   P.x = Msg.LP.Lo;
   P.y = Msg.LP.Hi;
   RECT rect = {P.x, P.y,
   P.x + SizeMan, P.y + SizeMan};
   InvalidateRect(HWindow, &rect, NULL);
}

void TMyWindow::WMRButtonDown(RTMessage Msg)
{  RButtonPressed = 1;
   P.x = Msg.LP.Lo;
```

```
        P.y = Msg.LP.Hi;
        RECT rect = {P.x, P.y,
        P.x + SizeWoman, P.y + SizeWoman};
        InvalidateRect(HWindow, &rect, NULL);
}

int PASCAL WinMain(HANDLE hInstance, HANDLE hPrevInstance,
    LPSTR lpCmdLine, int nCmdShow)
{   hInstGlob = hInstance;
    TApp App("Bitmap, cursor and icon",
    hInstance, hPrevInstance, lpCmdLine, nCmdShow);
    App.Run();
    return App.Status;
}
```

In Sections 7.3 and 7.4 we have seen how to use a device memory context and function *StretchBlt*. As you can see from the above program text, the same concepts are used here in a slightly different notation, which we will not discuss in detail. The main thing to remember is that we cannot directly copy a bitmap to a normal device context, but, instead, we successively have to

- create a memory device context (using *CreateCompatibleDC*)
- select a bitmap into a memory device context (using *SelectObject*)
- copy a rectangle from the memory device context to the normal device context (using *StretchBlt*, or a similar function to be discussed in Chapter 9)

You may be interested in a comparison of the sizes of the executable files. Curiously enough, they differ considerably. The sizes shown below apply to executable files obtained by using the make files briefly discussed at the end of Section 7.2 and based on the medium memory model:

File	Size in bytes
BM.EXE	10752 (Microsoft Visual C++)
BM.EXE	10240 (with Borland C++)
BMMFC.EXE	24576 (Microsoft Foundation Classes)
BMOWL.EXE	61440 (Borland ObjectWindows Library)

The code produced by the Microsoft and Borland compilers is very small and almost the same in size as long as we do not use their class libraries. If we do, the code is considerably larger, especially with the Borland ObjectWindows Library. The above comparatively large size of file BMOWL.EXE is characteristic of OWL applications. Of course, all this may change with future compiler versions. I should also mention that I have not explored any compiler options for code optimization. As mentioned in Section 1.2, an attractive aspect of make files is that all compiler and link options are explicit, so if you are familiar with these options you can clearly see which I used and possibly explain the above differences in file sizes. As we know, the Microsoft Visual C++ concept of 'external make file' enables us to combine the convenience of an integrated environment with the explicitness of a make file.

Since the above figures depend on so many circumstances, we should be very careful with them. I therefore included this comparison only in one chapter, which happens to be the present one.

7.6 Questions

7.1   Why are some variables, such as *LButtonPressed*, given the *static* attribute in program BM and made class members in the programs BMMFC and BMOWL?

7.2   How can we load a cursor, an icon, and a bitmap?

7.3   What is a memory device context used for and how is it created?

7.4   How can we display an icon in the client rectangle?

7.5   What happens if we replace the style *CS_HREDRAW | CS_VREDRAW* with *NULL*?

8

Interactive Line Drawing

8.1 Problem Definition

We now want to write a program for interactive line drawing. The user should be able to draw lines in the same way as is done with many commercial draw packages, such as the Microsoft Draw program, and as is illustrated by Figure 7.1. Initially, there is a so-called *crosshair* mouse cursor in the form of a very large plus sign. We move the cursor to the position that is to be the start point of the line and we press the left mouse button and keep it pressed down. We then *drag* the cursor, that is, we move the mouse, with the left mouse button kept down. While doing this, we see a straight line drawn from the start point just defined to the current cursor position. Moving the cursor causes this line to change, just like an elastic string with a fixed start point and a moving end point. When we want the line to be fixed as it appears on the screen, we simply release the left mouse button. After this, any mouse movements no longer change the line just drawn.

8.2 General Aspects

We need some more Windows messages to implement this idea. Besides *WM_LBUTTONDOWN*, we will also use *WM_LBUTTONUP* and *WM_MOUSEMOVE*. Their meanings are obvious, as are the names of the corresponding MFC functions *OnLButtonDown*, *OnLButtonUp* and *OnMouseMove*, which are members of the *CWnd* class, available with the MFC to derive our own window class *CMyWindow* from.

Displaying the crosshair cursor is the easiest part. We only have to use the identifier *IDC_CROSS* instead of *IDC_ARROW*, used so far.

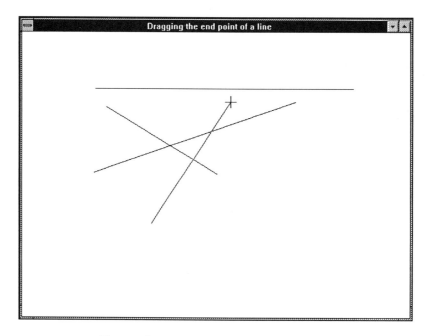

Figure 7.1. *Lines produced with program DRAG*

We had better not draw lines in response to *WM_PAINT* messages, by using the *InvalidateRect* function. If we did, we would have to define a rectangle to be invalidated, and anything already present inside that rectangle would then be erased. One solution would be to store both end points of all lines drawn so far and to draw these lines each time a *WM_PAINT* message is sent. However, this would take too much time, because *WM_MOUSEMOVE* messages will be sent very frequently, and if each of these were to generate a *WM_PAINT* message resulting in redrawing the entire client rectangle, all lines drawn so far would have to be redrawn each time we moved the mouse a little. This would be an enormous waste of time. We can do much better by updating the screen directly in response to *WM_MOUSEMOVE* messages.

While we are moving the mouse with the left button kept down, there is a line on the screen that changes all the time because of its moving end point. Actually, we have to erase an old line and draw a new one for each small movement of the mouse. However, we must not erase lines in the normal way, that is, by turning all their black pixels white. If we did, any point of intersection of two lines would be erased if one of these two lines were erased, leaving a small hole in the remaining line. We will therefore draw and erase lines simply by inverting their pixels, until a line has its final form. In other words, we will use two drawing modes. As long as we are dealing with *WM_MOUSEMOVE* messages while the left mouse button is kept down, we will invert pixels, using the drawing mode identified by the constant *R2_NOT*. The end of this process is signaled by a *WM_LBUTTONUP* message. Then the last version of the line is inverted once more, after which all its pixels are made black by using the drawing mode *R2_COPYPEN*. The name of the function that sets a drawing mode is *SetROP*2, where *ROP* stands for *raster operation*. Besides *R2_NOT* and *R2_COPYPEN* there are several other drawing modes, which you can find in the *Microsoft Windows Programmer's Reference* or elsewhere.

Make files

We can use the make files of Chapter 5 here, provided we replace all occurrences of *gr* with *drag*.

8.3 C Solution

The files for a C solution to our dragging and line-drawing problem are listed below:

File DRAG.H:

```
// DRAG.H:
long FAR PASCAL _export WndProc(HWND hWnd, UINT message,
     WPARAM wParam, LPARAM lParam);
int PASCAL WinMain(HANDLE hInstance, HANDLE hPrevInstance,
    LPSTR lpCmdLine, int nCmdShow);
```

File DRAG.C:

```
// DRAG.C: Interactive line drawing.

#include <windows.h>
#include "drag.h"

int Drawing;
HANDLE hInst;

int PASCAL WinMain(HANDLE hInstance, HANDLE hPrevInstance,
    LPSTR lpCmdLine, int nCmdShow)
{   char szAppName[]="drag";
    int xScreen, yScreen;
    WNDCLASS wndclass;
    HWND hWnd;
    MSG msg;
    xScreen = GetSystemMetrics(SM_CXSCREEN);
    yScreen = GetSystemMetrics(SM_CYSCREEN);
    if (!hPrevInstance)
    {   wndclass.style = NULL;
        wndclass.lpfnWndProc = WndProc;
        wndclass.cbClsExtra = 0;
        wndclass.cbWndExtra = 0;
        wndclass.hInstance = hInstance;
        wndclass.hIcon = LoadIcon(NULL, IDI_APPLICATION);
```

```
        wndclass.hCursor = LoadCursor(NULL, IDC_CROSS);
        wndclass.hbrBackground = GetStockObject(WHITE_BRUSH);
        wndclass.lpszMenuName = NULL;
        wndclass.lpszClassName = szAppName;
          // Name used in call to CreateWindow.
        if (!RegisterClass(&wndclass)) return FALSE;
    }
    hInst = hInstance;
    hWnd = CreateWindow(
        szAppName,
        "Dragging the end point of a line",
                                    // Text for window title bar.
        WS_OVERLAPPEDWINDOW,        // Window style.
        0,                          // Initial x position
        0,                          // Initial y position.
        xScreen,                    // Width.
        yScreen,                    // Height.
        NULL,                       // Parent window handle.
        NULL,                       // Window menu handle.
        hInstance,                  // Program instance handle.
        NULL                        // Create parameters.
    );
    Drawing = 0;
    ShowWindow(hWnd, nCmdShow);
    UpdateWindow(hWnd);
    while (GetMessage(&msg, NULL, 0, 0))
    {  TranslateMessage(&msg);      // Translates virtual key codes
       DispatchMessage(&msg);       // Dispatches message to window
    }
    return msg.wParam;      // Returns the value from PostQuitMessage
}

long FAR PASCAL _export WndProc(HWND hWnd, UINT message,
      WPARAM wParam, LPARAM lParam)
{  HDC hDC;
   static POINT Pbegin, Pend;
   switch (message)
   {
   case WM_LBUTTONDOWN:
      Pbegin.x = LOWORD(lParam);
      Pbegin.y = HIWORD(lParam);
      Pend = Pbegin;
      Drawing = 1;
      break;
   case WM_MOUSEMOVE:
      if (Drawing)
      {  hDC = GetDC(hWnd);
         SetROP2(hDC, R2_NOT);      // Erase old line:
         MoveTo(hDC, Pbegin.x, Pbegin.y);
         LineTo(hDC, Pend.x, Pend.y);
```

```
            Pend.x = LOWORD(lParam);
            Pend.y = HIWORD(lParam);  // Draw new line:
            MoveTo(hDC, Pbegin.x, Pbegin.y);
            LineTo(hDC, Pend.x, Pend.y);
            ReleaseDC(hWnd, hDC);
         }
         break;
      case WM_LBUTTONUP:
         hDC = GetDC(hWnd);
         SetROP2(hDC, R2_NOT);          // Erase old line:
         MoveTo(hDC, Pbegin.x, Pbegin.y);
         LineTo(hDC, Pend.x, Pend.y);
         Pend.x = LOWORD(lParam);
         Pend.y = HIWORD(lParam);

         // Draw new line:
         SetROP2(hDC, R2_COPYPEN);
         MoveTo(hDC, Pbegin.x, Pbegin.y);
         LineTo(hDC, Pend.x, Pend.y);

         ReleaseDC(hWnd, hDC);
         Drawing = 0;
         break;
      case WM_DESTROY:
         PostQuitMessage(0); break;
      default:
         return DefWindowProc(hWnd, message, wParam, lParam);
   }
   return 0L;
}
```

A line that is being drawn has a fixed end point *Pbegin* and a moving one *Pend*. Both are set equal to the current cursor position when the left mouse button is pressed down. A nonzero value of the variable *Drawing* indicates that a line is being drawn, which means that the left mouse button is kept down. For each *WM_MOUSEMOVE* message, we erase the old line between *Pbegin* and *Pend*, then update *Pend* and finally draw a new line between *Pbegin* and the new *Pend*. These erase and draw operations are done in the same way. The three statements

```
SetROP2(hDC, R2_NOT);
MoveTo(hDC, Pbegin.x, Pbegin.y);
LineTo(hDC, Pend.x, Pend.y);
```

simply invert each pixel on the straight line between *Pbegin* and *Pend*. In other words, each such pixel turns white if it is black and vice versa.

Note the use of *GetDC* and *ReleaseDC*, instead of *BeginPaint* and *EndPaint* which we would use in response to a *WM_PAINT* message.

8.4 MFC Solution

Using C++ and the MFC, we need only a small program to achieve what we have discussed and implemented in the previous sections:

File DRAGMFC.H:

```
// DRAGMFC.H:
class CApp: public CWinApp
{ public:
    BOOL InitInstance();
};


class CMyWindow: public CFrameWnd
{ CPoint Pbegin, Pend;
    int Drawing;
public:
    CMyWindow();
    afx_msg void OnLButtonDown(UINT nFlags, CPoint point);
    afx_msg void OnMouseMove(UINT nFlags, CPoint point);
    afx_msg void OnLButtonUp(UINT nFlags, CPoint point);
    DECLARE_MESSAGE_MAP()
};
```

File DRAGMFC.CPP:

```
// DRAGMFC.CPP: Dragging the end point of a line

#include <afxwin.h>
#include "dragmfc.h"

BOOL CApp::InitInstance()
{ m_pMainWnd = new CMyWindow();
    m_pMainWnd->ShowWindow(m_nCmdShow);
    m_pMainWnd->UpdateWindow();
    return TRUE;
}

CApp App;

CMyWindow::CMyWindow()
{ int xScreen = GetSystemMetrics(SM_CXSCREEN),
        yScreen = GetSystemMetrics(SM_CYSCREEN);
    RECT rect = {0, 0, xScreen, yScreen};
    CString ClassName = AfxRegisterWndClass(
        NULL,  // No repainting when the size changes
        AfxGetApp()->LoadStandardCursor(IDC_CROSS),
        HBRUSH(GetStockObject(WHITE_BRUSH)),
        NULL);
```

```
        Create(ClassName, "Dragging the end point of a line",
               WS_OVERLAPPEDWINDOW, rect, NULL, NULL);
        Drawing = 0;
}

BEGIN_MESSAGE_MAP(CMyWindow, CFrameWnd)
    ON_WM_LBUTTONDOWN()
    ON_WM_MOUSEMOVE()
    ON_WM_LBUTTONUP()
END_MESSAGE_MAP()

void CMyWindow::OnLButtonDown(UINT nFlags, CPoint point)
{   Pbegin = Pend = point;
    Drawing = 1;
}

void CMyWindow::OnMouseMove(UINT nFlags, CPoint point)
{   if (Drawing)
    {   CClientDC dc(this);
        dc.SetROP2(R2_NOT);        // Erase old line:
        dc.MoveTo(Pbegin);
        dc.LineTo(Pend);
        Pend = point;              // Draw new line:
        dc.MoveTo(Pbegin);
        dc.LineTo(Pend);
    }
}

void CMyWindow::OnLButtonUp(UINT nFlags, CPoint point)
{   CClientDC dc(this);
    dc.SetROP2(R2_NOT);            // Erase old line:
    dc.MoveTo(Pbegin);
    dc.LineTo(Pend);
    Pend = point;
    dc.SetROP2(R2_COPYPEN);        // Draw new line, final version:
    dc.MoveTo(Pbegin);
    dc.LineTo(Pend);
    Drawing = 0;
}
```

Note the statement

```
CClientDC dc(this);
```

occurring in both *OnMouseMove* and *OnLButtonUp*. Like *CPaintDC*, class *CClientDC* is
derived from class *CDC* (see Figure B4 in Appendix B). The difference between these two
derived classes is that *CPaintDC* must be used in the *OnPaint* function and *CClientDC*
elsewhere. *CPaintDC* constructors and destructors call the API functions *BeginPaint* and

EndPaint, respectively, while those of *CClientDC* call *GetDC* and *ReleaseDC* instead. Thus, we must not confuse the columns for *CPaintDC* and *CClientDC* in this table:

	CPaintDC	*CClientDC*
Related message	*WM_PAINT*	Other, e.g. *WM_MOUSEMOVE*
API function called by constructor	*BeginPaint*	*GetDC*
API function called by destructor	*EndPaint*	*ReleaseDC*

Note that *Pbegin*, *Pend* and *Drawing* are private members of the *CMyWindow* class. This is possible because we use them only in member functions of this class.

In Section 6.4, we used the functions *AfxRegisterWndClass* and *Create* in the *CMy-Window* constructor to specify a background color. Here we use the same functions to specify a cursor other than the default one.

8.5 OWL Solution

The files for an OWL solution to the problem defined in Section 8.1 are listed below. Note the way we override the virtual functions *GetWindowClass* and *GetClassName* to define a crosshair cursor. Recall that we briefly discussed these two functions at the beginning of Section 7.5 and that we saw a list of standard cursors in Section 7.2:

File DRAGOWL.H:

```
// DRAGOWL.H:
class TApp: public TApplication
{  public:
     TApp(LPSTR Name, HANDLE hInstance, HANDLE hPrevInstance,
       LPSTR lpCmdLine, int nCmdShow)
       : TApplication(Name, hInstance, hPrevInstance, lpCmdLine,
       nCmdShow){}
     virtual void InitMainWindow();
};

class TMyWindow: public TWindow
{  POINT Pbegin, Pend;
   int Drawing;
public:
   TMyWindow(PTWindowsObject AParent, LPSTR ATitle);
   virtual void GetWindowClass(WNDCLASS _FAR &AWndClass);
   virtual LPSTR GetClassName();
   virtual void WMLButtonDown(RTMessage Msg)
     = [WM_FIRST + WM_LBUTTONDOWN];
   virtual void WMLButtonUp(RTMessage Msg)
     = [WM_FIRST + WM_LBUTTONUP];
   virtual void WMMouseMove(RTMessage Msg)
     = [WM_FIRST + WM_MOUSEMOVE];
};
```

File DRAGOWL.CPP:

```cpp
// DRAGOWL.CPP: Interactive line drawing
#define WIN31
#include <owl.h>
#include "dragowl.h"

void TApp::InitMainWindow()
{   TWindow *pWin;
    MainWindow = pWin = new TMyWindow(NULL, Name);
    pWin->Attr.X = 0;
    pWin->Attr.Y = 0;
    pWin->Attr.W = GetSystemMetrics(SM_CXSCREEN);
    pWin->Attr.H = GetSystemMetrics(SM_CYSCREEN);
}

void TMyWindow::GetWindowClass(WNDCLASS _FAR &AWndClass)
{   TWindow::GetWindowClass(AWndClass);
    AWndClass.hCursor = LoadCursor(NULL, IDC_CROSS);
}

LPSTR TMyWindow::GetClassName()
{   return "TMyWindow";
}

TMyWindow::TMyWindow(PTWindowsObject AParent, LPSTR ATitle)
     : TWindow(AParent, ATitle)
{   Drawing = 0;
}

void TMyWindow::WMLButtonDown(RTMessage Msg)
{   Pbegin.x = Pend.x = Msg.LP.Lo;
    Pbegin.y = Pend.y = Msg.LP.Hi;
    Drawing = 1;
}

void TMyWindow::WMMouseMove(RTMessage Msg)
{   if (Drawing)
    {   HDC hDC = GetDC(HWindow);
        SetROP2(hDC, R2_NOT);     // Erase old line:
        MoveTo(hDC, Pbegin.x, Pbegin.y);
        LineTo(hDC, Pend.x, Pend.y);
        Pend.x = Msg.LP.Lo;
        Pend.y = Msg.LP.Hi; // Draw new line:
        MoveTo(hDC, Pbegin.x, Pbegin.y);
        LineTo(hDC, Pend.x, Pend.y);
        ReleaseDC(HWindow, hDC);
    }
}
```

```
void TMyWindow::WMLButtonUp(RTMessage Msg)
{  HDC hDC = GetDC(HWindow);
   SetROP2(hDC, R2_NOT);       // Erase old line:
   MoveTo(hDC, Pbegin.x, Pbegin.y);
   LineTo(hDC, Pend.x, Pend.y);
   Pend.x = Msg.LP.Lo;
   Pend.y = Msg.LP.Hi;
   SetROP2(hDC, R2_COPYPEN);  // Draw new line, final version:
   MoveTo(hDC, Pbegin.x, Pbegin.y);
   LineTo(hDC, Pend.x, Pend.y);
   Drawing = 0;
   ReleaseDC(HWindow, hDC);
}

int PASCAL WinMain(HANDLE hInstance, HANDLE hPrevInstance,
   LPSTR lpCmdLine, int nCmdShow)
{  TApp App("Dragging the end point of a line",
   hInstance, hPrevInstance, lpCmdLine, nCmdShow);
   App.Run();
   return App.Status;
}
```

8.6 Questions

The following questions refer to those programming styles (C, MFC, OWL) in which you are interested.

8.1   How can we replace the normal cursor with a crosshair cursor?
8.2   Why did we draw lines directly in response to the *WM_MOUSEMOVE* rather than to *WM_PAINT* message (in combination with *InvalidateRect*)?
8.3   Which special drawing mode is used and why?
8.4   The programs of this chapter did not internally store the lines that were drawn. What serious drawback does this approach have with regard to size changes of the window? If we stored both end points of each line segment in an array, for example, we would be able to avoid this drawback. How?

9

Animation

9.1 Problem Definition

In this section we will discuss how to write a program for animation. We will generate stars, appearing beside each other on lines that make angles of 45° with the window edges. This problem is reminiscent of the well-known example of a bouncing ball (which would be less suitable for an illustration in this book because of there being only one ball). Instead of such a ball, we use a star with five vertices, and instead of *moving* this object, we *copy* it in a special way. Starting with an empty client rectangle, the number of visible stars initially increases, but an already existing star is erased if a new one happens to obtain the same position. We will use yellow stars on a (dark) blue background. Figure 9.1 may give you an impression of the screen at a given moment, when there are two instances of the program running, along with our line-drawing program of Chapter 8. When we change the size of the window (by dragging an edge or a corner), we start again with an empty client rectangle. All stars on the screen will have the same size, which is proportional to the size of the window. More precisely, each star will fit into a circle, the diameter of which is equal to one tenth of either the client rectangle's height or its width, whichever is smaller. Since the bit-block transfer routine that we will be using is based on rectangles, we will actually use a small blue square of $L \times L$ pixels, with a yellow star inside it, where L is two pixels larger than the diameter just mentioned. Any two neighboring stars will lie exactly L pixels apart with regard to both x and y. Stars will appear only in the largest rectangle whose width and height are both a multiple of L, and which lies inside the client rectangle. The situation is similar to a chessboard, with squares in fixed positions. The stars will therefore never partially overlap: they will be placed either beside each other or at exactly the same position.

There will be a new star (or a disappearing one) every tenth of a second. This applies to every program instance. For example, both windows shown in Figure 9.1 on the right change ten times per second, even when we are drawing lines in the window on the left. A new aspect of this chapter is the use of a *timer*, which makes this possible. We will also see how to use special *raster operations*, which are important for animation applications.

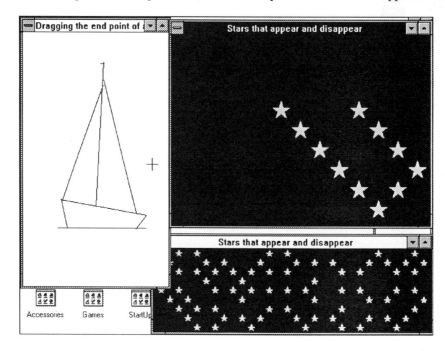

Figure 9.1. Appearing and disappearing stars

9.2 General Aspects

Perhaps the most surprising aspect of the program to be developed is that it continues even when another window is active. In Figure 9.1 neither window is static: stars appear and disappear in both. Immediately after starting any of our applications, each covers the entire screen because of the way we create the main window in our programs (using *xScreen* and *yScreen* as the window dimensions). In order to see more windows at the same time, we have to reduce each window size for this program (by dragging an edge or a corner). Also, we may have to use the Alt+Tab key combination to make an active window visible. Animation in several windows as shown in Figure 9.1 is rather spectacular, especially for those who are used to DOS applications. Fortunately, it is easy to program. We can simply use the *WM_TIMER* message, sent by Windows every 100 ms, provided that we initialize the timer by means of the following call:

```
SetTimer(hWnd, 1, 100, NULL);
```

The second argument, 1, identifies the timer (since there could be more than one timer in use). The third argument, 100, is the time-out value, in milliseconds. We could have used a pointer to a callback function (obtained by using *MakeProcInstance*, see Chapter 3) as the fourth argument. As we will instead use the *WM_TIMER* message in the *WndProc* function, we do not need such a function and write therefore *NULL* for this argument. When our program terminates, we must not forget the following call, by way of cleaning up:

```
KillTimer(hWnd, 1);
```

Strictly speaking, all this applies only to C programs, as discussed in Section 9.3, but the changes required when using class libraries are obvious, as we will see in Sections 9.4 and 9.5.

Recall that in Chapter 7 we loaded bitmaps from external sources. Instead, we will now build one, representing a star, internally. This is a somewhat complicated and possibly time-consuming action, but, fortunately, it needs to be done only in response to *WM_SIZE* messages. As in Chapter 7, we will be using a memory-device context for this purpose. Copying bits each time a *WM_TIMER* message is sent can then be done very fast by using the *BitBlt* function. This function, for 'bit-block transfer', is similar to *StretchBlt*, used in Chapter 7. However, *BitBlt* simply copies a bitmap from a memory device context to a normal device context, without altering its size.

Ternary raster operations

The actual action of displaying a star on the screen is now done by the following bit block transfer:

```
BitBlt(hDC, x, y, L, L, hdcMem, 0, 0, 0x00960169L);
           // 00960169 is the code for DSPxx (Postfix), that is,
           // Dest xor Source xor Pattern (where Pattern means Brush)
           // Result = Pattern (= blue) if Source = Destination
           // See the Microsoft Windows Programmer's Reference
```

As with *StretchBlt*, the first five arguments denote the destination. As for the source, we specify only its device context, *hdcMem*, and its upper-left corner $(0, 0)$. What remains is a *long int* value specifying the raster operation to be performed. The value $0x00960169L$ used here can be found in the *Microsoft Windows Programmer's Reference*. There are as many as 256 distinct raster operation codes, so finding the one we need is by no means a simple matter. In general, the result R of a bit-block transfer depends on three factors:

- the source S
- the destination D
- the 'pattern' P, which is simply the currently selected brush

If we only wanted to copy a bitmap from its source to its destination, we would use the symbolic constant *SRCCOPY* for this final argument. This identifier actually represents the value 0x00CC0020, and in this case we simply have $R = S$. In other words, with the *SRC-COPY* raster operation, the result depends only on the source, while the destination and the pattern are ignored. In our application, the source consists of a yellow star in a blue square, so there are yellow and blue pixels in it. For each of these, the corresponding pixels in the destination may also be either blue or yellow. With a blue brush as the pattern P, we can now use the following table to show how we want the resulting pixels to depend on S, D and P:

Source S	Destination D	Pattern P	Result R
blue	blue	blue	blue
yellow	yellow	blue	blue
yellow	blue	blue	yellow
blue	yellow	blue	yellow

The first of the four lines in the above table is obvious: when we move a blue source to a blue destination, the result will be blue. The second line indicates that whenever a new star coincides with an existing one (both the source and the destination being yellow) the old star disappears (the result being blue). The third line applies to a new star being created on a blue background, which results in a new (yellow) star. Finally, the fourth line expresses that a piece of blue sky in the source cannot obscure a yellow star in the destination. This situation will not really occur in our problem because a new square (containing a star) and an existing one either exactly coincide or do not overlap at all.

In general, the result is derived from the source, the destination and the pattern by means of the following Boolean operations (where the symbols between parentheses will be discussed shortly):

Bitwise AND (&, a)
Bitwise OR (|, o)
Bitwise Exclusive OR (^, x)
Bitwise NOT (¬, n)

It is not immediately clear how we can apply these operations to the colors blue and yellow in the above table. Yet we must express R in terms of S, D and P by means of these operations. When carefully inspecting the above table, we observe that R is apparently equal to the color that occurs either once or three times in the variables S, D and P. This reminds us of the way we can find the result of an exclusive OR operation: using only 0 and 1, the value of $A \wedge B$ is equal to 1 if and only if the value 1 occurs exactly once in A and B, as follows from

$$0 \wedge 0 = 0$$
$$0 \wedge 1 = 1$$
$$1 \wedge 0 = 1$$
$$1 \wedge 1 = 0$$

Extending this to three variables, we find that $A \wedge B \wedge C$ is equal to 1 if and only if the value 1 occurs either once or three times in the variables A, B and C. Also, this expression is equal to 0 if the value 0 occurs either once or three times in the variables A, B and C. In short, $A \wedge B \wedge C$ is equal to the value that occurs either once or three times in the variables A, B and C. Since we want R to be the color that occurs either once or three times in S, D and P, we boldly write

$$R = S \wedge D \wedge P \tag{9.1}$$

At first, this does not seem to make sense, since it is not clear how to associate blue and yellow with truth values or with bits. However, like any other information stored in computers, colors are coded as sequences of bits. If we were using only black and white, we could assign 0 to black and 1 to white. Now that we are using blue and yellow, the simplest possible codes are either 1 for blue and 0 for yellow or, alternatively, 0 for blue and 1 for yellow. Both cases yield the desired value of R, as shown in the following table, the rows of which correspond with those of the previous one:

1 = blue, 0 = yellow	0 = blue, 1 = yellow
$(S = 1, D = 1, P = 1) \Rightarrow R = 1$	$(S = 0, D = 0, P = 0) \Rightarrow R = 0$
$(S = 0, D = 0, P = 1) \Rightarrow R = 1$	$(S = 1, D = 1, P = 0) \Rightarrow R = 0$
$(S = 0, D = 1, P = 1) \Rightarrow R = 0$	$(S = 1, D = 0, P = 0) \Rightarrow R = 1$
$(S = 1, D = 0, P = 1) \Rightarrow R = 0$	$(S = 0, D = 1, P = 0) \Rightarrow R = 1$

For example, according to the last equation in the first column, a blue source ($S = 1$), a yellow destination ($D = 0$) and a blue brush ($P = 1$) gives a yellow result ($R = 0$).

We also obtain the correct value (blue or yellow) if we use color codes of several bits. Recall that we are dealing with a *bitwise* exclusive OR operator. This means that the first bit of the result follows from the first bits of the three operands, and so on. For example, if we have blue = 0101 and yellow = 0011, then the second line of the above tables (with $S =$ yellow and $D = P =$ blue) would lead to

$$R = S \wedge D \wedge P = 0011 \wedge 0101 \wedge 0101 = 0101 (= \text{blue})$$

Instead of directly using $S \wedge D \wedge P$, we first have to convert this to *Reverse Polish*, also known as *postfix*, because it is listed in this form in the table that we need to consult. As you can find, for example, in my book *Programs and Data Structures in C*, postfix is useful for compiler construction, and it has the advantage that parentheses are not needed. The main point to remember is that an operator is placed *after* both operands instead of in between. For example, the postfix expression for $a + b$ is $a\ b\ +$, and that of $a * (b + c) + d$ is $a\ b\ c + * d +$. In view of what follows, we write the right-hand side of Eq. (9.1) as

$$D \wedge (P \wedge S)$$

This is allowed because the $\wedge$ operator (like +, but unlike –) is symmetric and associative. Writing this latest form in Reverse Polish, we obtain

$D\ P\ S\ {\wedge}\ {\wedge}$

Finally, to obtain the form in which it appears in the *Microsoft Windows Programmer's Reference*, we must replace any operator symbols &, |, ^ and ¬ (for *AND*, *OR*, *Exclusive OR* and *NOT*) with *a*, *o*, *x* and *n*, respectively. The final form for our example is therefore written as

$D\ P\ S\ x\ x$

In the reference book just mentioned this code occurs in a very large table, some lines of which are shown below:

Boolean Function in Hex	Hex ROP	Boolean Function in Reverse Polish	Common Name
96	00960169	*DPSxx*	-
CC	00CC0020	*S*	*SRCCOPY*
EE	00EE0086	*DSo*	*SRCPAINT*

The second column shows the hexadecimal raster-operation code to be used as the final argument of *BitBlt*.

The Boolean function in HEX

A given Reverse Polish form, such as *DPSxx*, is not easy to find in this table, because there are 256 of them (ranging from 00 to *FF*), and they are listed in increasing order of the values in the first column, which is referred to as 'Boolean function in HEX'. It would therefore be much better if we could find this rather intriguing code (96 in our example). Fortunately, this can be done once we have found Eq. (9.1). All we need to do is to write all possible values of the triple P, S, D, together with R in a table of eight rows. These rows must be in ascending order (000, 001, ..., 111) of the first three columns. The corresponding R values then form the binary equivalent of the desired code of two hexadecimal digits. In our example, we extend our previous tables of four lines, which is not difficult because on each row R is simply the bit value that occurs either once or three times in the preceding columns:

P	S	D	R
0	0	0	0
0	0	1	1
0	1	0	1
0	1	1	0
1	0	0	1
1	0	1	0
1	1	0	0
1	1	1	1

We now turn the column of *R* clockwise through 90°. In other words, starting at the bottom, we write the eight bits of column *R* in a row, obtaining

1 0 0 1   0 1 1 0
  9   6

Note that the hexadecimal code 96 (the *Boolean function in Hex*) found in this way also occurs as 0096 at the beginning of the *Hex ROP* code 00960169 that we actually use. This is not a coincidence, but this principle applies to all 256 codes.

Some of the 256 codes have been given a mnemonic constant, which in the *Programmer's Reference* are included in a fourth column under the heading *Common Name*. Two of these, mentioned in Section 7.2, and occurring in the above table, are *SRCCOPY* and *SRCPAINT*.

Make files

After replacing all occurrences of *gr* with *stars*, we can use the make files of Chapter 5.

9.3 C Solution

After the rather long discussion in the previous section, it is now time to look at the programs that put all this into practice:

File STARS.H:

```
//STARS.H:
long FAR PASCAL _export WndProc(HWND hWnd, UINT message,
      WPARAM wParam, LPARAM lParam);
int PASCAL WinMain(HANDLE hInstance, HANDLE hPrevInstance,
    LPSTR lpCmdLine, int nCmdShow);
```

File STARS.C:

```
// STARS.C: Stars that appear and disappear (animation).
#include <windows.h>
#include <math.h>
#include "stars.h"
HBRUSH hbgBrush;

int PASCAL WinMain(HANDLE hInstance, HANDLE hPrevInstance,
    LPSTR lpCmdLine, int nCmdShow)
{  static char szAppName[]="stars";
   int xScreen, yScreen;
   WNDCLASS wndclass;
   HWND hWnd;
   MSG msg;
```

```
      xScreen = GetSystemMetrics(SM_CXSCREEN);
      yScreen = GetSystemMetrics(SM_CYSCREEN);
      hbgBrush = CreateSolidBrush(RGB(0, 0, 255));
      if (!hPrevInstance)
      {  wndclass.style = CS_HREDRAW | CS_VREDRAW;
         wndclass.lpfnWndProc = WndProc;
         wndclass.cbClsExtra = 0;
         wndclass.cbWndExtra = 0;
         wndclass.hInstance = hInstance;
         wndclass.hIcon = NULL;
         wndclass.hCursor = LoadCursor(NULL, IDC_ARROW);
         wndclass.hbrBackground = hbgBrush;
         wndclass.lpszMenuName =  NULL;
         wndclass.lpszClassName = szAppName;
         if (!RegisterClass(&wndclass)) return FALSE;
      }
      hWnd = CreateWindow(
         szAppName,
         "Stars that appear and disappear", // Text for window title bar.
         WS_OVERLAPPEDWINDOW,               // Window style.
         0,                                 // Initial x position
         0,                                 // Initial y position.
         xScreen,                           // Width.
         yScreen,                           // Height.
         NULL,                              // Parent window handle.
         NULL,                              // Window menu handle.
         hInstance,                         // Program instance handle.
         NULL);                             // Create parameters.
      SetTimer(hWnd, 1, 100, NULL);
      ShowWindow(hWnd, nCmdShow);
      UpdateWindow(hWnd);
      while (GetMessage(&msg, NULL, 0, 0))
      {  TranslateMessage(&msg);     // Translates virtual key codes
         DispatchMessage(&msg);      // Dispatches message to window
      }
      DeleteObject(hbgBrush);
      return msg.wParam;      // Returns the value from PostQuitMessage
   }


long FAR PASCAL _export WndProc(HWND hWnd, UINT message,
      WPARAM wParam, LPARAM lParam)
{  BOOL xout, yout;
   HDC hDC, hdcMem;
   HBRUSH hBrush;
   HPEN hPen;
   COLORREF yellow = RGB(255, 255, 0);
   static HANDLE hBitmap;
   int xScreen, yScreen, R, h, k, nHor, nVert, TotHor, TotVert;
   static int L, x, y, deltaX, deltaY, xmin, xmax, ymin, ymax;
```

```
POINT pentagon[5];
const double pi = 3.1415926535;
double angle;
switch (message)
{
case WM_SIZE:
   xScreen = LOWORD(lParam);
   yScreen = HIWORD(lParam);
   R = (xScreen < yScreen ? xScreen : yScreen)/20;
   h = R + 1;
   L = 2 * h;              // Side of square
   nHor = xScreen/L;       // nHor stars on a horizontal line
   nVert = yScreen/L;      // nVert stars in a column
   TotHor = nHor * L;      // Largest multiple of L fitting in xScreen
   TotVert = nVert * L;    // Largest multiple of L fitting in yScreen
   xmin = (xScreen - TotHor)/2; xmax = xmin + TotHor - L;
   ymin = (yScreen - TotVert)/2; ymax = ymin + TotVert - L;
   x = xmin + (nHor/3) * L;    // Just some start position
   y = ymin + (nVert/4) * L;
   deltaX = deltaY = L;        // Step size
   for (k=0; k<5; k++)             // Vertices of pentagon, relative to
   { angle = pi/2 + k * 4 * pi/5;   // upper left corner of bitmap
      pentagon[k].x = h + (int)(R * cos(angle));
      pentagon[k].y = h - (int)(R * sin(angle));
   }
   if (hBitmap) DeleteObject(hBitmap);
   hDC = GetDC(hWnd);
   SelectObject(hDC, hbgBrush);
   Rectangle(hDC, 0, 0, xScreen, yScreen);
   hdcMem = CreateCompatibleDC(hDC);
   hBitmap = CreateCompatibleBitmap(hDC, L, L);
   ReleaseDC(hWnd, hDC);
   SelectObject(hdcMem, hBitmap);
   SelectObject(hdcMem, GetStockObject(NULL_PEN));
   SelectObject(hdcMem, hbgBrush);
   Rectangle(hdcMem, 0, 0, L+1, L+1);
   hBrush = CreateSolidBrush(yellow);
   hPen = CreatePen(PS_SOLID, 1, yellow);
   SelectObject(hdcMem, hBrush);
   SelectObject(hdcMem, hPen);
   SetPolyFillMode(hdcMem, WINDING);
   Polygon(hdcMem, pentagon, 5);
   DeleteDC(hdcMem);
   DeleteObject(hBrush);
   DeleteObject(hPen);
   break;
case WM_TIMER:
   if (!hBitmap) break;
   hDC = GetDC(hWnd);
```

```
        hdcMem = CreateCompatibleDC(hDC);
        SelectObject(hdcMem, hBitmap);
        SelectObject(hDC, hbgBrush);

        xout = (x + deltaX > xmax || x + deltaX < xmin);
        yout = (y + deltaY > ymax || y + deltaY < ymin);
        if (xout) deltaX = -deltaX;
        if (yout) deltaY = -deltaY;
        if (!(xout && yout)) {x += deltaX; y += deltaY;}
        BitBlt(hDC, x, y, L, L, hdcMem, 0, 0, 0x00960169L);
        ReleaseDC(hWnd, hDC);
        DeleteDC(hdcMem);
        break;
    case WM_DESTROY:
        if (hBitmap) DeleteObject(hBitmap);
        KillTimer(hWnd, 1);
        PostQuitMessage(0);
        break;
    default:
        return DefWindowProc(hWnd, message, wParam, lParam);
    }
    return 0L;
}
```

The time-consuming computation of the vertices of a star takes place only in response to *WM_SIZE* messages. We use graphics functions such as *Polygon* here as if we were displaying objects directly on the screen. Instead, we use a memory device context to build a bitmap to be used later very frequently in response to *WM_TIMER* messages. Since a star is a polygon with edges that intersect, we must use a special filling mode for polygons, identified by the name *WINDING*. We indicate that we want to use this mode by the following function call:

```
SetPolyFillMode(hdcMem, WINDING);
```

The default polygon-filling mode, *ALTERNATE*, would not fill the pentagon that lies inside the star.

We normally update the position (x, y) of each new star by increasing x by *deltaX* and y by *deltaY*. However, if the new position found in this way lies outside the rectangle characterized by *xmin*, *xmax*, *ymin* and *ymax*, we change the sign of *deltaX* or *deltaY* just before we update x and y, which means that the x- or y-component of the direction in which the stars propagate is reversed. There is one exception, however. When dealing with a star that lies in one of the four corners of the client rectangle, that is, if the signs of both *deltaX* and *deltaY* are changing at the same time, we leave x and y unchanged, because otherwise that star would not be erased. It would then remain in the corner, while its neighbors disappear because of stars being placed twice in the same positions. With the above exception, such corner positions are also visited twice, so that those stars disappear in the same way as the others.

9.4 MFC Solution

With the MFC, we write an *OnTimer* function, which is automatically called each time a *WM_TIMER* message is sent to the window. You can find a call to *SetTimer* in the *On-Create* function, which is called when a *WM_CREATE* message is sent to the window. Analogously, there is a call to *KillTimer* in the *OnClose* function, called in response to a *WM_CLOSE* message. As usual, all variables shared by message-response functions are implemented as members of class *CMyWindow*.

File STARSMFC.H:

```
// STARSMFC.H:

class CApp: public CWinApp
{  public:
   BOOL InitInstance();
};

class CMyWindow: public CFrameWnd
{  int L, x, y, deltaX, deltaY, xmin, xmax, ymin, ymax, started;
   CBitmap bitmap;
   CBrush bgBrush;
   COLORREF blue, yellow;
public:
   CMyWindow();
   afx_msg int OnCreate(LPCREATESTRUCT);
   afx_msg void OnClose();
   afx_msg void OnSize(UINT nType, int cx, int cy);
   afx_msg void OnTimer(UINT nIDEvent);
   DECLARE_MESSAGE_MAP()
};
```

File STARSMFC.CPP:

```
// STARSMFC.CPP: Stars that appear and disappear

#include <afxwin.h>
#include <math.h>
#include "starsmfc.h"

BOOL CApp::InitInstance()
{  m_pMainWnd = new CMyWindow();
   m_pMainWnd->ShowWindow(m_nCmdShow);
   m_pMainWnd->UpdateWindow();
   return TRUE;
}

CApp App;
```

```
CMyWindow::CMyWindow()
{  int xScreen = GetSystemMetrics(SM_CXSCREEN),
       yScreen = GetSystemMetrics(SM_CYSCREEN);
   blue = RGB(0, 0, 255); yellow = RGB(255, 255, 0);
   bgBrush.CreateSolidBrush(blue);
   RECT rect = {0, 0, xScreen, yScreen};
   CString ClassName = AfxRegisterWndClass(
      CS_HREDRAW | CS_VREDRAW,
      NULL,
      HBRUSH(bgBrush.m_hObject),
      NULL);
   Create(ClassName, "Stars that appear and disappear",
         WS_OVERLAPPEDWINDOW, rect, NULL, NULL);
}

BEGIN_MESSAGE_MAP(CMyWindow, CFrameWnd)
   ON_WM_CREATE()
   ON_WM_CLOSE()
   ON_WM_SIZE()
   ON_WM_TIMER()
END_MESSAGE_MAP()

int CMyWindow::OnCreate(LPCREATESTRUCT)
{  started = 0;
   SetTimer(1, 100, NULL);
   return 0;
}

void CMyWindow::OnClose()
{  KillTimer(1);
   bgBrush.DeleteObject();
   if (started) bitmap.DeleteObject();
   PostQuitMessage(0);
}

void CMyWindow::OnSize(UINT nType, int cx, int cy)
{  int R, h, k, nHor, nVert, TotHor, TotVert;
   POINT pentagon[5];
   const double pi = 3.1415926535;
   COLORREF yellow = RGB(255, 255, 0),
            blue = RGB(0, 0, 255);
   double angle;
   CBrush fgBrush, *pOldBrush;
   CPen bgPen, fgPen, *pOldPen;
   CBitmap *pOldBitmap;
   R = min(cx, cy)/20;
   h = R + 1;
   L = 2 * h;
   nHor = cx/L;                   // nHor stars on a horizontal line
   nVert = cy/L;                  // nVert stars in a column
```

```
      TotHor = nHor * L;          // Largest multiple of L fitting in cx
      TotVert = nVert * L;        // Largest multiple of L fitting in cy
      xmin = (cx - TotHor)/2; xmax = xmin + TotHor - L;
      ymin = (cy - TotVert)/2; ymax = ymin + TotVert - L;
      x = xmin + (nHor/3) * L; // Just some start position
      y = ymin + (nVert/4) * L;
      deltaX = deltaY = L;
      for (k=0; k<5; k++)         // Vertices of pentagon
      {  angle = pi/2 + k * 4 * pi/5;
         pentagon[k].x = h + int(R * cos(angle));
         pentagon[k].y = h - int(R * sin(angle));
      }
      CClientDC dc(this);
      CDC dcMem;
      dcMem.CreateCompatibleDC(&dc);
      if (started) bitmap.DeleteObject();
      bitmap.CreateCompatibleBitmap(&dc, L, L);
      pOldBitmap = dcMem.SelectObject(&bitmap);

      bgPen.CreateStockObject(NULL_PEN);
      pOldPen = dcMem.SelectObject(&bgPen);
      pOldBrush = dcMem.SelectObject(&bgBrush);
      dcMem.Rectangle(0, 0, L+1, L+1);  // Blue square as background

      fgPen.CreatePen(PS_SOLID, 1, yellow);
      dcMem.SelectObject(&fgPen);
      fgBrush.CreateSolidBrush(yellow);
      dcMem.SelectObject(&fgBrush);
      dcMem.SetPolyFillMode(WINDING);
      dcMem.Polygon(pentagon, 5);

      dcMem.SelectObject(pOldBitmap);
      dcMem.SelectObject(pOldPen);
      dcMem.SelectObject(pOldBrush);
      fgPen.DeleteObject();
      fgBrush.DeleteObject();
      started = 1;
   }

void CMyWindow::OnTimer(UINT nIDEvent)
{  if (!started) return;
   CClientDC dc(this);
   CDC dcMem;
   dcMem.CreateCompatibleDC(&dc);
   CBitmap *pOldBitmap = dcMem.SelectObject(&bitmap);
   CBrush *pOldBrush = dc.SelectObject(&bgBrush);

   BOOL xout = (x + deltaX > xmax || x + deltaX < xmin);
   BOOL yout = (y + deltaY > ymax || y + deltaY < ymin);
```

```
    if (xout) deltaX = -deltaX;
    if (yout) deltaY = -deltaY;
    if (!(xout && yout)) {x += deltaX; y += deltaY;}

    dc.BitBlt(x, y, L, L, &dcMem, 0, 0, 0x00960169L);
    dcMem.SelectObject(pOldBitmap);
    dc.SelectObject(pOldBrush);
}
```

In function *OnSize* we find

```
    CClientDC dc(this);
```

The object *dc* is a normal device context, based on the current window. We need it here only to make *dcMem* compatible with it. This is then declared as follows:

```
    CDC dcMem;
```

Object *dCMem* is a memory device context. We need it because we can select a bitmap only into a memory device context, not in a normal device context. We initialize *dcMem* as follows:

```
    dcMem.CreateCompatibleDC(&dc);
```

This statement makes the memory device context *dcMem* compatible with the normal device context *dc*.

The *bitmap* object is a member of the *CMyWindow* class, as you can see in the following line, which occurs in the header file STARSMFC.H:

```
    CBitmap bitmap;
```

We give *bitmap* its required size and make it compatible with the bitmap of the normal device context *dc* by the following function call, occurring in the *OnSize* function:

```
    bitmap.CreateCompatibleBitmap(&dc, L, L);
```

Remember, we can select a bitmap only in a memory device context, not in a normal device context. We will see how the bitmap is deleted in a moment. The $L \times L$ bitmap is now selected into the memory device context *dcMem*:

```
    pOldBitmap = dcMem.SelectObject(&bitmap);
```

We store the address of the old bitmap in the pointer *pOldBitmap*, so that we can restore the old situation later.

Drawing on a memory device context does not display anything on the screen. It is nevertheless a useful activity because we can transfer the drawing produced in this way to the normal device context very quickly and at any location. We first draw a blue square as a background:

```
bgPen.CreateStockObject(NULL_PEN);
pOldPen = dcMem.SelectObject(&bgPen);
pOldBrush = dcMem.SelectObject(&bgBrush);
dcMem.Rectangle(0, 0, L+1, L+1);
```

A yellow star is then drawn (and filled) in the middle of this square:

```
fgPen.CreatePen(PS_SOLID, 1, yellow);
dcMem.SelectObject(&fgPen);
fgBrush.CreateSolidBrush(yellow);
dcMem.SelectObject(&fgBrush);
dcMem.SetPolyFillMode(WINDING);
dcMem.Polygon(pentagon, 5);
```

After this we restore the old situation to avoid having *dcMem* destroyed (by its destructor) while there are still objects of our own selected into it:

```
dcMem.SelectObject(pOldBitmap);
dcMem.SelectObject(pOldPen);
dcMem.SelectObject(pOldBrush);
fgPen.DeleteObject();
fgBrush.DeleteObject();
```

Besides pens and brushes, a *bitmap* is also selected into *dcMem*. This is made a class member because we need it both in *OnSize* and in *OnTimer*. There is also a class member *started*, which is initially 0 and made 1 when *bitmap* is selected into the memory device context. This explains the statement

```
if (started) bitmap.DeleteObject();
```

occurring in both the *OnSize* and the *OnClose* functions.

So much for the function *OnSize*. We now turn to *OnTimer*, which is called very frequently. On each call the yellow star inside the blue square, which we have just drawn on the memory device context, is now copied to the normal device context. We begin by defining a (normal) device context *dc* and a memory device context *dcMem*, which is made compatible with *dc*:

```
CClientDC dc(this);
CDC dcMem;
dcMem.CreateCompatibleDC(&dc);
```

We then select *bitmap* (created and filled in *OnSize*) into *dcMem*, and we do the same with the background brush, since this will be the 'pattern' *P*, as discussed in Section 9.2:

```
CBitmap *pOldBitmap = dcMem.SelectObject(&bitmap);
CBrush *pOldBrush = dc.SelectObject(&bgBrush);
```

We update *x* and *y* as discussed at the end of Section 9.3. Then we perform the actual bit-block transfer that changes the screen:

```
dc.BitBlt(x, y, L, L, &dcMem, 0, 0, 0x00960169L);
```

Finally, we restore the old situation, so that our own bitmap and background brush are no longer selected in *dcMem* when this memory device context goes out of scope:

```
dcMem.SelectObject(pOldBitmap);
dc.SelectObject(pOldBrush);
```

9.5 OWL Solution

As usual, the OWL solution is similar to the C solution with regard to the use of handles, while its classes and member functions are similar to the MFC solution. Note how we create the background brush in function *TApp::InitMainWindow*, and delete it in the *WMClose* function. As we need this brush in function *GetWindowClass*, it might look more logical to assign the appropriate value to *hBgBrush* in this function instead of in *InitMainWindow*. However, if we do, that value would be assigned only to the first instance of our program. If we start the program twice, as was done to produce Figure 9.1, the stars in the second window would then not have the correct colors because *hBgBrush* would then not have been assigned a value. (Recall that the result *R* of a bit-block transfer depends on a source *S*, a destination *D* and a pattern *P*, which is the current brush, as we have seen in Section 9.2.) This illustrates the fact that the *GetWindowClass* function is called only for the first program instance, not for the second. Remember, when we have started the program twice, there are two windows, but there is only one window class; in other words, the window is registered only once. There is no such problem with the version listed below:

File STARSOWL.H:

```
// STARSOWL.H:

class TApp: public TApplication
{ public:
    TApp(LPSTR Name, HANDLE hInstance, HANDLE hPrevInstance,
        LPSTR lpCmdLine, int nCmdShow)
      : TApplication(Name, hInstance, hPrevInstance, lpCmdLine,
                     nCmdShow){}
    virtual void InitMainWindow();
};
```

```
class TMyWindow: public TWindow
{  int L, x, y, deltaX, deltaY, xmin, xmax, ymin, ymax, started;
   HBITMAP hBitmap;
   COLORREF yellow;
public:
   HBRUSH hBgBrush;
   TMyWindow(PTWindowsObject AParent, LPSTR ATitle)
     : TWindow(AParent, ATitle){}
   virtual void GetWindowClass(WNDCLASS _FAR &AWndClass);
   virtual LPSTR GetClassName();
   virtual void WMCreate(RTMessage Msg) =
      [WM_FIRST + WM_CREATE];
   virtual void WMClose(RTMessage Msg) =
      [WM_FIRST + WM_CLOSE];
   virtual void WMTimer(RTMessage Msg)=
      [WM_FIRST + WM_TIMER];
   virtual void WMSize(RTMessage Msg);
};
```

File STARSOWL.CPP:

```
// STARSOWL.CPP: Stars that appear and disappear

#define WIN30
#include <owl.h>
#include <math.h>
#include "starsowl.h"

inline int min(int x, int y){return x < y ? x : y;}

void TApp::InitMainWindow()
{  TMyWindow *p;
   MainWindow = p = new TMyWindow(NULL, Name);
   p->Attr.X = 0;
   p->Attr.Y = 0;
   p->Attr.W = GetSystemMetrics(SM_CXSCREEN);
   p->Attr.H = GetSystemMetrics(SM_CYSCREEN);
   p->hBgBrush = CreateSolidBrush(RGB(0, 0, 255));  // Blue background
}

void TMyWindow::GetWindowClass(WNDCLASS _FAR &AWndClass)
{  TWindow::GetWindowClass(AWndClass);
   AWndClass.hbrBackground = hBgBrush;
}

LPSTR TMyWindow::GetClassName()
{  return "TMyWindow";
}
```

```
void TMyWindow::WMCreate(RTMessage)
{  started = 0;
   hBitmap = 0;
   yellow = RGB(255, 255, 0);
   SetTimer(HWindow, 1, 100, NULL);
}

void TMyWindow::WMClose(RTMessage)
{  KillTimer(HWindow, 1);
   DeleteObject(hBgBrush);
   if (hBitmap) DeleteObject(hBitmap);
   PostQuitMessage(0);
}

void TMyWindow::WMSize(RTMessage Msg)
{  int R, h, k, nHor, nVert, TotHor, TotVert,
   cx = Msg.LP.Lo, cy = Msg.LP.Hi;
   POINT pentagon[5];
   const double pi = 3.1415926535;
   double angle;
   HBRUSH hFgBrush, hOldBrush;
   HPEN hBgPen, hFgPen, hOldPen;
   HBITMAP hOldBitmap;
   R = min(cx, cy)/20;
   h = R + 1;
   L = 2 * h;
   nHor = cx/L;            // nHor stars on a horizontal line
   nVert = cy/L;           // nVert stars in a column
   TotHor = nHor * L;      // Largest multiple of L fitting in cx
   TotVert = nVert * L;    // Largest multiple of L fitting in cy
   xmin = (cx - TotHor)/2; xmax = xmin + TotHor - L;
   ymin = (cy - TotVert)/2; ymax = ymin + TotVert - L;
   x = xmin + (nHor/3) * L;  // Just some start position
   y = ymin + (nVert/4) * L;
   deltaX = deltaY = L;
   for (k=0; k<5; k++)                    // Vertices of pentagon
   {  angle = pi/2 + k * 4 * pi/5;
      pentagon[k].x = h + int(R * cos(angle));
      pentagon[k].y = h - int(R * sin(angle));
   }
   HDC hDC = GetDC(HWindow);
   HDC hdcMem = CreateCompatibleDC(hDC);
   if (hBitmap) DeleteObject(hBitmap);
   hBitmap = CreateCompatibleBitmap(hDC, L, L);
   ReleaseDC(HWindow, hDC);
   hOldBitmap = SelectObject(hdcMem, hBitmap);

   hBgPen = GetStockObject(NULL_PEN);
   hOldPen = SelectObject(hdcMem, hBgPen);
```

```
        hOldBrush = SelectObject(hdcMem, hBgBrush);
        Rectangle(hdcMem, 0, 0, L+1, L+1);  // Blue square as background

        hFgPen = CreatePen(PS_SOLID, 1, yellow);
        SelectObject(hdcMem, hFgPen);
        hFgBrush = CreateSolidBrush(yellow);
        SelectObject(hdcMem, hFgBrush);

        SetPolyFillMode(hdcMem, WINDING);
        Polygon(hdcMem, pentagon, 5);

        SelectObject(hdcMem, hOldBitmap);
        SelectObject(hdcMem, hOldPen);
        SelectObject(hdcMem, hOldBrush);
        DeleteObject(hFgPen);
        DeleteObject(hFgBrush);
        DeleteDC(hdcMem);
        started = 1;
}


void TMyWindow::WMTimer(RTMessage)
{   if (!started) return;
    HDC hDC = GetDC(HWindow);
    HDC hdcMem = CreateCompatibleDC(hDC);
    HBITMAP hOldBitmap = SelectObject(hdcMem, hBitmap);
    HBRUSH hOldBrush = SelectObject(hDC, hBgBrush);

    BOOL xout = (x + deltaX > xmax || x + deltaX < xmin);
    BOOL yout = (y + deltaY > ymax || y + deltaY < ymin);
    if (xout) deltaX = -deltaX;
    if (yout) deltaY = -deltaY;
    if (!(xout && yout)) {x += deltaX; y += deltaY;}

    BitBlt(hDC, x, y, L, L, hdcMem, 0, 0, 0x00960169L);
    SelectObject(hdcMem, hOldBitmap);
    SelectObject(hDC, hOldBrush);
    ReleaseDC(HWindow, hDC);
    DeleteDC(hdcMem);
}


int PASCAL WinMain(HANDLE hInstance, HANDLE hPrevInstance,
    LPSTR lpCmdLine, int nCmdShow)
{   TApp App("Stars that appear and disappear",
    hInstance, hPrevInstance, lpCmdLine, nCmdShow);
    App.Run();
    return App.Status;
}
```

9.6 Questions

9.1   How can we use a timer? Which functions are involved?

9.2   Show that the Boolean function *DSo* (in Reverse Polish) for the ternary raster operation *SRCPAINT* gives *EE* as its hexadecimal code (see the end of Section 9.2).

9.3   What is done in response to *WM_SIZE* messages, and what in response to *WM_TIMER* messages?

9.4   When a *WM_SIZE* message is sent, we do not draw anything on the normal device context. Why do we nevertheless need such a device context in this case?

10

Dialog Boxes for File Names

10.1 Problem Definition

With many applications we have to open a file, the name of which is to be supplied by the user. Since most users do not like entering file names by typing them, it is desirable that the files of the current directory are listed in a dialog box and that we can select them by clicking. We will discuss a demonstration program, which first produces a window with a menu bar consisting only of a *File* menu, as shown in Figure 10.1 (in a window the height of which was reduced by the user). Clicking *File*, or typing Alt+F, produces an extremely simple menu, consisting only of an *Open* menu item. If we click this, we obtain a more interesting screen, of which Figure 10.2 is an example.

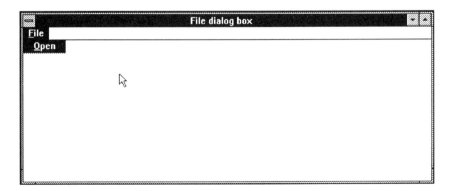

Figure 10.1. File menu

The user can then supply a file name in several ways. We will not discuss the use of this dialog box in detail because it is similar to those of most professional Windows applications, and therefore well known. Instead, we will focus on the programming aspects. For example, we must know how, in our program, we can supply a list of file types and file-name extensions which are to be used for the small window, titled *List Files of Type*, at the bottom left of the *Open* window in Figure 10.2.

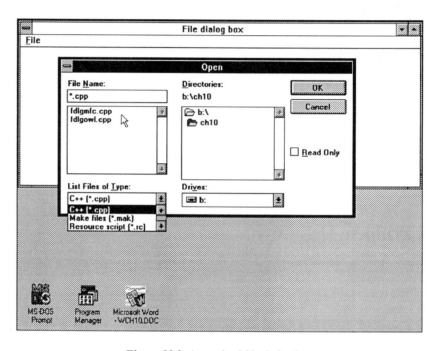

Figure 10.2. A standard file dialog box

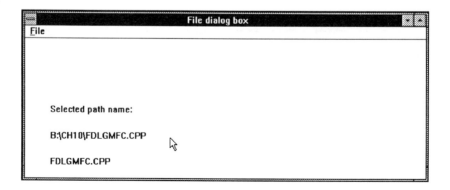

Figure 10.3. Screen after selecting a file

The name selected by the user will be available both as a complete path name and as only a file name. We will demonstrate this simply by displaying these names, as shown in Figure 10.3.

We will restrict ourselves to reading the name of a file from the dialog box. Using such a file name to read data from the file can be done by using standard C functions, such as *fopen* and *fscanf*. We may also use the file name for output. In that case, the word *Open* in the title bar of Figure 10.2 may be undesirable. Fortunately, a minor program modification will cause this word to be replaced with *Save As*, which will be what we want in the case of output. We will discuss this at the end of Sections 10.3, 10.4 and 10.5.

10.2 General Aspects

With early versions of Windows we had to solve this problem by means of a very general concept, called a *combo box*. Such a solution is rather complicated because there are so many options to choose from. With Windows 3.1, we can use the so-called *common dialog box* library, which provides facilities for frequently occurring dialog boxes, such as the one we need here. We will take this newer approach to solve our problem. As usual with menus (see Chapter 4), we will use a resource script file, and we will define the constant *IDM_OPEN* in a header file and use it in the program. Also, we will refer in our program to the menu structure by using the name, *FMenu*, which precedes the keyword *MENU* in the resource script file.

The file types and their extensions (also known as *filters*) to be used in the dialog box will be specified in our program in a very long, null-terminated character string, for which we will use

```
"All files (*.*)|*.*|"
"Header files (*.h)|*.h|"
"C++ (*.cpp)|*.cpp|"
"Make files (*.mak)|*.mak|"
"Resource script (*.rc)|*.rc|"
"Module definition (*.def)|*.def|"
"Word for Windows (*.doc)|*.doc||"
```

Remember, we can write a very long string in our program by writing several of them, each surrounding by double quotes in the normal way and separated only by white-space characters. For example, we can write the string *"ABCDE"* as *"ABC" "DE"*. The above seven lines therefore constitute only one string. This string consists of seven pairs, such as, for example,

```
C++ (*.cpp)|*.cpp|
```

on the third of the above seven lines. This pair indicates that, possibly by means of a scroll bar, it will be possible to select

```
C++ (*.cpp)
```

in the *List Files of Type* box at the bottom left. If we do this, the text

```
*.cpp
```

will occur in the *File Name* box at the top left, while all files of the current directory that
have file-name extension .CPP will appear in the file list, center left (as shown in Figure
10.2). The vertical bar serving as a delimiter is used twice in each pair, and there is an
additional one at the very end of the string.

10.3 C Solution

The following files show how we can write a C program to solve our problem:

File FDLG.RC:

```
// FDLG.RC:

#include <windows.h>
#include "fdlg.h"

FMenu MENU
BEGIN
    POPUP "&File"
    BEGIN
        MENUITEM "&Open", IDM_OPEN
    END
END
```

File FDLG.H:

```
// FDLG.H:

#define IDM_OPEN 1001
long FAR PASCAL _export WndProc(HWND hWnd, UINT message,
        WPARAM wParam, LPARAM lParam);
int PASCAL WinMain(HANDLE hInstance, HANDLE hPrevInstance,
    LPSTR lpCmdLine, int nCmdShow);
```

File FDLG.C:

```
// FDLG.C: File dialog box
#include <windows.h>
#include <commdlg.h>
#include <string.h>
#include "fdlg.h"
```

```
int PASCAL WinMain(HANDLE hInstance, HANDLE hPrevInstance,
    LPSTR lpCmdLine, int nCmdShow)
{   char szAppName[]="fdlg";
    int xScreen, yScreen;
    WNDCLASS wndclass;
    HWND hWnd;
    MSG msg;

    xScreen = GetSystemMetrics(SM_CXSCREEN);
    yScreen = GetSystemMetrics(SM_CYSCREEN);

    if (!hPrevInstance)
    {   wndclass.style = CS_HREDRAW | CS_VREDRAW;
        wndclass.lpfnWndProc = WndProc;
        wndclass.cbClsExtra = 0;
        wndclass.cbWndExtra = 0;
        wndclass.hInstance = hInstance;
        wndclass.hIcon = LoadIcon(NULL, IDI_APPLICATION);
        wndclass.hCursor = LoadCursor(NULL, IDC_ARROW);
        wndclass.hbrBackground = GetStockObject(WHITE_BRUSH);
        wndclass.lpszMenuName = "FMenu";
        wndclass.lpszClassName = szAppName;
           // Name used in call to CreateWindow.
        if (!RegisterClass(&wndclass)) return FALSE;
    }

    hWnd = CreateWindow(
        szAppName,
        "File dialog box",              // Text for window title bar.
        WS_OVERLAPPEDWINDOW,            // Window style.
        0,                              // Initial x position
        0,                              // Initial y position.
        xScreen,                        // Width.
        yScreen,                        // Height.
        NULL,                           // Parent window handle.
        NULL,                           // Window menu handle.
        hInstance,                      // Program instance handle.
        NULL                            // Create parameters.
    );

    ShowWindow(hWnd, nCmdShow);
    UpdateWindow(hWnd);

    while (GetMessage(&msg, NULL, 0, 0))
    {   TranslateMessage(&msg);      // Translates virtual key codes
        DispatchMessage(&msg);       // Dispatches message to window
    }
    return msg.wParam;      // Returns the value from PostQuitMessage
}
```

```
long FAR PASCAL _export WndProc(HWND hWnd, UINT message,
        WPARAM wParam, LPARAM lParam)
{ HDC hDC;
  PAINTSTRUCT ps;
  OPENFILENAME ofn;
  char szFilter[256], chReplace;
  static char szFile[256]="", szFileTitle[256]="";
  static int MenuUsed = 0;
  UINT i, cbString;
  switch (message)
  {
  case WM_COMMAND:
     if (wParam == IDM_OPEN)
     { strcpy(szFilter,
        "All files (*.*)|*.*|"
        "Header files (*.h)|*.h|"
        "C++ (*.cpp)|*.cpp|"
        "Make files (*.mak)|*.mak|"
        "Resource script (*.rc)|*.rc|"
        "Module definition (*.def)|*.def|"
        "Word for Windows (*.doc)|*.doc||");
        cbString = strlen(szFilter);
        chReplace = szFilter[cbString-1];
        for (i=0; szFilter[i]; i++)
            if (szFilter[i] == chReplace) szFilter[i] = '\0';

        memset(&ofn, 0, sizeof(OPENFILENAME));
        ofn.lStructSize = sizeof(OPENFILENAME);
        ofn.hwndOwner = hWnd;
        ofn.lpstrFilter = szFilter;
        ofn.nFilterIndex = 1;
        ofn.lpstrFile = szFile;
        ofn.nMaxFile = sizeof(szFile);
        ofn.lpstrFileTitle = szFileTitle;
        ofn.nMaxFileTitle = sizeof(szFileTitle);
        ofn.lpstrInitialDir = NULL; // szDirName;
        GetOpenFileName(&ofn);
        MenuUsed = 1;
        InvalidateRect(hWnd, NULL, TRUE);
        break;
     }
  case WM_PAINT:
     hDC = BeginPaint(hWnd, &ps);
     if (MenuUsed)
     { TextOut(hDC, 40, 100, "Selected path name:", 19);
       TextOut(hDC, 40, 140, szFile, strlen(szFile));
       TextOut(hDC, 40, 180, szFileTitle, strlen(szFileTitle));
     }
     EndPaint(hWnd, &ps);
```

```
            break;
        case WM_DESTROY:
            PostQuitMessage(0); break;
        default:
            return DefWindowProc(hWnd, message, wParam, lParam);
    }
    return 0L;
}
```

File FDLG.MAK:

```
# FDLG.MAK; usage (with Microsoft C++): nmake -f fdlg.mak
fdlg.exe: fdlg.obj gen.def fdlg.res
        link /nod fdlg, fdlg, nul, libw+mlibcew+commdlg.lib, \
            gen.def
        rc fdlg.res
fdlg.res: fdlg.rc fdlg.h
        rc -r fdlg.rc
fdlg.obj: fdlg.c fdlg.h
        cl -c -AM -G2sw -Ow -W3 -Zp -Tp fdlg.c
# File GEN.DEF can be found in Section 1.2
```

File FDLGB.MAK:

```
# FDLGB.MAK; usage (with Borland C++): make -f fdlgb.mak
fdlg.exe: fdlg.obj gen.def fdlg.res
        tlink /n /Tw /L\borlandc\lib cOwm fdlg, fdlg, nul,\
            import mathwm cwm, gen.def
        rc fdlg.res
fdlg.res: fdlg.rc fdlg.h
        rc -r fdlg.rc
fdlg.obj: fdlg.c fdlg.h
        bcc -c -mm -w-par -P -2 -W fdlg.c
# File GEN.DEF can be found in Section 1.2
```

Note the library name COMMDLG.LIB, occurring in the *link* command of the make file FDLG.MAK for the Microsoft compiler. Although we have already used this library in connection with the Microsoft Foundation Classes, this is the first time we use it for a plain C program.

When the *OPEN* command in the menu is selected, the standard function *strcpy* copies the very long string just discussed to character array *szFilter*, as you can see in the eight lines that follow the line

```
if (wParam == IDM_OPEN)
```

in function *WndProc*. Then the following fragment replaces all occurrences of character | with null-characters ('\0'):

```
cbString = strlen(szFilter);
chReplace = szFilter[cbString-1];
for (i=0; szFilter[i]; i++)
   if (szFilter[i] == chReplace) szFilter[i] = '\0';
```

We now see that we could have used any other special character instead of the 'wildcard' |
we have been using. We must now fill the structure *ofn* of type *OPENFILENAME*. For
example, the following statement places the address of our array *szFilter* in it:

```
ofn.lpstrFilter = szFilter;
```

After filling *ofn*, the call

```
GetOpenFileName(&ofn);
```

does the actual work of obtaining the desired file name from the user. After this call, the
selected file name is stored in *szFile*, and any file title in *szFileTitle*. Note that we have
made this possible by placing the addresses of these arrays in members of structure *ofn*
before we called *GetOpenFileName*.

  If, in the title bar of the dialog box, we prefer the text *Save As* to *Open* because the
name to be entered will refer to an output file, then replacing this function name *Get-
OpenFileName* with *GetSaveFileName* is all we have to do.

10.4 MFC Solution

With the MFC we use the class *CFileDialog* to solve our problem by means of the common dialog box library. When using this library, we must use the header file AFXDLGS.H
in addition to AFXWIN.H, so we write the following two lines at the beginning of our
program:

```
#include <afxwin.h>
#include <afxdlgs.h>
```

Instead of calling function *GetOpenFileName* (or *GetSaveFileName*), we define an object
of type *CFileDialog* using a constructor with arguments. The final argument of this constructor is the very string we have been using as array *szFilter* in Section 10.3. After all,
this MFC solution too is based on the common dialog box library. Figure 10.4 shows that
class *CFileDialog*, like some classes to be discussed later, is derived from class *CDialog*,
which in turn is derived from class *CWnd*. (You may also encounter class *CModalDialog*
in existing programs, but this class is no longer required according to the new Visual C++
class hierarchy.)

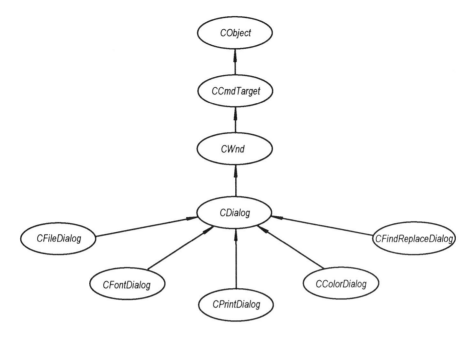

Figure 10.4. CFileDialog and some other dialog classes

The following resource script file is almost entirely about our extremely simple menu, not about file dialog box, which is more interesting:

File FDLGMFC.RC:

```
// FDLGMFC.RC:
#include <windows.h>
#include "fdlgmfc.h"
FILEMENU MENU
BEGIN
    POPUP "&File"
    BEGIN
        MENUITEM "&Open", IDM_OPEN
    END
END
```

File FDLGMFC.H:

```
// FDLGMFC.H
#define IDM_OPEN 1001
class CApp: public CWinApp
{  public:
    BOOL InitInstance();
};
```

```
class CMyWindow: public CFrameWnd
{  CString PathName, FileTitle;
   int MenuUsed;
public:
   CMyWindow();
   afx_msg void OnOpen();
   afx_msg void OnPaint();
   DECLARE_MESSAGE_MAP()
};
```

File FDLGMFC.CPP:

```
// FDLGMFC.CPP: Demonstration of a file dialog box
#include <afxwin.h>
#include <afxdlgs.h>
#include "fdlgmfc.h"

BOOL CApp::InitInstance()
{  m_pMainWnd = new CMyWindow();
   m_pMainWnd->ShowWindow(m_nCmdShow);
   m_pMainWnd->UpdateWindow();
   return TRUE;
}

CApp App;

CMyWindow::CMyWindow()
{  int xScreen = GetSystemMetrics(SM_CXSCREEN),
       yScreen = GetSystemMetrics(SM_CYSCREEN);
   RECT rect = {0, 0, xScreen, yScreen};
   Create(NULL, "File dialog box",
   WS_OVERLAPPEDWINDOW, rect, NULL, "FILEMENU");
   MenuUsed = 0;
}

BEGIN_MESSAGE_MAP(CMyWindow, CFrameWnd)
   ON_WM_PAINT()
   ON_COMMAND(IDM_OPEN, OnOpen)
END_MESSAGE_MAP()

void CMyWindow::OnOpen()
{  CFileDialog FileDialog(
   TRUE,    // TRUE = Open, FALSE = Save As (text for title bar)
   NULL, NULL,
   NULL,
   "All files (*.*)|*.*|"
   "Header files (*.h)|*.h|"
   "C++ (*.cpp)|*.cpp|"
   "Make files (*.mak)|*.mak|"
   "Resource script (*.rc)|*.rc|"
```

```
      "Module definition (*.def)|*.def|"
      "Word for Windows (*.doc)|*.doc||");
   FileDialog.DoModal();
   PathName = FileDialog.GetPathName();
   FileTitle = FileDialog.GetFileTitle();
   MenuUsed = 1;
   InvalidateRect(NULL, TRUE);
}

void CMyWindow::OnPaint()
{  CPaintDC dc(this);
   if (MenuUsed)
   {  dc.TextOut(40, 100, "Selected path name:");
      dc.TextOut(40, 140, PathName);
      dc.TextOut(40, 180, FileTitle);
   }
}
```

File FDLGMFC.MAK:

```
# FDLGMFC.MAK; usage (with Microsoft C++): nmake -f fdlgmfc.mak
fdlgmfc.exe: fdlgmfc.obj gen.def fdlgmfc.res
      link /nod fdlgmfc,fdlgmfc,nul,\
         mafxcw+libw+mlibcew+commdlg+shell, gen.def
      rc fdlgmfc.res
fdlgmfc.res: fdlgmfc.rc fdlgmfc.h
      rc -r fdlgmfc.rc
fdlgmfc.obj: fdlgmfc.cpp fdlgmfc.h
      cl -c -AM -G2sw -Ow -W3 -Zp fdlgmfc.cpp
# File GEN.DEF can be found in Section 1.2
```

Note the first argument of the *CFileDialog* constructor in the *OnOpen* function. As indicated by comment, we should replace *TRUE* with *FALSE* here if we want the user to enter the name of an output file. The text in the title bar of the dialog box would then be *Save As* instead of *Open*.

10.5 OWL Solution

The common dialog box library, on which this chapter is based, was not available until Windows 3.1. In earlier Windows versions the use of API functions for file dialog boxes was much more complex. There were, however, facilities for this purpose available for ObjectWindows programmers. In other words, programming file dialog boxes was easier with Borland C++ than with Microsoft C(++) with Windows 3.0. We can still use these facilities (based on the OWL class *TFileDialog*). However, now that the common dialog box library is available, we may as well use it here in combination with ObjectWindows. A drawback of the older, specific OWL solution is that it provides for only one 'mask', such as *.* or *.*cpp*, as an allowed file-name extension, instead of the more general method based on a long string (consisting of seven program lines in our example). Ignoring the *TFileDialog* class, we will therefore again use the common dialog box library. This also has the advantage of making this section consistent with Sections 10.3 and 10.4:

File FDLGOWL.RC:

```
// FDLGOWL.RC:
#include <windows.h>
#include "fdlgowl.h"

FILEMENU MENU
BEGIN
    POPUP "&File"
    BEGIN
        MENUITEM "&Open", IDM_OPEN
    END
END
```

File FDLGOWL.H:

```
// FDLGOWL.H
#define IDM_OPEN 1001
class TApp: public TApplication
{  public:
    TApp(LPSTR Name, HANDLE hInstance, HANDLE hPrevInstance,
        LPSTR lpCmdLine, int nCmdShow)
        : TApplication(Name, hInstance, hPrevInstance, lpCmdLine,
                        nCmdShow){}
    virtual void InitMainWindow();
};

class TMyWindow: public TWindow
{  public:
    char szFile[256], szFileTitle[256];
    int MenuUsed;
    TMyWindow(PTWindowsObject AParent, LPSTR ATitle);
    void OnOpen(RTMessage Msg) = [CM_FIRST + IDM_OPEN];
    virtual void Paint(HDC hDC, PAINTSTRUCT&);
};
```

File FDLGOWL.CPP:

```
// FDLGOWL.CPP: A file dialog box.
#define WIN31
#include <owl.h>
#include <commdlg.h>
#include <string.h>
#include "fdlgowl.h"
```

```
void TApp::InitMainWindow()
{  TMyWindow *p;
   MainWindow = p = new TMyWindow(NULL, Name);
   p->Attr.X = 0;
   p->Attr.Y = 0;
   p->Attr.W = GetSystemMetrics(SM_CXSCREEN);
   p->Attr.H = GetSystemMetrics(SM_CYSCREEN);
   p->szFile[0] = '\0';
   p->szFileTitle[0] = '\0';
   p->MenuUsed = 0;
}


TMyWindow::TMyWindow(PTWindowsObject AParent, LPSTR ATitle)
     : TWindow(AParent, ATitle)
{  AssignMenu("FILEMENU");
}


void TMyWindow::OnOpen(RTMessage)
{  char szFilter[256], chReplace;
   OPENFILENAME ofn;
   int i, cbString;
   strcpy(szFilter,
   "All files (*.*)|*.*|"
   "Header files (*.h)|*.h|"
   "C++ (*.cpp)|*.cpp|"
   "Make files (*.mak)|*.mak|"
   "Resource script (*.rc)|*.rc|"
   "Module definition (*.def)|*.def|"
   "Word for Windows (*.doc)|*.doc||");
   cbString = strlen(szFilter);
   chReplace = szFilter[cbString-1];

   for (i=0; szFilter[i]; i++)
      if (szFilter[i] == chReplace) szFilter[i] = '\0';

   memset(&ofn, 0, sizeof(OPENFILENAME));
   ofn.lStructSize = sizeof(OPENFILENAME);
   ofn.hwndOwner = HWindow;
   ofn.lpstrFilter = szFilter;
   ofn.nFilterIndex = 1;
   ofn.lpstrFile = szFile;
   ofn.nMaxFile = sizeof(szFile);
   ofn.lpstrFileTitle = szFileTitle;
   ofn.nMaxFileTitle = sizeof(szFileTitle);
   ofn.lpstrInitialDir = NULL; // szDirName;
   ::GetOpenFileName(&ofn); // Or ::GetSaveFileName for output
   MenuUsed = 1;
   InvalidateRect(HWindow, NULL, TRUE);
}
```

```
    void TMyWindow::Paint(HDC hDC, PAINTSTRUCT&)
    {  if (MenuUsed)
       {  TextOut(hDC, 40, 100, "Selected path name:", 19);
          TextOut(hDC, 40, 140, szFile, strlen(szFile));
          TextOut(hDC, 40, 180, szFileTitle, strlen(szFileTitle));
       }
    }

    int PASCAL WinMain(HANDLE hInstance, HANDLE hPrevInstance,
       LPSTR lpCmdLine, int nCmdShow)
    {  TApp App("File dialog box",
       hInstance, hPrevInstance, lpCmdLine, nCmdShow);
       App.Run();
       return App.Status;
    }
```

File FDLGOWL.MAK:

```
    # FDLGOWL.MAK; usage (with Borland C++): make -f fdlgowl.mak
    fdlgowl.exe: fdlgowl.obj fdlgowl.res
         bcc -mm -WE -L\borlandc\owl\lib;\borlandc\classlib\lib \
            fdlgowl.obj owlwm.lib tclassm.lib
         rc fdlgowl.res
    fdlgowl.res: fdlgowl.rc
         rc -r -i\borlandc\owl\include fdlgowl.rc
    fdlgowl.obj: fdlgowl.cpp fdlgowl.h
         bcc -c -mm -WE \
            -I\borlandc\owl\include;\borlandc\classlib\include \
            fdlgowl.cpp
```

Nearly at the end of function *OnOpen* we find the call to *GetOpenFileName*, which causes the text *Open* to appear in the title bar of the dialog box. We could call *GetSaveFileName* instead if we wanted to replace *OnOpen* with *Save As*.

10.6 Questions

10.1   Why are some local variables in function *WndProc* (in program FDLG.C) given the *static* attribute?

10.2   What is variable *MenuUsed* for in all three programs?

10.3   We could have displayed the path and file names immediately when they become available instead of only after *WM_PAINT* messages. If we did this without precautions, what would happen if a long file name is entered first and a short one later? And what happens in both cases if the user changes the window size when the client rectangle shows some text, such as in Figure 10.3?

10.4   What happens with the text shown in Figure 10.3 if the height of the client rectangle is made less than 180 pixels? And what if the original height is then restored?

11

Fonts

11.1 Problem Definition

So far, we have used the *system font* to display text. It is often required to use other fonts, with regard not only to typeface but also to size and style. There is a way to achieve this, which is very convenient both to the user and to the programmer. As in Chapter 10, the method we will use is based on the 'common dialog box library'.

Before dealing with the programming aspects of fonts, let us first have a look at some fonts themselves. Figure 11.1 shows nine of them. They were produced by a program to be discussed shortly. Each of the nine lines shows a different font. These fonts are all so-called *TrueType* fonts, which have several advantages over older fonts. Being based on mathematical rules, they are scalable and their appearance on the screen closely resembles the way they are printed. If you are unfamiliar with fonts, you should note that *Arial* is a sans-serif typeface, also known as *Helvetica* or *Swiss*. As you can see, the forms of the characters are simpler than those of the others. A very common typeface is *Times*, which is here called *Times New Roman*. Most of the text in this book is printed in this typeface. Most fonts are proportional. For example, the capital letter W takes much more space than the lower case letter i. An exception is the *Courier* typeface, the TrueType version of which is called *Courier New*. It depends on your printer which typefaces are available to you.

Font sizes are measured in *points* (pt), one point being 1/72 inch. Since room is included for special accents, as used, for example, in Ä, characters are not as high as we might expect. Depending on the typeface, the height of a capital letter such as I (or a digit, such as 1) lies between 65% and 75% of the font size. For example, the height of a 72 pt capital letter is not 72/72 = 1 inch but rather about 0.7 inch (= 0.7 × 25.4 ≈ 18 mm). The character height in Figure 11.1 is much less than 20 pt, but this is because this illustration is much smaller than its original on the screen. Obviously, the real size of characters on a video display also depends on the monitor type.

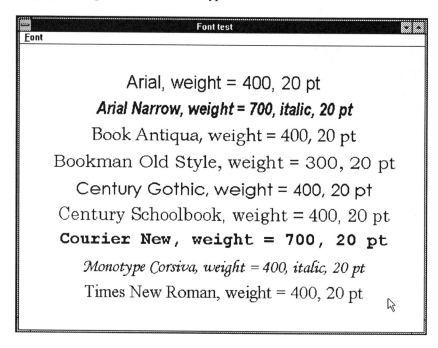

Figure 11.1. Some fonts

The programs to be discussed in this chapter will enable the user to select the fonts that will be used. This is not obvious because we could also have produced the client area of Figure 11.1 using only output operations. In that case the fonts would have been chosen by the programmer. We now see that we can distinguish two aspects:

1 Reading information about a font selected by the user.
2 Displaying text in the selected font.

Our programs will illustrate not only the second but also the first of these two points. Thanks to the common dialog box library, this is not as difficult as you may think. We will provide the user with a dialog box, as shown in Figure 11.2, to select fonts. A sample piece of text in the chosen font will then be displayed on a new line. Due to limited space on the screen, this can be done only nine times, as shown in Figure 11.1. Each line shows the name of the font, its *weight*, indicating whether or not the user has selected *Bold*, the name *italic* if this applies, and the point size. As you can see in Figure 11.1, the weight is 700 if the font is in boldface. Otherwise it is 400, except for *Bookman Old Style* where it is 300.

Note that Figure 11.1 is the final result, obtained after repeatedly choosing fonts by means of the dialog box shown in Figure 11.2.

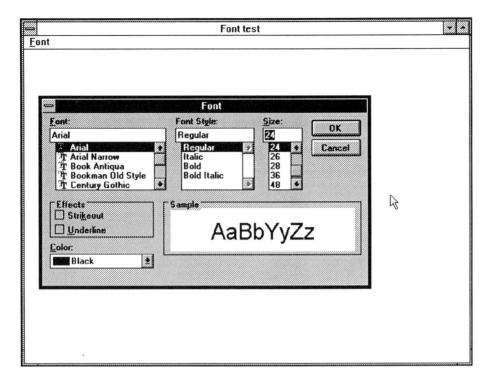

Figure 11.2. *Dialog box to select a font*

11.2 General Aspects

The dialog box shown in Figure 11.2 is very convenient. Not only are there lists of type-faces, sizes and styles from which the user can choose, but such a choice is also immediately visualized by a sample of the chosen font in the dialog box itself. If the font is not what the user wants, it can be changed before the dialog box is left. Surprisingly, this dialog box is easy to program. To keep our programs as simple as possible, we will display text in the chosen font as soon as the font is selected. This means that there will be no provision to repaint the screen: if and when the user changes the size of the window, the entire client area is cleared. We will simply use a current *y*-coordinate (which we will call *LineNr* in our programs), indicating the vertical position for the next line of text. Starting with 0, this variable is increased by 40 pixels for each line of text. The text on each line will appear in its center.

Make files

After replacing all occurrences of *fdlg* with *font*, we can use the make files of Chapter 10.

11.3 C Solution

In the program listed below, the *WndProc* function is the most interesting part. Traditionally, a structure *lf* of type *LOGFONT* is used as a *logical-font descriptor*. It contains such members as *lfHeight*, *lfWeight* and *lfItalic*. To use the common dialog box library, we also need structure *cf*, of type *CHOOSEFONT*, which is closely related to the dialog box.

File FONT.RC:

```
// FONT.RC:
#include <windows.h>
#include "font.h"
FontMenu MENU
BEGIN
    MENUITEM "&Font", IDM_FONT
END
```

File FONT.H:

```
// FONT.H:
#define IDM_FONT 1000
long FAR PASCAL _export WndProc(HWND hWnd, UINT message,
        WPARAM wParam, LPARAM lParam);
int PASCAL WinMain(HANDLE hInstance, HANDLE hPrevInstance,
    LPSTR lpCmdLine, int nCmdShow);
```

File FONT.C:

```
// FONT.C: Font dialog box
#include <windows.h>
#include <commdlg.h>
#include <stdio.h>
#include <string.h>
#include "font.h"

int xScreen, yScreen, LineNr;

int PASCAL WinMain(HANDLE hInstance, HANDLE hPrevInstance,
    LPSTR lpCmdLine, int nCmdShow)
{   char szAppName[]="font";
    WNDCLASS wndclass;
    HWND hWnd;
    MSG msg;
    xScreen = GetSystemMetrics(SM_CXSCREEN);
    yScreen = GetSystemMetrics(SM_CYSCREEN);
    LineNr = 0;
    if (!hPrevInstance)
    {   wndclass.style = CS_HREDRAW | CS_VREDRAW;
        wndclass.lpfnWndProc = WndProc;
```

```
          wndclass.cbClsExtra = 0;
          wndclass.cbWndExtra = 0;
          wndclass.hInstance = hInstance;
          wndclass.hIcon = LoadIcon(NULL, IDI_APPLICATION);
          wndclass.hCursor = LoadCursor(NULL, IDC_ARROW);
          wndclass.hbrBackground = GetStockObject(WHITE_BRUSH);
          wndclass.lpszMenuName = "FontMenu";
          wndclass.lpszClassName = szAppName;
             // Name used in call to CreateWindow.
          if (!RegisterClass(&wndclass)) return FALSE;
      }
      hWnd = CreateWindow(
          szAppName,
          "Font test",                    // Text for window title bar.
          WS_OVERLAPPEDWINDOW,            // Window style.
          0,                              // Initial x position
          0,                              // Initial y position.
          xScreen,                        // Width.
          yScreen,                        // Height.
          NULL,                           // Parent window handle.
          NULL,                           // Window menu handle.
          hInstance,                      // Program instance handle.
          NULL                            // Create parameters.
      );
      ShowWindow(hWnd, nCmdShow);
      UpdateWindow(hWnd);
      while (GetMessage(&msg, NULL, 0, 0))
      {  TranslateMessage(&msg);      // Translates virtual key codes
         DispatchMessage(&msg);       // Dispatches message to window
      }
      return msg.wParam;       // Returns the value from PostQuitMessage
}

long FAR PASCAL _export WndProc(HWND hWnd, UINT message,
        WPARAM wParam, LPARAM lParam)
{  HDC hDC;
   HFONT hFont, hOldFont;
   LOGFONT lf;
   CHOOSEFONT cf;
   char buf[100];
   switch (message)
   {
   case WM_COMMAND:
      if (wParam == IDM_FONT)
      {  // Let the user select a font:
         memset(&cf, 0, sizeof(CHOOSEFONT));
         cf.lStructSize = sizeof(CHOOSEFONT);
         cf.hwndOwner = hWnd;
         cf.lpLogFont = &lf;
```

```
              cf.Flags = CF_SCREENFONTS | CF_EFFECTS;
              cf.rgbColors = RGB(255, 0, 0);  // Red
              cf.nFontType = SCREEN_FONTTYPE;
              ChooseFont(&cf);
              // Display the selected font:
              hDC = GetDC(hWnd);
              sprintf(buf, "%s, weight = %d, %s%d pt",
                 lf.lfFaceName, lf.lfWeight,
                 (lf.lfItalic ? "italic, " : ""),
                 cf.iPointSize/10);
              hFont = CreateFontIndirect(&lf);
              hOldFont= SelectObject(hDC, hFont);
              SetTextColor(hDC, cf.rgbColors);
              SetTextAlign(hDC, TA_CENTER);
              TextOut(hDC, xScreen/2, LineNr += 40, buf, strlen(buf));
              SelectObject(hDC, hOldFont);
              DeleteObject(hFont);
              ReleaseDC(hWnd, hDC);
          }
          break;
      case WM_DESTROY:
          PostQuitMessage(0); break;
      default:
          return DefWindowProc(hWnd, message, wParam, lParam);
      }
      return 0L;
   }
```

The following statement places the address of *lf* in *cf*:

```
   cf.lpLogFont = &lf;
```

This explains that, in the following call, function *ChooseFont* has access not only to *cf* but also to *lf*:

```
   ChooseFont(&cf);
```

This explains that after this call we can use the contents of *lf* both to copy data from it by using *sprintf* and to 'create' the font by calling *CreateFontIndirect*:

```
   sprintf(buf, "%s, weight = %d, %s%d pt",
      lf.lfFaceName, lf.lfWeight,
      (lf.lfItalic ? "italic, " : ""),
      cf.iPointSize/10);
   hFont = CreateFontIndirect(&lf);
```

This font, with handle *hFont*, is then selected into the device context, in the same way as can be done with a brush, for example.

It may at first seem confusing that we should need both structures *lf* and *cf*. But remember, there are some aspects that essentially belong to the dialog box, not to the font. This is the case, for example, with the *color* to be displayed in the bottom-left corner of the dialog box (see Figure 11.2). In the current version of the program, the color *red* is initially displayed here as a result of the following statement:

```
cf.rgbColors = RGB(255, 0, 0);   // Red
```

The user can change this color, using *black*, for example, as was done in Figure 11.2. This selection results only in assigning a new value to the *rgbColors* member of *cf*; it does not alter anything in *lf* which is used in *ChooseFont*. This explains that we must really indicate that we want to use the selected color by means of the following statement:

```
SetTextColor(hDC, cf.rgbColors);
```

The user's color selection would not have any effect on the actual output if we omitted this statement.

11.4 MFC Solution

The MFC solution seems at first very different from the C solution we have just seen. However, there is an analogy, as we will see shortly. The Microsoft foundation class *CFontDialog*, like *CFileDialog*, is derived from *CDialog*, as we have already seen in Figure 10.4 of the last chapter. We will also use class *CFont*, which is similar to the classes *CPen*, *CBrush*, *CPalette* and *CBitmap* in that it is derived from *CGdiObject*, as you can see in Figure B3 in Appendix B.

File FONTMFC.RC:

```
// FONTMFC.RC:
#include <windows.h>
#include "fontmfc.h"

FontMenu MENU
BEGIN
    MENUITEM "&Font", IDM_FONT
END
```

File FONTMFC.H:

```
// FONTMFC.H:
#define IDM_FONT 1000
class CApp: public CWinApp
{  public:
    BOOL InitInstance();
};
```

```
class CMyWindow: public CFrameWnd
{  public:
   int LineNr, xScreen, yScreen;
   CMyWindow();
   afx_msg void OnFont();
   DECLARE_MESSAGE_MAP()
};
```

File FONTMFC.CPP:

```
//FONTMFC.CPP: Test font dialog
#include <afxwin.h>
#include <afxdlgs.h>
#include "fontmfc.h"

CMyWindow::CMyWindow()
{  xScreen = GetSystemMetrics(SM_CXSCREEN);
   yScreen = GetSystemMetrics(SM_CYSCREEN);
   LineNr = 0;
   RECT rect = {0, 0, xScreen, yScreen};
   Create(NULL, "Font test",
          WS_OVERLAPPEDWINDOW, rect, NULL, "FontMenu");
}

BOOL CApp::InitInstance()
{  m_pMainWnd = new CMyWindow();
   m_pMainWnd->ShowWindow(m_nCmdShow);
   m_pMainWnd->UpdateWindow();
   return TRUE;
}

BEGIN_MESSAGE_MAP(CMyWindow, CFrameWnd)
   ON_COMMAND(IDM_FONT, OnFont)
END_MESSAGE_MAP()

CApp App;

void CMyWindow::OnFont()
{  CFontDialog F(NULL);
   F.m_cf.rgbColors = RGB(255, 0, 0);  // Red
   if (F.DoModal() == IDCANCEL) return;
   CFont Font, *pOldFont;
   char buf[100];
   sprintf(buf, "%s, weight = %d, %s%d pt",
      F.m_lf.lfFaceName, F.m_lf.lfWeight,
      (F.m_lf.lfItalic ? "italic, " : ""),
      F.m_cf.iPointSize/10);
   Font.CreateFontIndirect(&F.m_lf);
   CClientDC dc(this);
   pOldFont = dc.SelectObject(&Font);
```

```
      dc.SetTextColor(F.m_cf.rgbColors);
      dc.SetTextAlign(TA_CENTER);
      dc.TextOut(xScreen/2, LineNr += 40 , buf);
      dc.SelectObject(pOldFont);
      Font.DeleteObject();
   }
```

We can clearly see how program FONTMFC.CPP is related to FONT.C, by considering the variables and types occurring in the following table:

In FONT.C	In FONTMFC.CPP	Used for
LOGFONT lf;	*CFont Font;*	*Font description*
CHOOSEFONT cf;	*CFontDialog F(NULL);*	*Dialog box*

There is an *m_cf* member of type *CHOOSEFONT* in the *CFontDialog* object *F*, which we use to set the initial color:

```
   F.m_cf.rgbColors = RGB(255, 0, 0);  // Red
```

The call

```
   F.DoModal()
```

does most of the work. It is similar to the call to *ChooseFont* in program FONT.C.

Object F also contains the member *m_lf*, of type *LOGFONT*, so after calling *DoModal*, we can use

```
   F.m_lf.lfFaceName
```

to copy the typeface name to *buf* in the call to *sprintf*.

11.5 OWL Solution

The following solution for the ObjectWindows Library is very closely related to program FONT.C, discussed in Section 11.3:

File FONTOWL.RC:

```
// FONTOWL.RC:
#include <windows.h>
#include "fontowl.h"
FontMenu MENU
BEGIN
   MENUITEM "&Font", IDM_FONT
END
```

File FONTOWL.H:

```
// FONTOWL.H:
#define IDM_FONT 1001
class TApp: public TApplication
{ public:
    TApp(LPSTR Name, HANDLE hInstance, HANDLE hPrevInstance,
         LPSTR lpCmdLine, int nCmdShow)
       : TApplication(Name, hInstance, hPrevInstance, lpCmdLine,
                      nCmdShow){}
    virtual void InitMainWindow();
};

class TMyWindow: public TWindow
{ public:
    int LineNr;
    TMyWindow(PTWindowsObject AParent, LPSTR ATitle);
    void OnFont(RTMessage Msg) = [CM_FIRST + IDM_FONT];
};
```

File FONTOWL.CPP:

```
// FONTOWL.CPP: A font dialog box.
#define WIN31
#include <owl.h>
#include <commdlg.h>
#include <string.h>
#include <stdio.h>
#include "fontowl.h"

void TApp::InitMainWindow()
{ TMyWindow *p;
    MainWindow = p = new TMyWindow(NULL, Name);
    p->Attr.X = 0;
    p->Attr.Y = 0;
    p->Attr.W = GetSystemMetrics(SM_CXSCREEN);
    p->Attr.H = GetSystemMetrics(SM_CYSCREEN);
    p->LineNr = 0;
}

TMyWindow::TMyWindow(PTWindowsObject AParent, LPSTR ATitle)
     : TWindow(AParent, ATitle)
{ AssignMenu("FontMenu");
}

void TMyWindow::OnFont(RTMessage)
{ HDC hDC;
    HFONT hFont, hOldFont;
    LOGFONT lf;
```

```
        CHOOSEFONT cf;
        char buf[100];
        // Let the user select a font:
        memset(&cf, 0, sizeof(CHOOSEFONT));
        cf.lStructSize = sizeof(CHOOSEFONT);
        cf.hwndOwner = HWindow;
        cf.lpLogFont = &lf;
        cf.Flags = CF_SCREENFONTS | CF_EFFECTS;
        cf.rgbColors = RGB(255, 0, 0);   // Red
        cf.nFontType = SCREEN_FONTTYPE;
        ChooseFont(&cf);
        // Display the selected font:
        hDC = GetDC(HWindow);
        sprintf(buf, "%s, weight = %d, %s%d pt",
            lf.lfFaceName, lf.lfWeight,
            (lf.lfItalic ? "italic, " : ""),
            cf.iPointSize/10);
        hFont = CreateFontIndirect(&lf);
        hOldFont= SelectObject(hDC, hFont);
        SetTextColor(hDC, cf.rgbColors);
        SetTextAlign(hDC, TA_CENTER);
        TextOut(hDC, Attr.W/2, LineNr += 40, buf, strlen(buf));
        SelectObject(hDC, hOldFont);
        DeleteObject(hFont);
        ReleaseDC(HWindow, hDC);
    }

int PASCAL WinMain(HANDLE hInstance, HANDLE hPrevInstance,
    LPSTR lpCmdLine, int nCmdShow)
{ TApp App("Font test",
    hInstance, hPrevInstance, lpCmdLine, nCmdShow);
    App.Run();
    return App.Status;
}
```

11.6 Questions

11.1 Do the words *font* and *typeface* have the same meaning?

11.2 Why do we use both a *LOGFONT* and a *CHOOSEFONT* structure in program FONT.C?

11.3 Which function generates a font dialog box in FONT.C and in FONTOWL.CPP? Which in FONTMFC.CPP?

11.4 Is *color* a font attribute? In which structure can we specify a color? What is the color box in the bottom-left corner of the font dialog box for?

11.5 How can we specify that a chosen color is to be used for subsequent text output?

12

Printing

12.1 Problem Definition

It would be no good if output operations were restricted to the video display. We have already seen in Chapter 10 that there are other possibilities: after reading a file name from a file dialog box, the standard output functions such as *fopen* and *fprintf* enable us to write output to files. We could then use such files later to print their data. However, this is normally not what we want. With many applications it is desirable that we send output to the printer, and that several fonts as well as graphics can be used. In this chapter we will see how this can be done in the same way as it is done by editors, text processors, and draw programs, as far as these run under Windows. Actually, we will *not* send output directly to the printer, but rather to the Print Manager, which is part of Windows. But as this does not make much difference from the user's point of view, it is as if we are printing directly from our program.

With most commercial programs that run under Windows, the user initiates printing by means of a dialog box. The common dialog box library provides us with facilities for such a print dialog box, similar to the file dialog box and the font dialog box used in Chapters 10 and 11. We will discuss a program which initially shows only a very simple menu, which (after a reduction of the window height by the user) is shown in Figure 12.1, with *File* selected. If we then select the *Print* menu item, a dialog box such as the one shown in Figure 12.2 is displayed. After clicking the *OK* button, the line

```
A single line of text.
```

will be printed, starting at about two inches from both the left and the top edges of the paper. We will do this by using the *TextOut* function, with which we are already familiar.

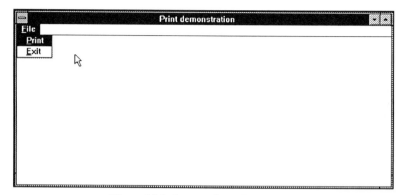

*Figure 12.1. Screen after selecting **File***

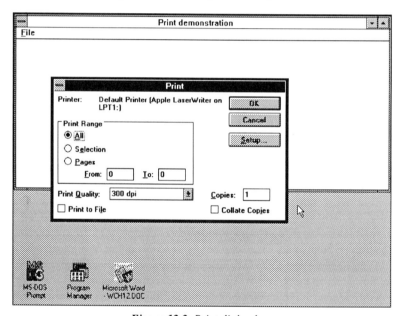

Figure 12.2. Print dialog box

Although not demonstrated here, we can select a special font as discussed in Chapter 11, and apply this to the text to be printed, provided that our printer can accept it. We can also use graphics output functions, such as, for example, *Polygon*, again provided that our printer has graphics capabilities.

If the user gives a print command while the printer is not ready, the dialog box of Figure 12.3 appears. We can then either switch the printer on and 'press' the *Retry* button, or cancel this command and delete the print job from the print queue by using Windows' Print Manager. Note that the icon of the print manager can be seen at the bottom in Figure 12.3. After selecting the print manager, either by clicking this icon or by means of the

Alt+Tab key combination, the window shown in Figure 12.4 appears. Clicking the *Delete* button deletes the print job.

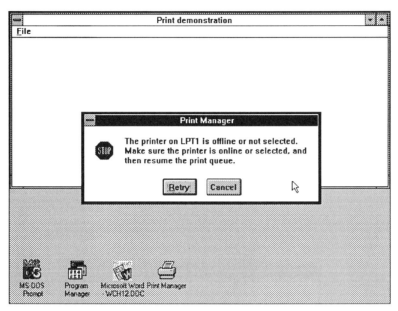

Figure 12.3. *Dialog box appearing if printer is not ready*

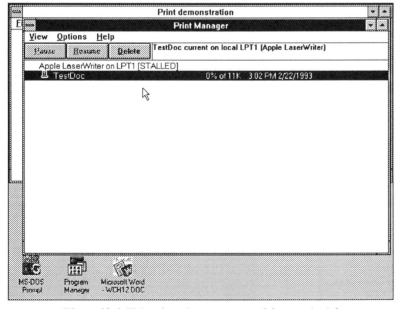

Figure 12.4. *Using the print-manager to delete a print job*

Note that we are *not* dealing with a screen dump in this chapter. If we were, only text and graphics visible on the screen could be printed, with a rather low resolution, depending on the video display. Instead, we have control over the printer directly from our program, and the print quality depends only on the printer we are using, not on the resolution of the screen.

Except for the simplicity of the above single line of text (which you could easily replace with more interesting material), this way of sending output to the printer will appeal to most users.

12.2 General Aspects

We program a print dialog box by using a structure *pd* of type *PRINTDLG*. After declaring and initializing *pd*, we call the function *PrintDlg*, with the address of *pd* as its argument. This function modifies the contents of *pd*. It places a device handle in *pd.hDC*, which we can then use like a device-context handle for a normal window.

Make files

We can use the make files of Chapter 10, after replacing all occurrences of *fdlg* with *print*.

12.3 C Solution

In the previous section, I deliberately simplified our discussion about using a device context for the printer. Before applying *TextOut* or any other well-known output function to the printer, we have to start a print job by calling the functions *StartDoc* and *StartPage*. Similarly, we have to call the functions *EndPage* and *EndDoc* after the (final) output operation, and we should clean things up by calling *DeleteDC* and *GlobalFree*. Let us first have a look at the program text:

File PRDLG.RC:

```
// PRDLG.RC:
#include <windows.h>
#include "prdlg.h"

PRDLG MENU
BEGIN
   POPUP "&File"
   BEGIN
      MENUITEM "&Print", IDM_PRINT
      MENUITEM "&Exit", IDM_EXIT
   END
END
```

File PRDLG.H:

```
// PRDLG.H:
#define IDM_PRINT 1001
#define IDM_EXIT  1002
long FAR PASCAL _export WndProc(HWND hWnd, UINT message,
      WPARAM wParam, LPARAM lParam);
int PASCAL WinMain(HANDLE hInstance, HANDLE hPrevInstance,
    LPSTR lpCmdLine, int nCmdShow);
```

File PRDLG.C:

```
// PRDLG.C: Demonstrates printing
#include <windows.h>
#include <commdlg.h>
#include <string.h>
#include "prdlg.h"

int PASCAL WinMain(HANDLE hInstance, HANDLE hPrevInstance,
    LPSTR lpCmdLine, int nCmdShow)
{   char szAppName[]="prdlg";
    WNDCLASS wndclass;
    HWND hWnd;
    MSG msg;
    int xScreen = GetSystemMetrics(SM_CXSCREEN),
        yScreen = GetSystemMetrics(SM_CYSCREEN);
    if (!hPrevInstance)
    {   wndclass.style = CS_HREDRAW | CS_VREDRAW;
        wndclass.lpfnWndProc = WndProc;
        wndclass.cbClsExtra = 0;
        wndclass.cbWndExtra = 0;
        wndclass.hInstance = hInstance;
        wndclass.hIcon = LoadIcon(NULL, IDI_APPLICATION);
        wndclass.hCursor = LoadCursor(NULL, IDC_ARROW);
        wndclass.hbrBackground = GetStockObject(WHITE_BRUSH);
        wndclass.lpszMenuName = "PRDLG";
            // Reference to menu name in file PRDLG.RC
        wndclass.lpszClassName = szAppName;
        if (!RegisterClass(&wndclass)) return FALSE;
    }
    hWnd = CreateWindow(
        szAppName,
        "Print demonstration",          // Text for window title bar.
        WS_OVERLAPPEDWINDOW,            // Window style.
        0,                              // Initial x position
        0,                              // Initial y position.
        xScreen,                        // Width.
        yScreen,                        // Height.
        NULL,                           // Parent window handle.
        NULL,                           // Window menu handle.
```

```
        hInstance,                      // Program instance handle.
        NULL                            // Create parameters.
    );
    ShowWindow(hWnd, nCmdShow);
    UpdateWindow(hWnd);
    while (GetMessage(&msg, NULL, 0, 0))
    { TranslateMessage(&msg);       // Translates virtual key codes
      DispatchMessage(&msg);        // Dispatches message to window
    }
    return msg.wParam;      // Returns the value from PostQuitMessage
}

long FAR PASCAL _export WndProc(HWND hWnd, UINT message,
        WPARAM wParam, LPARAM lParam)
{ PRINTDLG pd;
  DOCINFO DocInfo;
  char *TextSample = "A single line of text.";
  switch (message)
  { case WM_COMMAND:
      if (wParam == IDM_PRINT)
      { memset(&pd, 0, sizeof(PRINTDLG));
        pd.lStructSize = sizeof(PRINTDLG);
        pd.hwndOwner = hWnd;
        pd.Flags = PD_RETURNDC;
        if (PrintDlg(&pd) != 0)
        { DocInfo.cbSize = sizeof(DOCINFO);
          DocInfo.lpszDocName = "TestDoc";
          DocInfo.lpszOutput = (LPSTR) NULL;
          StartDoc(pd.hDC, &DocInfo);
          StartPage(pd.hDC);
          TextOut(pd.hDC, 600, 600, TextSample, strlen(TextSample));
          EndPage(pd.hDC);
          EndDoc(pd.hDC);
          DeleteDC(pd.hDC);
          if (pd.hDevMode != NULL) GlobalFree(pd.hDevMode);
          if (pd.hDevNames != NULL) GlobalFree(pd.hDevNames);
        } else MessageBox(hWnd, "Print attempt failed", "", IDOK);
        return 0;
      } else
      if (wParam == IDM_EXIT)
      { SendMessage(hWnd, WM_CLOSE, 0, 0L);
        return 0;
      }
    case WM_DESTROY:
        PostQuitMessage(0); break;
    default:
        return DefWindowProc(hWnd, message, wParam, lParam);
  }
  return 0L;
}
```

There are two actions to be distinguished. First, we have to display a print dialog box. After initializing *pd*, which includes placing the constant *PD_RETURNDC* in *pd.Flags*, we use the following call:

```
PrintDlg(&pd)
```

Thanks to the constant just mentioned, *pd.hDC* has now been assigned a device-context handler for the printer. We need this for the second action, which is printing a 'document'. We first have to place suitable values in the three members of structure *DocInfo*, which has type *DOCINFO*:

```
DocInfo.cbSize = sizeof(DOCINFO);
DocInfo.lpszDocName = "TestDoc";
DocInfo.lpszOutput = (LPSTR) NULL;
```

The document name, for which we use *TestDoc* here, is a means to identify this print job. The *Print Manager* displays this name so we can use it to remove the print job from the print queue, if we want to do so before it is finished. The document name must not be longer than 32 characters, including the terminating null character.

The *lpszOutput* member of *DocName* is set to *NULL* if we really want to use the printer. Instead of *NULL*, we can use the name of a file if we want to redirect a print job to a file. We can then start the print job by calling *StartDoc*:

```
StartDoc(pd.hDC, &DocInfo);
```

For each page being printed, we use *StartPage* before and *EndPage* after all print operations for it. Instead of only one call to *TextOut*, there will normally be many more calls to output functions. As the program text shows, we finally have to do some cleaning- up chores, consisting of calls to *EndDoc*, *DeleteDC* and *GlobalFree*.

12.4 MFC Solution

The MFC solution to our printing problem contains a function *CMyWindow::OnPrint* which is similar to what we have seen in program PRDLG.C. Instead of a *PRINTDLG* object and the *PrintDlg* function, we now use a *CPrintDialog* object *pd* and its member function *DoModal*:

File PRDLGMFC.RC:

```
// PRDLGMFC.RC:
#include <windows.h>
#include "prdlgmfc.h"

PRDLGMFC MENU
```

```
BEGIN
   POPUP "&File"
   BEGIN
      MENUITEM "&Print", IDM_PRINT
      MENUITEM "&Exit", IDM_EXIT
   END
END
```

File PRDLGMFC.H:

```
// PRDLGMFC.H
#define IDM_PRINT 1001
#define IDM_EXIT 1002
class CApp: public CWinApp
{  public:
   BOOL InitInstance();
};

class CMyWindow: public CFrameWnd
{  public:
   CMyWindow();
   afx_msg void OnPrint();
   afx_msg void OnExit();
   DECLARE_MESSAGE_MAP()
};
```

File PRDLGMFC.CPP:

```
// PRDLGMFC.CPP: Demonstrates a menu
#include <afxwin.h>
#include <afxdlgs.h>
#include <stdio.h>
#include "prdlgmfc.h"

BOOL CApp::InitInstance()
{  m_pMainWnd = new CMyWindow();
   m_pMainWnd->ShowWindow(m_nCmdShow);
   m_pMainWnd->UpdateWindow();
   return TRUE;
}

CApp App;

CMyWindow::CMyWindow()
{  int xScreen = GetSystemMetrics(SM_CXSCREEN),
       yScreen = GetSystemMetrics(SM_CYSCREEN);
   RECT rect = {0, 0, xScreen, yScreen};
   Create(NULL, "Print demonstration",
   WS_OVERLAPPEDWINDOW, rect, NULL, "PRDLGMFC");
}
```

```
BEGIN_MESSAGE_MAP(CMyWindow, CFrameWnd)
   ON_COMMAND(IDM_PRINT, OnPrint)
   ON_COMMAND(IDM_EXIT, OnExit)
END_MESSAGE_MAP()

void CMyWindow::OnPrint()
{  DOCINFO DocInfo;
   CPrintDialog pd(FALSE);
   char *TextSample = "A single line of text.";
   pd.m_pd.Flags = PD_RETURNDC;
   if (pd.DoModal() != IDCANCEL)
   {  DocInfo.cbSize = sizeof(DOCINFO);
      DocInfo.lpszDocName = "TestDoc";
      DocInfo.lpszOutput = (LPSTR) NULL;
      StartDoc(pd.m_pd.hDC, &DocInfo);
      StartPage(pd.m_pd.hDC);
      TextOut(pd.m_pd.hDC, 600, 600, TextSample, strlen(TextSample));
      EndPage(pd.m_pd.hDC);
      EndDoc(pd.m_pd.hDC);
      DeleteDC(pd.m_pd.hDC);
      if (pd.m_pd.hDevMode != NULL) GlobalFree(pd.m_pd.hDevMode);
      if (pd.m_pd.hDevNames != NULL) GlobalFree(pd.m_pd.hDevNames);
   } else MessageBox("Print attempt failed", "", IDOK);
}

void CMyWindow::OnExit()
{  PostQuitMessage(0);
}
```

Note the notation

```
pd.m_pd.hDC
```

which often occurs in this program. This means that our *CPrintDialog* object *pd* has a member *m_pd*, which we can use as the *PRINTDLG* object *pd* occurring in program PRDLG.C.

12.5 OWL Solution

As usual, the OWL solution is based on classes, like the MFC solution, but is also very similar to the C solution, especially with regard to the use of handles:

File PRDLGOWL.RC:

```
// PRDLGOWL.RC:
#include <windows.h>
#include "prdlgowl.h"
```

```
PRDLGMFC MENU
BEGIN
   POPUP "&File"
   BEGIN
      MENUITEM "&Print", IDM_PRINT
      MENUITEM "&Exit", IDM_EXIT
   END
END
```

File PRDLGOWL.H:

```
// PRDLGOWL.H:
#define IDM_PRINT 1001
#define IDM_EXIT 1002
class TApp: public TApplication
{  public:
   TApp(LPSTR Name, HANDLE hInstance, HANDLE hPrevInstance,
       LPSTR lpCmdLine, int nCmdShow)
     : TApplication(Name, hInstance, hPrevInstance, lpCmdLine,
                   nCmdShow){}
   virtual void InitMainWindow();
};

class TMyWindow: public TWindow
{  public:
   char szFile[256], szFileTitle[256];
   int MenuUsed;
   TMyWindow(PTWindowsObject AParent, LPSTR ATitle);
   void OnPrint(RTMessage Msg) = [CM_FIRST + IDM_PRINT];
   void OnExit(RTMessage Msg) = [CM_FIRST + IDM_EXIT];
};
```

File PRDLGOWL.CPP:

```
// PRDLGOWL.CPP: A file dialog box.
#define WIN31
#include <owl.h>
#include <commdlg.h>
#include <string.h>
#include "prdlgowl.h"

void TApp::InitMainWindow()
{  TMyWindow *p;
   MainWindow = p = new TMyWindow(NULL, Name);
   p->Attr.X = 0;
   p->Attr.Y = 0;
   p->Attr.W = GetSystemMetrics(SM_CXSCREEN);
   p->Attr.H = GetSystemMetrics(SM_CYSCREEN);
}
```

```
TMyWindow::TMyWindow(PTWindowsObject AParent, LPSTR ATitle)
     : TWindow(AParent, ATitle)
{  AssignMenu("PRDLGMFC");
}

void TMyWindow::OnPrint(RTMessage)
{  PRINTDLG pd;
   DOCINFO DocInfo;
   char *TextSample = "A single line of text.";
   memset(&pd, 0, sizeof(PRINTDLG));
   pd.lStructSize = sizeof(PRINTDLG);
   pd.hwndOwner = HWindow;
   pd.Flags = PD_RETURNDC;
   if (PrintDlg(&pd) != 0)
   {  DocInfo.cbSize = sizeof(DOCINFO);
      DocInfo.lpszDocName = "TestDoc";
      DocInfo.lpszOutput = (LPSTR) NULL;
      StartDoc(pd.hDC, &DocInfo); StartPage(pd.hDC);
      TextOut(pd.hDC, 600, 600, TextSample, strlen(TextSample));
      EndPage(pd.hDC); EndDoc(pd.hDC);
      DeleteDC(pd.hDC);
      if (pd.hDevMode != NULL) GlobalFree(pd.hDevMode);
      if (pd.hDevNames != NULL) GlobalFree(pd.hDevNames);
   } else MessageBox(HWindow, "Print attempt failed", "", IDOK);
}

void TMyWindow::OnExit(RTMessage)
{  PostQuitMessage(0);
}

int PASCAL WinMain(HANDLE hInstance, HANDLE hPrevInstance,
   LPSTR lpCmdLine, int nCmdShow)
{  TApp App("Print demonstration",
   hInstance, hPrevInstance, lpCmdLine, nCmdShow);
   App.Run();
   return App.Status;
}
```

12.6 Questions

12.1   Can we print in a Windows program without using a dialog box?

12.2   What is a *PRINTDLG* structure for?

12.3   What is a *DOCINFO* structure for?

12.4   The following functions, in alphabetic order, are related to a document: EndDoc, EndPage, StartDoc, StartPage. In which order do they occur in our programs?

12.5   Which arguments do we use with these four functions?

13

The Towers of Hanoi in Action

13.1 Problem Definition

Most examples in this book are extremely simple and possibly not very interesting from an algorithmic point of view. This chapter is different in that it is about an interesting and well-known programming problem, known as *The Towers of Hanoi*. You can find programs to solve this problem in many books on programming and computer science. These programs are instructive because they demonstrate recursion in a very elegant way. Let us first define the original problem and show its conventional solution (which can also be found as Exercise 43 in my book *C++ for Programmers*):

There are three pegs, A, B, C, on which disks with holes in their centers can be placed. These disks have all different diameters. A larger disk must never be placed on top of a smaller one. There are *n* disks, numbered 1, 2, ... , *n*, from the smallest to the largest. Initially all these disks, in their proper order, are on peg A, so that pegs B and C are empty. The problem is to move all disks, one by one, from peg A to peg C, never placing a larger disk on a smaller one; peg B may be used as auxiliary. Write a program that reads *n* and prints the solution to this problem. For example, if *n* = 2, a conventional program with typewriter-like output would 'print' the following lines:

```
Disk 1 from peg A to peg B.
Disk 2 from peg A to peg C.
Disk 1 from peg B to peg C.
```

Such a conventional, non-Windows program, written in C++ and copied from the book mentioned above, is shown below:

```
// HANOI.CPP: Solution to the Towers of Hanoi problem.
#include <iostream.h>

void Hanoi(char src, char aux, char dest, int n)
/* A tower of n disks is moved from peg src to
   peg dest; peg aux may be used temporarily.
*/
{ if (n > 0)
  { Hanoi(src, dest, aux, n-1);
    cout << "Disk " << n << " from peg " <<
            src << " to peg " << dest << '.' << endl;
    Hanoi(aux, src, dest, n-1);
  }
}

int main()
{ int n;
  cout << endl;
  cout << "Enter n, the number of disks: ";
  cin >> n;
  Hanoi('A', 'B', 'C', n);
  cout << endl;
  return 0; s
}
```

This program is based on the idea that moving a tower consisting of the disks 1, 2, ... , n from A to C consists of no work at all if n is zero, and can be divided into the following three subproblems if n is greater than zero:

1 Move a tower consisting of the disks 1, 2, ... , $n-1$ from A to B.
2 Move disk n from A to C.
3 Move a tower consisting of the disks 1, 2, ... , $n-1$ from B to C.

Since the steps 1 and 3 are similar but simpler than the original problem, it is natural to solve this with recursion.

We now want to write a specific *Windows program* for this problem. Instead of a simple line of text, we will use a dialog box as shown in Chapter 3 for the input of N, the number of disks. More interestingly, the output will display the situation of the pegs and the disks for each move. This example is therefore another application of *animation*, a subject discussed in Chapter 9. Obviously, the moves must not occur as frequently as possible, but in a pace that we as human beings can follow, say, one move every 1.5 s. In this way we have some time to predict each next move and see if such predictions are right.

With a tower of N disks, there will be exactly $2^N - 1$ moves. During the process of moving disks, we may as well display both the current move number and this total number of moves, say, in the top-left corner of the client rectangle.

An attractive aspect of using a timer is that only very small time slices are assigned to our program. This means that other applications (or other instances of the same one) can run at the same time. Figure 13.1 shows two windows, each displaying an instance of our program. Note that although these two windows have different dimensions, the towers as well as the text fit nicely into them. Running this program yourself on your computer gives you a better impression than this figure, not only because you can see them move but also because the disks have different colors.

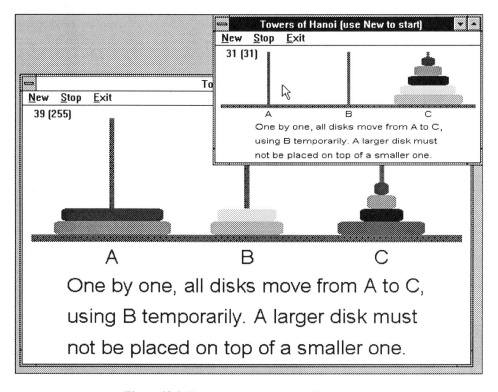

Figure 13.1. Two instances running at the same time

13.2 General Aspects

Since disks will be moved only once every 1500 ms, speed is not a critical factor for this problem. There is therefore no need to use bit-block transfer operations as we did in Chapters 7 and 9. Instead, we can simply fill rectangles for the pegs and the board on which they stand and rounded rectangles for the disks. The functions to be used for them are *Rectangle* and *RoundRect*, respectively. We will use six different colors for the disks, and a different one, imitating the color of wood, for the pegs and the board. Actually, we implement a disk move by three fill operations. Suppose that some disk is to move from peg A to peg B. We then do the following:

1   Using the color of this disk, we fill a rounded rectangle for its new position on peg B.
2   Using the white background color, we fill a rectangle to replace the old disk on peg A.
3   Using the color of wood, we fill a smaller rectangle to restore the portion of peg A
     inside the white rectangle just filled.

The word *fill* in this discussion actually means *draw and fill*: when filling a rectangle with
a brush of a certain color, we also draw it, using a pen of the same color. This is done
automatically if such a pen has been selected into the device context.

The API functions *Rectangle* and *RoundRect* have quite a few parameters. As usual, the
first is a device-context handle. This is followed by the coordinate pairs of the top-left and
bottom-right corners. Then *RoundRect* has two additional parameters, denoting the width
and the height of an ellipse, of which one fourth part is used for each rectangle corner.

When the user changes the size of the window, the current state of the three towers
must be redrawn to a different scale. We therefore need a data structure, which we have to
update for each move. We will limit the number of disks to $NMAX = 20$. This is not a
serious restriction because, first, this limit can easily be increased and, second, it would
take more than 400 hours for our program to complete all the steps required to move a
tower of 20 disks. (Remember, with N disks, we need $2^N - 1$ moves, each taking 1.5 s.)
This limitation enables us to use a two-dimensional array, *Stack*, to represent the three
towers internally. This array can be regarded as three *stacks*, because each tower is really a
stack of disks: only at the top of each tower can we insert and remove disks. We will use a
second array, *StPtr*, of three elements. There will be N disks, where $N \leq NMAX$. The
precise meaning of the arrays just mentioned can best be shown by means of this program
fragment, which describes the initial situation:

```
static int Stack[3][NMAX], StPtr[3];
for (i=N; i>0; i--) Stack[0][N-i] = i;
StPtr[0] = N; StPtr[1] = StPtr[2] = 0;
```

Internally, we use the integers $j = 0, 1, 2$ instead of the letters A, B and C, while the
integers $i = 1, 2, ... , N$ denote the disks. In the initial situation, we have $i = Stack[0][0] = N$
(largest disk, at the bottom of tower 0) and $i = Stack[0][N - 1] = 1$ (smallest disk, at the
top). At any time, there are $StPtr[j]$ disks on tower j. The number of the largest of these
disks can be found as $Stack[j][0]$, and that of the smallest as $Stack[j]$ $[StPtr - 1]$.

Each of the three stack pointers $StPtr[j]$ 'points to' the first free location of stack j.
Suppose that a disk is to be moved from tower $jSrc$ to tower $jDest$. This can only mean that
the uppermost disk of tower $jSrc$ is placed on top of the disks that are already on tower
$jDest$. The following statements find the number i of that disk as well as the vertical positions $kSrc$ and $kDest$ of the source and destination. They also update our arrays in accor-
dance with this move:

```
kSrc = --StPtr[jSrc];   // j = horizontal position (0=A, 1=B, 2=C)
kDest = StPtr[jDest]++; // k = vertical position (0 = lowest)
Stack[jDest][kDest] = i = Stack[jSrc][kSrc];
                        // i = disk number (1 = smallest)
```

The most interesting aspect of this problem is related to its recursive nature. Since our program will be based on a timer, a short recursive function, as shown in Section 13.1, will not be useful here. This is because we have to specify all actions that are to be done when Windows sends a *WM_TIMER* message. After the following line in function *WndProc*, we have to write a program fragment for one disk move:

```
case WM_TIMER:
```

In other words, it is now Windows, not a recursive function, that triggers each next move. The function *Hanoi* that we will use here is therefore not recursive, and it is called any time a *WM_TIMER* message is received. Its task is to find the source and the destination pegs to be used for the next disk move. As we have seen, the recursive function *Hanoi* in Section 13.1 shows three actions. In our new, nonrecursive function with the same name, we replace the recursive calls with calls to the function *Push*, which places the arguments of such recursive calls onto a *linked stack*. As you may know, a linked stack is a linked list for which only two operations, *Push* and *Pop*, are defined. The *Push* operation adds an element (also known as a *node*) to the linked stack at its beginning, while *Pop* extracts an element from the stack, also at its beginning. Besides a pointer to the next node, there are three *int* members, *jSrc*, *jDest*, *n*, in each node. If *n* is positive, these members mean that a tower consisting of the disks 1, 2, ..., *n* is to be moved from peg *jSrc* to *jDest*. If *n* is negative, its absolute value is the number of a single disk that is to be moved from *jSrc* to *jDest*. Thus there are two cases, to be distinguished by the sign of node member *n*.

At the very beginning, there is only one node, with members *jSrc* = 0, *jDest* = 2, *n* = *N*, indicating that the entire tower of *N* disks is to be moved from A to C. Function *Hanoi* mainly consists of a loop, which first calls *Pop*, to see if there is any work to be done. If there is and it finds a positive *n* value in the node popped from the linked stack, it splits the work that is to be done into three simpler tasks, in about the same way as discussed in Section 13.1. These simpler tasks are translated into *Push* calls. In other words, after popping one node from the linked stack, three new nodes are pushed to it. However, when a negative *n* is found, there are no such calls to *Push* and the loop terminates because a single disk is to be moved. Function *Hanoi* then returns to its caller, which is function *WndProc*.

Since we are dealing with a linked *stack* (not a *queue*), the operations that are pushed last will be popped first. Without a special precaution, we would therefore obtain the disk moves in the wrong order. A simple remedy is to perform the three *Push* calls (resulting from a single *Pop*) in the opposite order. You can see how this is done by carefully comparing the three calls to *Push* in the function below with the three actions in the recursive function used in Section 13.1:

```
int Hanoi(int *pSrc, int *pDest)
{  // Find source and destination pegs for next move:
   int n;
   for (;;)
   {  if (!Pop(pSrc, pDest, &n)) return 0; // No work to be done
      if (n < 0) break; // Single disk found; disk number i = abs(n)
```

```
if (n > 0)
{   int jAux = 3 - *pSrc - *pDest;   // 0 + 1 + 2 = 3
    Push(jAux, *pDest, n-1);
        // Third action (first pushed to linked stack):
        // tower of n-1 disks from jAux to jDest
    Push(*pSrc, *pDest, -n);
        // Second action:
        // only disk n from jSrc to jDest
        // (negative means one disk)
    Push(*pSrc, jAux, n-1);
        // First action (last pushed to linked stack):
        // tower of n-1 disks from jSrc to jAux.
}
}
return 1;
}
```

Remember that the above function will be called every 1.5 s. Although it is somewhat
similar to the function *Hanoi* of Section 13.1, both its task and the way it works are essentially different.

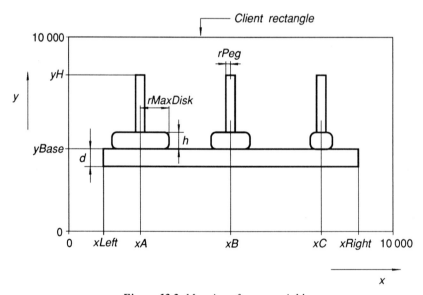

Figure 13.2. *Meaning of some variables*

The meaning of some variables

Figure 13.2 shows the meaning of the variables *xLeft, xRight, xA, xB, xC, yBase, yH, h, d,
rMaxDisk* and *rPeg*, used in function *WndProc*. It also shows that both *x* and *y* range from

0 to 10 000, regardless of the actual size of the window. Recall that $i = 1$ denotes the smallest disk, and $i = N$ the largest. Then disk i has radius

$$r_i = \frac{i}{N} \cdot r_{MaxDisk}$$

Using type *long* for temporary results, we write this formula in the program as follows:

```
ri = (int)((long)i * rMaxDisk/N);
```

Make files

We can use the same make files as those in Chapter 3, provided we replace all occurrences of *inp* with *hanoi*.

13.3 C Solution

Program file HANOI.C is much larger than the programs we have seen so far. Such large programs are usually divided into several modules, but it is presented here as one file because this is more consistent with the structure of this book.

File HANOI.RC:

```
// HANOI.RC:
#include <windows.h>
#include "hanoi.h"
N_INPUT DIALOG 20, 20, 200, 60
STYLE DS_MODALFRAME | WS_SYSMENU
CAPTION "Number of disks? (e.g. 5)"
BEGIN
    EDITTEXT ID_INPUT, 5, 10, 50, 12
    DEFPUSHBUTTON "OK", ID_OK, 95, 30, 30, 15, WS_GROUP
END
MainMenu MENU
BEGIN
    MENUITEM "&New", IDM_NEW
    MENUITEM "&Stop", IDM_STOP
    MENUITEM "&Exit", IDM_EXIT
END
```

File HANOI.H:

```
// HANOI.H:
#define IDM_NEW 1001
#define IDM_STOP 1002
#define IDM_EXIT 1003
```

```
#define ID_INPUT 1004
#define ID_OK 1005
long FAR PASCAL _export WndProc(HWND hWnd, UINT message,
    WPARAM wParam, LPARAM lParam);
int PASCAL WinMain(HANDLE hInstance, HANDLE hPrevInstance,
    LPSTR lpCmdLine, int nCmdShow);
BOOL FAR PASCAL _export InputProc(HWND hDlg, UINT message,
    WPARAM wParam, LPARAM lParam);
```

File HANOI.C:

```
// HANOI.C: Towers of Hanoi
#include <windows.h>
#include <stdlib.h>
#include <string.h>
#include <stdio.h>
#include "hanoi.h"
#define NMAX 20
enum {WAITING, STARTING, BUSY} status;
int N;
COLORREF WoodColor;
const char* const pCaption="Towers of Hanoi (use New to start)";
HWND hWindow;
HANDLE hInstGlobal;
typedef
    struct node_tag{int jSrc, jDest; int n; struct node_tag *pNext;}
    NODE;
NODE *pStart=NULL;

void Push(int jSrc, int jDest, int n)
{  NODE *p=pStart;
   pStart = (NODE *) malloc(sizeof(NODE));
   if (pStart == NULL)
   {  MessageBox(hWindow, "Not enough memory",
      "Fatal error", MB_ICONSTOP);
      PostQuitMessage(0);
   }
   pStart->jSrc = jSrc; pStart->jDest = jDest;
   pStart->n = n; pStart->pNext = p;
}

int Pop(int *pSrc, int *pDest, int *pn)
{  NODE *p;
   if (pStart == NULL) return 0;
   *pSrc = pStart->jSrc; *pDest = pStart->jDest; *pn = pStart->n;
   p = pStart;
   pStart = pStart->pNext;
   free(p);
   return 1;
}
```

```
void CleanUp(void)
{  NODE *p;
   while (pStart != NULL)
   {  p = pStart;
      pStart = pStart->pNext;
      free(p);
   }
}

int Hanoi(int *pSrc, int *pDest)
{  //  Find source and destination pegs for next move:
   int n;
   for (;;)
   {  if (!Pop(pSrc, pDest, &n)) return 0;
      if (n < 0) break;
      if (n > 0)
      {  int jAux = 3 - *pSrc - *pDest;  // 0 + 1 + 2 = 3
         Push(jAux, *pDest, n-1);
            // Third action (first to linked stack):
            // tower of n-1 disks from jAux to jDest
         Push(*pSrc, *pDest, -n);
            // Second action:
            // only disk n from jSrc to jDest
            // (negative means one disk)
         Push(*pSrc, jAux, n-1);
            // First action (last to linked stack):
            // tower of n-1 disks from jSrc to jAux.
      }
   }
   return 1;
}

COLORREF GenColor(int i)
{  int red=0, green=0, blue=0;
   switch (i % 6)
   {  case 1: red = 255; break;
      case 2: green = 255; break;
      case 3: blue = 255; break;
      case 4: red = green = 255; break;
      case 5: green = blue = 255; break;
      case 0: blue = red = 255; break;
   }
   return RGB(red, green, blue);
}

int PASCAL WinMain(HANDLE hInstance, HANDLE hPrevInstance,
      LPSTR lpCmdLine, int nCmdShow)
{   char szAppName[]="hanoi";
    WNDCLASS wndclass;
```

```
        HWND hWnd;
        MSG msg;
        int xScreen = GetSystemMetrics(SM_CXSCREEN),
            yScreen = GetSystemMetrics(SM_CYSCREEN);
        WoodColor = RGB(120, 120, 0);
        hInstGlobal = hInstance;
        pStart = 0;
        status = WAITING;
        if (!hPrevInstance)
        {   wndclass.style = CS_HREDRAW | CS_VREDRAW;
            wndclass.lpfnWndProc = WndProc;
            wndclass.cbClsExtra = 0;
            wndclass.cbWndExtra = 0;
            wndclass.hInstance = hInstance;
            wndclass.hIcon = LoadIcon(NULL, IDI_APPLICATION);
            wndclass.hCursor = LoadCursor(NULL, IDC_ARROW);
            wndclass.hbrBackground = GetStockObject(WHITE_BRUSH);
            wndclass.lpszMenuName = "MainMenu";
                // Reference to menu name in file HANOI.RC
            wndclass.lpszClassName = szAppName;
                // Name used in call to CreateWindow.
            if (!RegisterClass(&wndclass)) return FALSE;
        }
        hWindow = hWnd = CreateWindow(
            szAppName,
            "",                         // Text for window title bar.
            WS_OVERLAPPEDWINDOW,        // Window style.
            0,                          // Initial x position
            0,                          // Initial y position.
            xScreen,                    // Width.
            yScreen,                    // Height.
            NULL,                       // Parent window handle.
            NULL,                       // Window menu handle.
            hInstance,                  // Program instance handle.
            NULL                        // Create parameters.
        );
        ShowWindow(hWnd, nCmdShow);
        UpdateWindow(hWnd);
        SetTimer(hWnd, 1, 1500, NULL);
        while (GetMessage(&msg, NULL, 0, 0))
        {   TranslateMessage(&msg);     // Translates virtual key codes
            DispatchMessage(&msg);      // Dispatches message to window
        }
        return msg.wParam;     // Returns the value from PostQuitMessage
}

const char * const pLine1 =
    "One by one, all disks move from A to C,";
const char * const pLine2 =
    "using B temporarily. A larger disk must";
```

```
const char * const pLine3 =
   "not be placed on top of a smaller one.";

long FAR PASCAL _export WndProc(HWND hWnd, UINT message,
      WPARAM wParam, LPARAM lParam)
{  static int Stack[3][NMAX], StPtr[3], xA, xB, xC, rMaxDisk,
     h, rPeg, yBase, yH, xScreen, yScreen;
   int xLeft, xRight, d;
   static long nCount, nTotalCount;
   FARPROC lpProcInput;
   char buf[25];
   HDC hDC;
   PAINTSTRUCT ps;
   HPEN hPen, hWoodPen, hOldPen, hDiskPen, hWhitePen;
   HBRUSH hBrush, hWoodBrush, hOldBrush, hDiskBrush, hWhiteBrush;
   HFONT hFont, hOldFont;
   int i, j, k, xText, xMargin;
   COLORREF DiskColor;
   switch (message)
   {
   case WM_SIZE:
      xScreen = LOWORD(lParam); yScreen = HIWORD(lParam);
      break;
   case WM_PAINT:
      hDC = BeginPaint(hWnd, &ps);
      SetMapMode(hDC, MM_ANISOTROPIC);
      SetViewportOrg(hDC, 0, yScreen);
      SetWindowExt(hDC, 10000, 10000);
      SetViewportExt(hDC, xScreen, -yScreen);
      yBase = 5000; yH = 9500;
      d = 300; xA = 2000; xB = 5000; xC = 8000;
      rMaxDisk = 1300; xLeft = 200; xRight = 9800; rPeg = 60;
      hWoodPen = CreatePen(PS_SOLID, 0, WoodColor);
      hWoodBrush = CreateSolidBrush(WoodColor);
      hOldPen = SelectObject(hDC, hWoodPen);
      hOldBrush = SelectObject(hDC, hWoodBrush);
      Rectangle(hDC, xLeft, yBase, xRight, yBase-d);
      Rectangle(hDC, xA-rPeg, yH, xA+rPeg, yBase);
      Rectangle(hDC, xB-rPeg, yH, xB+rPeg, yBase);
      Rectangle(hDC, xC-rPeg, yH, xC+rPeg, yBase);
      SelectObject(hDC, hOldPen);
      SelectObject(hDC, hOldBrush);
      DeleteObject(hWoodPen);
      DeleteObject(hWoodBrush);

      hFont = CreateFont(900, 200, 0, 0, 500, 0, 0, 0,
         ANSI_CHARSET, OUT_DEFAULT_PRECIS, CLIP_DEFAULT_PRECIS,
         DEFAULT_QUALITY, FF_SWISS, NULL);
      hOldFont = SelectObject(hDC, hFont);
```

```
         SetTextAlign(hDC, TA_CENTER);
         TextOut(hDC, xA, 4600, "A", 1);
         TextOut(hDC, xB, 4600, "B", 1);
         TextOut(hDC, xC, 4600, "C", 1);
         SetTextAlign(hDC, TA_LEFT);
         xText = LOWORD(GetTextExtent(hDC, pLine1, strlen(pLine1)));
         xMargin = (10000 - xText)/2;
         TextOut(hDC, xMargin, 3500, pLine1, strlen(pLine1));
         TextOut(hDC, xMargin, 2300, pLine2, strlen(pLine2));
         TextOut(hDC, xMargin, 1100, pLine3, strlen(pLine3));
         SelectObject(hDC, hOldFont);
         DeleteObject(hFont);
         for (j=0; j<3; j++)
         {  // Restore tower j:
            int xj = xA + j * (xB - xA);
            for (k=0; k<StPtr[j]; k++)
            {  int ri;
               i = Stack[j][k];
               // Draw disk i on tower j at position k
               // A: j=0; B: j=1; C: j=2;
               // (lowest disk has position 0):
               ri = (int)((long)i * rMaxDisk/N); // radius of disk i
               DiskColor = GenColor(i);
               hDiskPen = CreatePen(PS_SOLID, 0, DiskColor);
               hDiskBrush = CreateSolidBrush(DiskColor);
               hOldPen = SelectObject(hDC, hDiskPen);
               hOldBrush = SelectObject(hDC, hDiskBrush);
               RoundRect(hDC, xj-ri, yBase+(k+1)*h,
                              xj+ri, yBase+k*h, h/2, h/2);
               SelectObject(hDC, hOldPen);
               SelectObject(hDC, hOldBrush);
               DeleteObject(hDiskPen);
               DeleteObject(hDiskBrush);
            }
         }
         EndPaint(hWnd, &ps);
         break;
      case WM_TIMER:
         if (status == STARTING)
         {  h = (int)(9L * (yH - yBase)/(10*N));
            // Initial situation, with N disks on peg A:
            for (i=N; i>0; i--) Stack[0][N-i] = i;
            StPtr[0] = N; StPtr[1] = StPtr[2] = 0;
            status = BUSY;
            nCount = 0;
            nTotalCount = (1L << N) - 1;
            InvalidateRect(hWnd, NULL, TRUE);
         } else
         if (status == BUSY)
         {  int jSrc, jDest, dx=xB-xA, xScr, xDest, kSrc, kDest, ri;
```

```
        // Find source and destination pegs and move one disk:
        if (Hanoi(&jSrc, &jDest) == 0) status = WAITING; else
        { hDC = GetDC(hWnd);
          SetMapMode(hDC, MM_ANISOTROPIC);
          SetViewportOrg(hDC, 0, yScreen);
          SetWindowExt(hDC, 10000, 10000);
          SetViewportExt(hDC, xScreen, -yScreen);
          kSrc = --StPtr[jSrc];        // j = horizontal position
          kDest = StPtr[jDest]++;       // k = vertical position
          Stack[jDest][kDest] = i = Stack[jSrc][kSrc];
                                        // i = disk number
          ri = (int)((long)i * rMaxDisk/N); // radius of disk i
          DiskColor = GenColor(i);
          hPen = CreatePen(PS_SOLID, 0, DiskColor);
          hBrush = CreateSolidBrush(DiskColor);
          hOldPen = SelectObject(hDC, hPen);
          hOldBrush = SelectObject(hDC, hBrush);
          xScr = xA + jSrc * dx;
          xDest = xA + jDest * dx;
          // Disk to destination:
          RoundRect(hDC, xDest-ri, yBase+(kDest+1)*h,
                         xDest+ri, yBase+kDest*h, h/2, h/2);

          hWhitePen = GetStockObject(WHITE_PEN);
          hWhiteBrush = GetStockObject(WHITE_BRUSH);
          SelectObject(hDC, hWhitePen);
          SelectObject(hDC, hWhiteBrush);
          DeleteObject(hPen);
          DeleteObject(hBrush);
          // White rectangle to source:
          Rectangle(hDC, xScr-ri, yBase+(kSrc+1)*h,
                         xScr+ri, yBase+kSrc*h);
          hWoodPen = CreatePen(PS_SOLID, 0, WoodColor);
          hWoodBrush = CreateSolidBrush(WoodColor);
          SelectObject(hDC, hWoodPen);
          SelectObject(hDC, hWoodBrush);
          // Restore portion of the source peg:
          Rectangle(hDC, xScr-rPeg, yBase+(kSrc+1)*h,
                         xScr+rPeg, yBase+kSrc*h);
          SelectObject(hDC, hOldPen);
          SelectObject(hDC, hOldBrush);
          DeleteObject(hWoodPen);
          DeleteObject(hWoodBrush);
          sprintf(buf, "%5ld (%ld)", ++nCount, nTotalCount);
          TextOut(hDC, 50, 9900, buf, strlen(buf));
          ReleaseDC(hWnd, hDC);
        }
      } else SetWindowText(hWnd, pCaption); // Status = WAITING
      break;
```

```
    case WM_COMMAND:
        if (wParam == IDM_NEW)
        {  if (status != WAITING) break;
           lpProcInput =
              MakeProcInstance((FARPROC)InputProc, hInstGlobal);
           DialogBox(hInstGlobal, "N_INPUT", hWnd, lpProcInput);
           FreeProcInstance(lpProcInput);
        } else
        if (wParam == IDM_STOP)
        {  CleanUp();
           status = WAITING;
        } else
        if (wParam == IDM_EXIT)
        {  CleanUp();
           SendMessage(hWnd, WM_CLOSE, wParam, lParam);
        }
        break;
    case WM_DESTROY:
        KillTimer(hWnd, 1);
        PostQuitMessage(0);
        break;
    default:
        return DefWindowProc(hWnd, message, wParam, lParam);
    }
    return 0L;
}

BOOL FAR PASCAL _export InputProc(HWND hDlg, UINT message,
    WPARAM wParam, LPARAM lParam)
{  char buffer[25];
   int n;
   switch(message)
   {
   case WM_INITDIALOG:
      SetFocus(GetDlgItem(hDlg, ID_INPUT));
      return TRUE;
   case WM_COMMAND:
      if (wParam == ID_OK)
      {  GetDlgItemText(hDlg, ID_INPUT, buffer, 25);
         EndDialog(hDlg, TRUE);
         if (sscanf(buffer, "%d", &n) == 1 && n >= 1 && n <= NMAX)
         {  N = n;
            Push(0, 2, N);  // A = 0, B = 1, C = 2
            status = STARTING;
            SetWindowText(hWindow,
               "Towers of Hanoi");
         } else
         {  char buf[80];
            sprintf(buf, "N must be positive and not greater than %d",
               NMAX);
```

```
            MessageBox(hWindow, buf, "Error", MB_ICONSTOP);
        }
        return TRUE;
    }
    break;
  }
  return FALSE;
}
```

Despite its length, much of this program is similar to what we have seen in the preceding chapters. For example, a number is read in this program in the same way as in Chapter 3. A discussion of some new elements can be found in the first two sections of this chapter.

In the *WM_PAINT* case of function *WndProc*, we begin by setting up a logical coordinate system, with its origin in the lower-bottom corner, a *y*-axis pointing upwards, and maximum *x*- and *y*-values of 10000. Recall that we discussed this subject in Chapter 5. We then draw three pegs as well as the board on which they are attached. It depends on the values stored in array *StPtr* whether or not we supply the pegs with disks (in two nested for-loops). Initially, we do not. As long as no integer *N* has been read, the three elements of that array are zero. In other words, the number of disks on each peg is zero, and the nested for-loops do not produce any graphics output. However, this program fragment is also executed, both when the user changes the size of the window (by dragging an edge or a corner) and as a consequence of the call *InvalidateRect*(*hWnd, NULL, TRUE*), to be discussed in a moment. If this happens while there are already disks on any pegs, they are redrawn.

Text alignment

The letters A, B and C, denoting the three pegs, should be placed exactly below these pegs. The easiest way to do this is by using *centered* alignment of text, as shown by the following fragment, which can be found in the *WM_PAINT* case of function *WndProc*:

```
SetTextAlign(hDC, TA_CENTER);
TextOut(hDC, xA, 4600, "A", 1);
TextOut(hDC, xB, 4600, "B", 1);
TextOut(hDC, xC, 4600, "C", 1);
SetTextAlign(hDC, TA_LEFT);
```

Thanks to the first of these statements, the center of the letter A will have *xA* as its *x*-coordinate, and so on (see Figure 13.2). The final line of the above fragment restores the default situation, that is, *left* alignment of text. The reason for this will be clear in a moment.

An interesting new aspect is the computation of the width of a character string, expressed in logical coordinates. This is not trivial because we are using a proportional font. Fortunately, function *GetTextExtent* (called immediately after the above fragment) is very easy to use. It returns a value of type *long int* (normally referred to as *DWORD* in Windows programs). The macros *LOWORD* and *HIWORD* applied to this return value give the width and the height of the text, passed as the second argument. These dimensions are based on the currently selected font. In this way we can make the left and right margins for the longest of the three text lines (which happens to be the first) exactly equal, as you can see in Figure 13.1. If there had been only one text line or if *all three* lines had to be centered, we would have used centered text alignment, as discussed above. In our case this is undesirable because it is much more usual for a piece of text to be left-aligned. Remember that the size of the window may change, with a corresponding change of the font size. Under all circumstances, our program will center the first of the three lines of text, while at the same time these lines will be left-aligned. So much for text alignment.

Actions initiated by the timer

The *WM_PAINT* case, which we have just been discussing, is executed only when the program starts and because of any size changes. By contrast, the *WM_TIMER* case is executed every 1500 ms. Just after an integer N is entered, the variable *status* is equal to the value *STARTING*, and we draw N disks on peg A. This is done by assigning proper initial values to the arrays *Stack* and *StPtr*, as discussed in Section 13.2. After resetting the move counter *nCount* and computing *nTotalCount* ($= 2^N - 1$), the total number of moves, we perform the call *InvalidateRect(hWnd, NULL, TRUE)* to repaint the client rectangle, so that the disks are displayed.

Once the process of moving disks has been started, we have *status = BUSY*. This is the most interesting case because function *Hanoi* is called here to determine which disk move is next. We have discussed both this call and the three graphics fill operations to be performed for each disk move in Section 13.2.

13.4 MFC Solution

There is a very subtle difference between the files HANOIMFC.RC, shown below, and HANOI.RC of Section 13.3. Instead of *ID_OK*, we use the name *IDOK* here because this is a predefined name when we are using the MFC (see also Section 3.3). The linked stack is declared as class *LinkedStack* in the header file HANOIMFC.H. According to the principle of encapsulation (one of the pillars of object-oriented programming), the operations *Push*, *Pop* and *CleanUp* are implemented as member functions of this class.

File HANOIMFC.RC:

```
// HANOIMFC.RC:
#include <windows.h>
#include "hanoimfc.h"

N_INPUT DIALOG 20, 20, 200, 60
STYLE DS_MODALFRAME | WS_SYSMENU
CAPTION "Number of disks? (e.g. 5)"
BEGIN
    EDITTEXT ID_INPUT, 5, 10, 50, 12
```

```
      DEFPUSHBUTTON "OK", IDOK, 95, 30, 30, 15, WS_GROUP
END

MainMenu MENU
BEGIN
   MENUITEM "&New", IDM_NEW
   MENUITEM "&Stop", IDM_STOP
   MENUITEM "&Exit", IDM_EXIT
END
```

File HANOIMFC.H:

```
// HANOIMFC.H:
#define ID_INPUT 1000
#define IDM_NEW 2000
#define IDM_STOP 2001
#define IDM_EXIT 2002
#define NMAX 20

class CApp: public CWinApp
{  public:
   BOOL InitInstance();
};

class LinkedStack
{  struct NODE {int jSrc, jDest; int n; NODE *pNext;} *pStart;
public:
   LinkedStack(){pStart=NULL;}
   void Push(int jSrc, int jDest, int n);
   int Pop(int &jSrc, int &jDest, int &n);
   void CleanUp();
};

enum STATUS {WAITING, STARTING, BUSY};

class CMyWindow: public CFrameWnd
{  int xA, xB, xC, d, rMaxDisk, h, rPeg, yBase, yH, xLeft, xRight,
      N, xScreen, yScreen, Stack[3][NMAX], StPtr[3];
   STATUS status;
   long nCount, nTotalCount;
   COLORREF WoodColor;
public:
   CMyWindow();
   ~CMyWindow();
   int Hanoi(int &jSrc, int &jDest);
   afx_msg void OnPaint();
   afx_msg void OnSize(UINT nType, int cx, int cy);
   afx_msg void OnTimer(UINT nIDEvent);
   afx_msg void OnNewTower();
```

```
   afx_msg void OnStopMove();
   afx_msg void OnExit();
   DECLARE_MESSAGE_MAP()
};

class CInput: public CDialog
{ public:
   char buffer[25];
   CInput(CWnd *pParentWnd): CDialog("N_INPUT", pParentWnd){}
   afx_msg void OnOK();
};
```

File HANOIMFC.CPP:

```
// HANOIMFC.CPP: Towers of Hanoi
#include <afxwin.h>
#include <stdlib.h>
#include "hanoimfc.h"

CMyWindow *pWindow;

const char * const pCaption =
   "Towers of Hanoi (use New to start)";
LinkedStack s;

void LinkedStack::Push(int jSrc, int jDest, int n)
{  NODE *p=pStart;
   pStart = new NODE;
   if (pStart == NULL)
   {  pWindow->MessageBox("Not enough memory", "Fatal error",
                          MB_ICONSTOP);
      PostQuitMessage(0);
   }
   pStart->jSrc = jSrc; pStart->jDest = jDest; pStart->n = n;
   pStart->pNext = p;
}

int LinkedStack::Pop(int &jSrc, int &jDest, int &n)
{  if (pStart == NULL) return 0;
   jSrc = pStart->jSrc; jDest = pStart->jDest; n = pStart->n;
   NODE *p = pStart;
   pStart = pStart->pNext;
   delete p;
   return 1;
}

void LinkedStack::CleanUp()
{  NODE *p;
   while (pStart != NULL)
   {  p = pStart;
```

```
            pStart = pStart->pNext;
            delete p;
        }
    }

    int CMyWindow::Hanoi(int &jSrc, int &jDest)
    {   int n;
        for (;;)
        {   if (!s.Pop(jSrc, jDest, n)) return 0;
            if (n < 0) break;
                // jSrc, jDest and n (> 0) will be used in OnSize
            if (n > 0)
            {   int jAux = 3 - jSrc - jDest;  // 0 + 1 + 2 = 3
                s.Push(jAux, jDest, n-1);
                    // Third action (first to linked stack):
                    // tower of n-1 disks from jAux to jDest
                s.Push(jSrc, jDest, -n);
                    // Second action:
                    // only disk n from jSrc to jDest
                    //(negative means one disk)
                s.Push(jSrc, jAux, n-1);
                    // First action (last to linked stack):
                    // tower of n-1 disks from jSrc to jAux.
            }
        }
        return 1;
    }


    COLORREF GenColor(int i)
    {   int red=0, green=0, blue=0;
        switch (i % 6)
        {   case 1: red = 255; break;
            case 2: green = 255; break;
            case 3: blue = 255; break;
            case 4: red = green = 255; break;
            case 5: green = blue = 255; break;
            case 0: blue = red = 255; break;
        }
        return RGB(red, green, blue);
    }


    BOOL CApp::InitInstance()
    {   m_pMainWnd = new CMyWindow();
        m_pMainWnd->ShowWindow(m_nCmdShow);
        m_pMainWnd->UpdateWindow();
        return TRUE;
    }


    CApp App;
```

```
CMyWindow::CMyWindow()
{  xScreen = GetSystemMetrics(SM_CXSCREEN);
   yScreen = GetSystemMetrics(SM_CYSCREEN);
   RECT rect = {0, 0, xScreen, yScreen};
   status = WAITING;
   StPtr[0] = StPtr[1] = StPtr[2] = 0;
   Create(NULL, pCaption,
          WS_OVERLAPPEDWINDOW, rect, NULL, "MainMenu");
   WoodColor = RGB(120, 120, 0);
   pWindow = this;
   SetTimer(1, 1500, NULL);
}

CMyWindow::~CMyWindow()
{  KillTimer(1);
}

BEGIN_MESSAGE_MAP(CMyWindow, CFrameWnd)
   ON_WM_SIZE()
   ON_WM_PAINT()
   ON_WM_TIMER()
   ON_COMMAND(IDM_NEW, OnNewTower)
   ON_COMMAND(IDM_STOP, OnStopMove)
   ON_COMMAND(IDM_EXIT, OnExit)
END_MESSAGE_MAP()

void CMyWindow::OnNewTower()
{  int n;
   if (status != WAITING) return;
   CInput input(this);
   input.DoModal();
   if (sscanf(input.buffer, "%d", &n) == 1 && n >= 1 && n <= NMAX)
   {  N = n;
      s.Push(0, 2, N);  // A = 0, B = 1, C = 2
      status = STARTING;
      SetWindowText("Towers of Hanoi");
   }
   else
   {  char buf[80];
      sprintf(buf,
         "N must be positive and not greater than %d", NMAX);
      MessageBox(buf, "Error", MB_ICONSTOP);
   }
}

void CMyWindow::OnStopMove()
{  s.CleanUp();
   status = WAITING;
}
```

```
void CMyWindow::OnExit()
{  s.CleanUp();
   SendMessage(WM_CLOSE);
}

void CInput::OnOK()
{  GetDlgItemText(ID_INPUT, buffer, 25);
   EndDialog(IDOK);
}

void CMyWindow::OnPaint()
{  CPaintDC dc(this);
   int i, j, k, xMargin;
   const char * const pLine1 =
      "One by one, all disks move from A to C,";
   const char * const pLine2 =
      "using B temporarily. A larger disk must";
   const char * const pLine3 =
      "not be placed on top of a smaller one.";
   yBase = 5000; yH = 9500;
   d = 300; xA = 2000; xB = 5000; xC = 8000;
   rMaxDisk = 1300; xLeft = 200; xRight = 9800; rPeg = 40;
   dc.SetMapMode(MM_ANISOTROPIC);
   dc.SetViewportOrg(0, yScreen);
   dc.SetWindowExt(10000, 10000);
   dc.SetViewportExt(xScreen, -yScreen);
   CPen WoodPen, *OldPen;
   CBrush WoodBrush, *OldBrush;
   WoodPen.CreatePen(PS_SOLID, 0, WoodColor);
   WoodBrush.CreateSolidBrush(WoodColor);
   OldPen = dc.SelectObject(&WoodPen);
   OldBrush = dc.SelectObject(&WoodBrush);
   // Board:
   dc.Rectangle(xLeft, yBase, xRight, yBase-d);
   // Pegs:
   dc.Rectangle(xA-rPeg, yH, xA+rPeg, yBase);
   dc.Rectangle(xB-rPeg, yH, xB+rPeg, yBase);
   dc.Rectangle(xC-rPeg, yH, xC+rPeg, yBase);
   dc.SelectObject(OldPen);
   dc.SelectObject(OldBrush);
   WoodPen.DeleteObject();
   WoodBrush.DeleteObject();

   CFont Font, *OldFont;
   Font.CreateFont(900, 200, 0, 0, 500, 0, 0, 0, ANSI_CHARSET,
      OUT_DEFAULT_PRECIS, CLIP_DEFAULT_PRECIS,
      DEFAULT_QUALITY, FF_SWISS, NULL);
   OldFont = dc.SelectObject(&Font);
   dc.SetTextAlign(TA_CENTER);
   dc.TextOut(xA, 4600, "A");
```

```
      dc.TextOut(xB, 4600, "B");
      dc.TextOut(xC, 4600, "C");
      dc.SetTextAlign(TA_LEFT);
      int xText = dc.GetTextExtent(pLine1, strlen(pLine1)).cx;
      xMargin = (10000 - xText)/2;
      dc.TextOut(800, 3500, pLine1);
      dc.TextOut(800, 2300, pLine2);
      dc.TextOut(800, 1100, pLine3);
      dc.SelectObject(OldFont);
      Font.DeleteObject();

      for (j=0; j<3; j++)
      {  // Restore tower j:
         int xj = xA + j * (xB - xA);
         for (k=0; k<StPtr[j]; k++)
         {  i = Stack[j][k];
            // Draw disk i on tower j at position k
            // A: j=0; B: j=1; C: j=2
            // (lowest disk has position 0):
            int ri = int(long(i) * rMaxDisk/N); // Radius of disk i
            CPen DiskPen;
            CBrush DiskBrush;
            COLORREF DiskColor = GenColor(i);
            DiskPen.CreatePen(PS_SOLID, 0, DiskColor);
            DiskBrush.CreateSolidBrush(DiskColor);
            OldPen = dc.SelectObject(&DiskPen);
            OldBrush = dc.SelectObject(&DiskBrush);
            dc.RoundRect(xj-ri, yBase+(k+1)*h,
                         xj+ri, yBase+k*h, h/2, h/2);
            dc.SelectObject(OldPen);
            dc.SelectObject(OldBrush);
            DiskPen.DeleteObject();
            DiskBrush.DeleteObject();
         }
      }
   }

void CMyWindow::OnSize(UINT nType, int cx, int cy)
{  xScreen = cx; yScreen = cy;
}

void CMyWindow::OnTimer(UINT nIDEvent)
{  int i;
   if (status == STARTING)
   {  h = int(9L * (yH - yBase)/(10*N));
      // Initial situation, with N disks on peg A:
      for (i=N; i>0; i--) Stack[0][N-i] = i;
      StPtr[0] = N; StPtr[1] = StPtr[2] = 0;
      status = BUSY;
      nCount = 0;
```

```
      nTotalCount = (1L << N) - 1;
      InvalidateRect(NULL, TRUE);
   } else
if (status == BUSY)
{  int jSrc, jDest, dx=xB-xA, xScr, xDest, kSrc, kDest;
   if (Hanoi(jSrc, jDest) == 0) status = WAITING; else
   {  CClientDC dc(this);
      CPen WhitePen, WoodPen, *OldPen;
      CBrush WhiteBrush, WoodBrush, *OldBrush;
      dc.SetMapMode(MM_ANISOTROPIC);
      dc.SetViewportOrg(0, yScreen);
      dc.SetWindowExt(10000, 10000);
      dc.SetViewportExt(xScreen, -yScreen);
      kSrc = --StPtr[jSrc];              // j = horizontal position
      kDest = StPtr[jDest]++;            // k = vertical position
      Stack[jDest][kDest] = i = Stack[jSrc][kSrc];
                                         // i = disk number
      int ri = int(long(i) * rMaxDisk/N); // radius of disk i
      COLORREF DiskColor = GenColor(i);
      CPen DiskPen;
      CBrush DiskBrush;
      DiskPen.CreatePen(PS_SOLID, 0, DiskColor);
      DiskBrush.CreateSolidBrush(DiskColor);
      OldPen = dc.SelectObject(&DiskPen);
      OldBrush = dc.SelectObject(&DiskBrush);
      xScr = xA + jSrc * dx;
      xDest = xA + jDest * dx;
      // Disk to destination:
      dc.RoundRect(xDest-ri, yBase+(kDest+1)*h,
                   xDest+ri, yBase+kDest*h, h/2, h/2);
      WhitePen.CreateStockObject(WHITE_PEN);
      WhiteBrush.CreateStockObject(WHITE_BRUSH);
      dc.SelectObject(&WhitePen);
      dc.SelectObject(&WhiteBrush);
      DiskPen.DeleteObject();
      DiskBrush.DeleteObject();
      // White rectangle to source:
      dc.Rectangle(xScr-ri, yBase+(kSrc+1)*h,
                   xScr+ri, yBase+kSrc*h);
      WoodPen.CreatePen(PS_SOLID, 0, WoodColor);
      WoodBrush.CreateSolidBrush(WoodColor);
      dc.SelectObject(&WoodPen);
      dc.SelectObject(&WoodBrush);
      // Restore portion of source peg:
      dc.Rectangle(xScr-rPeg, yBase+(kSrc+1)*h,
                   xScr+rPeg, yBase+kSrc*h);
      dc.SelectObject(OldPen);
      dc.SelectObject(OldBrush);
      WoodPen.DeleteObject();
```

```
            WoodBrush.DeleteObject();
            char buf[25];
            sprintf(buf, "%5ld (%ld)", ++nCount, nTotalCount);
            dc.TextOut(50, 9900, buf);
        }
    } else SetWindowText(pCaption); // status = WAITING
}
```

The way a number is read by means of a dialog box was discussed in Section 3.4. Instead
of an API function *GetTextExtent*, discussed in Section 13.3, we now use a *CDC* member
function with the same name. The latter function is different in that it returns a *CSize*
object, which is a class with *int* members *cx* and *cy*. We can use these members instead of
applying the macros *LOWORD* and *HIWORD*, to obtain the width and the height of the
text, supplied as the first argument of *GetTextExtent*:

```
    int xText = dc.GetTextExtent(pLine1, strlen(pLine1)).cx;
```

As discussed in Section 13.3 and illustrated at the bottom of Figure 13.1, we use the text
width found in this way to combine left alignment with centering the longest of three lines
of text.

13.5 OWL Solution

As in the two preceding sections, you are referred to Chapter 3 for the way *N*, the number
of disks, is read by means of a dialog box. Recall that the ObjectWindows Library offers us
the class *TInputDialog*, which we use in connection with the function *ExecDialog*. You
can find how this is done in function *OnNewTower* in program file HANOIOWL.CPP.
The dimensions of the dialog box are then read from the file INPUTDIA.DLG, an *#include*
line for which must be present in our resource script file, as the first of the files listed
below shows. This way of reading input data is comparatively easy to program. However,
beware of forgetting to write the *#include* line just mentioned. Omitting this line leads to a
run-time error that is not very helpful in spotting the source of the trouble (as I have
experienced several times myself).

File HANOIOWL.RC:

```
// HANOIOWL.RC:
#include <windows.h>
#include <owlrc.h>
#include "inputdia.dlg"
#include "hanoiowl.h"
MainMenu MENU
BEGIN
    MENUITEM "&New", IDM_NEW
    MENUITEM "&Stop", IDM_STOP
```

```
      MENUITEM "&Exit", IDM_EXIT
   END
```

File HANOIOWL.H:

```
// HANOIOWL.H:
#define IDM_NEW 2000
#define IDM_STOP 2001
#define IDM_EXIT 2002
#define NMAX 20

class TApp: public TApplication
{  public:
   TApp(LPSTR Name, HANDLE hInstance, HANDLE hPrevInstance,
        LPSTR lpCmdLine, int nCmdShow)
      : TApplication(Name, hInstance, hPrevInstance, lpCmdLine,
                     nCmdShow){}
   virtual void InitMainWindow();
};

class LinkedStack
{  struct NODE {int jSrc, jDest; int n; NODE *pNext;} *pStart;
public:
   LinkedStack(){pStart=NULL;}
   void Push(int jSrc, int jDest, int n);
   int Pop(int &jSrc, int &jDest, int &n);
   void CleanUp();
};

enum STATUS {WAITING, STARTING, BUSY};

class TMyWindow: public TWindow
{  int xA, xB, xC, d, rMaxDisk, h, rPeg, yBase, yH, xLeft, xRight,
       N, xScreen, yScreen, Stack[3][NMAX], StPtr[3];
   STATUS status;
   long nCount, nTotalCount;
   COLORREF WoodColor;
public:
   TMyWindow(PTWindowsObject AParent, LPSTR ATitle);
   int Hanoi(int &jSrc, int &jDest);
   void Paint(HDC hDC, PAINTSTRUCT&);
   void WMSize(RTMessage Msg);
   void WMTimer(RTMessage Msg) = [WM_FIRST + WM_TIMER];
   void WMCreate(RTMessage Msg) = [WM_FIRST + WM_CREATE];
   void WMClose(RTMessage Msg) = [WM_FIRST + WM_CLOSE];
   void OnNewTower() = [CM_FIRST + IDM_NEW];
   void OnStopMove() = [CM_FIRST + IDM_STOP];
   void OnExit() = [CM_FIRST + IDM_EXIT];
};
```

File HANOIOWL.CPP:

```
// HANOIOWL.CPP: Towers of Hanoi
#define WIN31
#include <stdio.h>
#include <stdlib.h>
#include <string.h>
#include <owl.h>
#include <inputdia.h>
#include "hanoiowl.h"

const char * const pCaption =
   "Towers of Hanoi (use New to start)";
HANDLE hWin;
LinkedStack s;

void LinkedStack::Push(int jSrc, int jDest, int n)
{  NODE *p=pStart;
   pStart = new NODE;
   if (pStart == NULL)
   {  MessageBox(hWin, "Not enough memory", "Fatal error",
         MB_ICONSTOP);
      PostQuitMessage(0);
   }
   pStart->jSrc = jSrc; pStart->jDest = jDest; pStart->n = n;
   pStart->pNext = p;
}

int LinkedStack::Pop(int &jSrc, int &jDest, int &n)
{  if (pStart == NULL) return 0;
   jSrc = pStart->jSrc; jDest = pStart->jDest; n = pStart->n;
   NODE *p = pStart;
   pStart = pStart->pNext;
   delete p;
   return 1;
}

void LinkedStack::CleanUp()
{  NODE *p;
   while (pStart != NULL)
   {  p = pStart;
      pStart = pStart->pNext;
      delete p;
   }
}

int TMyWindow::Hanoi(int &jSrc, int &jDest)
{  int n;
   for (;;)
   {  if (!s.Pop(jSrc, jDest, n)) return 0;
```

```
         if (n < 0) break;
             // jSrc, jDest and n (> 0) will be used in OnSize
         if (n > 0)
         {  int jAux = 3 - jSrc - jDest;  // 0 + 1 + 2 = 3
            s.Push(jAux, jDest, n-1);
                // Third action (first to linked stack):
                // tower of n-1 disks from jAux to jDest
            s.Push(jSrc, jDest, -n);
                // Second action:
                // only disk n from jSrc to jDest
                //(negative means one disk)
            s.Push(jSrc, jAux, n-1);
                // First action (last to linked stack):
                // tower of n-1 disks from jSrc to jAux.
         }
      }
      return 1;
}

COLORREF GenColor(int i)
{  int red=0, green=0, blue=0;
   switch (i % 6)
   {  case 1: red = 255; break;
      case 2: green = 255; break;
      case 3: blue = 255; break;
      case 4: red = green = 255; break;
      case 5: green = blue = 255; break;
      case 0: blue = red = 255; break;
   }
   return RGB(red, green, blue);
}

TMyWindow::TMyWindow(PTWindowsObject AParent, LPSTR ATitle)
   : TWindow(AParent, ATitle)
{  AssignMenu("MainMenu");
}

void TMyWindow::WMCreate(RTMessage)
{  xScreen = GetSystemMetrics(SM_CXSCREEN);
   yScreen = GetSystemMetrics(SM_CYSCREEN);
   status = WAITING;
   WoodColor = RGB(120, 120, 0);
   StPtr[0] = StPtr[1] = StPtr[2] = 0;
   hWin = HWindow;
   SetTimer(HWindow, 1, 1500, NULL);
}

void TApp::InitMainWindow()
{  TWindow *pWin;
```

```
    MainWindow = pWin = new TMyWindow(NULL, Name);
    pWin->Attr.X = 0;
    pWin->Attr.Y = 0;
    pWin->Attr.W = GetSystemMetrics(SM_CXSCREEN);
    pWin->Attr.H = GetSystemMetrics(SM_CYSCREEN);
}

void TMyWindow::WMClose(RTMessage)
{   KillTimer(HWindow, 1);
    PostQuitMessage(0);
}

void TMyWindow::OnNewTower()
{   int n;
    char buffer[80]="";
    if (status != WAITING) return;
    TInputDialog *p=
       new TInputDialog(this, "Number of disks? (e.g. 5)",
          "", buffer, sizeof(buffer));
    if (GetApplication()->
    ExecDialog(p) == IDOK)
    {   if (sscanf(buffer, "%d", &n) == 1 && n >= 1 && n <= NMAX)
        {   N = n;
            s.Push(0, 2, N);  // A = 0, B = 1, C = 2
            status = STARTING;
            SetWindowText(HWindow, "Towers of Hanoi");
        } else
        {   sprintf(buffer,
                "N must be positive and not greater than %d", NMAX);
            MessageBox(HWindow, buffer, "Error", MB_ICONSTOP);
        }
    }
}


void TMyWindow::OnStopMove()
{   s.CleanUp();
    status = WAITING;
}

void TMyWindow::OnExit()
{   s.CleanUp();
    SendMessage(HWindow, WM_CLOSE, 0, 0L);
}

void TMyWindow::Paint(HDC hDC, PAINTSTRUCT&)
{   int i, j, k, xText, xMargin;
    COLORREF DiskColor;
    const char * const pLine1 =
       "One by one, all disks move from A to C,";
    const char * const pLine2 =
```

```
        "using B temporarily. A larger disk must";
const char * const pLine3 =
        "not be placed on top of a smaller one.";
SetMapMode(hDC, MM_ANISOTROPIC);
SetViewportOrg(hDC, 0, yScreen);
SetWindowExt(hDC, 10000, 10000);
SetViewportExt(hDC, xScreen, -yScreen);
yBase = 5000; yH = 9500;
d = 300; xA = 2000; xB = 5000; xC = 8000;
rMaxDisk = 1300; xLeft = 200; xRight = 9800; rPeg = 60;
HPEN hPen, hWoodPen, hOldPen, hDiskPen, hWhitePen;
HBRUSH hBrush, hWoodBrush, hOldBrush, hDiskBrush, hWhiteBrush;
hWoodPen = CreatePen(PS_SOLID, 0, WoodColor);
hWoodBrush = CreateSolidBrush(WoodColor);
hOldPen = SelectObject(hDC, hWoodPen);
hOldBrush = SelectObject(hDC, hWoodBrush);
Rectangle(hDC, xLeft, yBase, xRight, yBase-d);
Rectangle(hDC, xA-rPeg, yH, xA+rPeg, yBase);
Rectangle(hDC, xB-rPeg, yH, xB+rPeg, yBase);
Rectangle(hDC, xC-rPeg, yH, xC+rPeg, yBase);
SelectObject(hDC, hOldPen);
SelectObject(hDC, hOldBrush);
DeleteObject(hWoodPen);
DeleteObject(hWoodBrush);

HFONT hFont, hOldFont;
hFont = CreateFont(900, 200, 0, 0, 500, 0, 0, 0,
    ANSI_CHARSET, OUT_DEFAULT_PRECIS, CLIP_DEFAULT_PRECIS,
    DEFAULT_QUALITY, FF_SWISS, NULL);
hOldFont = SelectObject(hDC, hFont);
SetTextAlign(hDC, TA_CENTER);
TextOut(hDC, xA, 4600, "A", 1);
TextOut(hDC, xB, 4600, "B", 1);
TextOut(hDC, xC, 4600, "C", 1);
SetTextAlign(hDC, TA_LEFT);
xText = LOWORD(GetTextExtent(hDC, pLine1, strlen(pLine1)));
xMargin = (10000 - xText)/2;
TextOut(hDC, xMargin, 3500, pLine1, strlen(pLine1));
TextOut(hDC, xMargin, 2300, pLine2, strlen(pLine2));
TextOut(hDC, xMargin, 1100, pLine3, strlen(pLine3));
SelectObject(hDC, hOldFont);
DeleteObject(hFont);
for (j=0; j<3; j++)
{  // Restore tower j:
    int xj = xA + j * (xB - xA);
    for (k=0; k<StPtr[j]; k++)
    {  int ri;
        i = Stack[j][k];
        // Draw disk i on tower j at position k
```

```
        // A: j=0; B: j=1; C: j=2;
        // (lowest disk has position 0):
        ri = (int)((long)i * rMaxDisk/N); // radius of disk i
        DiskColor = GenColor(i);
        hDiskPen = CreatePen(PS_SOLID, 0, DiskColor);
        hDiskBrush = CreateSolidBrush(DiskColor);
        hOldPen = SelectObject(hDC, hDiskPen);
        hOldBrush = SelectObject(hDC, hDiskBrush);
        RoundRect(hDC, xj-ri, yBase+(k+1)*h,
                       xj+ri, yBase+k*h, h/2, h/2);
        SelectObject(hDC, hOldPen);
        SelectObject(hDC, hOldBrush);
        DeleteObject(hDiskPen);
        DeleteObject(hDiskBrush);
      }
   }
}


void TMyWindow::WMSize(RTMessage)
{  RECT rect;
   GetClientRect(HWindow, &rect);
   xScreen = rect.right; yScreen = rect.bottom;
}


void TMyWindow::WMTimer(RTMessage)
{  int i;
   HDC hDC = GetDC(HWindow);
   SetMapMode(hDC, MM_ANISOTROPIC);
   SetViewportOrg(hDC, 0, yScreen);
   SetWindowExt(hDC, 10000, 10000);
   SetViewportExt(hDC, xScreen, -yScreen);
   if (status == STARTING)
   {  h = (int)(9L * (yH - yBase)/(10*N));
      // Initial situation, with N disks on peg A:
      for (i=N; i>0; i--) Stack[0][N-i] = i;
      StPtr[0] = N; StPtr[1] = StPtr[2] = 0;
      status = BUSY;
      nCount = 0;
      nTotalCount = (1L << N) - 1;
      InvalidateRect(HWindow, NULL, TRUE);
   } else
   if (status == BUSY)
   {  int jSrc, jDest, dx=xB-xA, xScr, xDest, kSrc, kDest, ri;
      char buf[50];
      // Find source and destination pegs and move one disk:
      if (Hanoi(jSrc, jDest) == 0) status = WAITING; else
      {  COLORREF DiskColor;
         HPEN hWoodPen, hOldPen, hDiskPen, hWhitePen;
         HBRUSH hWoodBrush, hOldBrush, hDiskBrush, hWhiteBrush;
```

```
            kSrc = --StPtr[jSrc];           // j = horizontal position
            kDest = StPtr[jDest]++;          // k = vertical position
            Stack[jDest][kDest] = i = Stack[jSrc][kSrc];
                                            // i = disk number
            ri = (int)((long)i * rMaxDisk/N); // radius of disk i
            DiskColor = GenColor(i);
            hDiskPen = CreatePen(PS_SOLID, 0, DiskColor);
            hDiskBrush = CreateSolidBrush(DiskColor);
            hOldPen = SelectObject(hDC, hDiskPen);
            hOldBrush = SelectObject(hDC, hDiskBrush);
            xScr = xA + jSrc * dx;
            xDest = xA + jDest * dx;
            // Disk to destination:
            RoundRect(hDC, xDest-ri, yBase+(kDest+1)*h,
                        xDest+ri, yBase+kDest*h, h/2, h/2);
            hWhitePen = GetStockObject(WHITE_PEN);
            hWhiteBrush = GetStockObject(WHITE_BRUSH);
            SelectObject(hDC, hWhitePen);
            SelectObject(hDC, hWhiteBrush);
            DeleteObject(hDiskPen);
            DeleteObject(hDiskBrush);
            // White rectangle to source:
            Rectangle(hDC, xScr-ri, yBase+(kSrc+1)*h,
                        xScr+ri, yBase+kSrc*h);
            hWoodPen = CreatePen(PS_SOLID, 0, WoodColor);
            hWoodBrush = CreateSolidBrush(WoodColor);
            SelectObject(hDC, hWoodPen);
            SelectObject(hDC, hWoodBrush);
            // Restore portion of the source peg:
            Rectangle(hDC, xScr-rPeg, yBase+(kSrc+1)*h,
                        xScr+rPeg, yBase+kSrc*h);
            SelectObject(hDC, hOldPen);
            SelectObject(hDC, hOldBrush);
            DeleteObject(hWoodPen);
            DeleteObject(hWoodBrush);
            sprintf(buf, "%5ld (%ld)", ++nCount, nTotalCount);
            TextOut(hDC, 50, 9900, buf, strlen(buf));
        }
    } else SetWindowText(HWindow, pCaption); // Status = WAITING
    ReleaseDC(HWindow, hDC);
}


int PASCAL WinMain(HINSTANCE hInstance, HINSTANCE hPrevInstance,
    LPSTR lpCmdLine, int nCmdShow)
{ TApp App("pCaption", hInstance, hPrevInstance,
            lpCmdLine, nCmdShow);
    App.Run();
    return App.Status;
}
```

Note the following two lines, which occur in the header file HANOIOWL.H:

```
void WMClose(RTMessage Msg) = [WM_FIRST + WM_CLOSE];
void OnNewTower() = [CM_FIRST + IDM_NEW];
```

We must be careful with the constant in front of the plus sign: *WM_FIRST* is used for Windows messages, while *CM_FIRST* refers to 'commands', generated by means of a menu. This is another subtle point that may easily lead to an obscure error. Accidentally replacing *CM_FIRST* with *WM_FIRST* would not produce any compile-time error message. The *New* menu command would simply not work in this case because the function *OnNewTower* cannot be found.

13.6 Questions

13.1   What is the task of function *Hanoi* in Section 13.1? And in the rest of this chapter?

13.2   How can we use left alignment for text lines in such a way that the longest of these lines is centered?

13.3   How can we draw and fill a rounded rectangle?

13.4   What are stacks used for and how are they implemented in this chapter?

13.5   Which mapping mode is used in this chapter? Why not use the same one as in Chapter 5?

Answers to Questions

1.1 When programming in plain C, *sending a message to a window* means that Windows calls the window procedure (consistently called *WndProc* in this book) of that window. A handle to the window is passed as the first parameter, the message in question as the second. The *message loop* (based on the API functions *GetMessage*, *TranslateMessage*, and *DispatchMessage*) causes Windows to perform the calls just mentioned.

When programming with class libraries, a member function of a (C++) class for the window is called, as we will see in Chapter 2.

1.2 C: We can specify a title for the title bar as the second argument of the function *CreateWindow*.

MFC: We can specify the title as the second argument of function *Create*, called in the constructor of *CMyWindow* (which is derived from the *CFrameWnd*).

OWL: We can do this in function *TApp::InitMainWindow*, when generating a *TMyWindow* object, using the *new* operator (where *TApp* is derived from *TApplication*, and *TMyWindow* from *TWindow*).

All this applies to the initial setting of titles. We will see in Chapter 3 that we can also use function *SetWindowText* to change the contents of the title bar.

1.3 The name *WinMain* is obligatory, while we may consistently replace *WndProc* with another name.

1.4 We can terminate program execution by means of the call *PostQuitMessage*(0).

1.5 The width and the height of the screen are returned by the API function *GetSystemMetrics* (see the *WinMain* function in Section 1.3, for example).

1.6   *DefWindowProc* is the 'default window procedure'. It deals with all messages that we ignore in our own program. There are many more messages than those discussed in this book. For example, a *WM_KEYDOWN* message is sent when we press a key on the keyboard.

1.7   *ShowWindow* specifies how a window is to be displayed; *UpdateWindow* sends a *WM_PAINT* message to the window.

1.8   Our class *CMyWindow* is directly derived from the Microsoft Foundation class *CFrameWnd*.

1.9   Our class *CApp* is directly derived from the Foundation class *CWinApp*.

1.10   Constructor *CMyWindow* is activated in function *CApp::InitInstance*.

1.11   Function *CApp::InitInstance* is called in the *WinMain* function of the Foundation classes (by using the pointer *afxCurrentWinApp*).

1.12   The executable files based on the Microsoft Foundation Classes are somewhat larger than those based on plain C but smaller than those based on the Borland ObjectWindows Library. (This is discussed at the end of Section 7.5.)

1.13   In Section 1.5 we used the ObjectWindows classes *TApplication* and *TWindow*. As Figure 1.6 shows, they are derived from other ObjectWindows classes and we derive our own classes *TApp* and *TMyWindow* from them.

1.14   See the previous answer.

1.15   The flow of control in program WTESTOWL is as follows:
    1   Windows calls function *WinMain*.
    2   *WinMain* calls *App.Run*.
    3   *App.Run* calls *TApp::InitMainWindow*
    4   *TApp::InitMainWindow* calls the *TMyWindow* constructor
    5   After returning to *App::Run*, this function starts the main message loop.

1.16   Left as an exercise for the reader.

1.17   See 1.12.

2.1   The client rectangle of a window is the part (below the title bar) that we use.

2.2   The API function *MessageBox* has the following four arguments:
    -   A handle of the parent window (that is, of the window in which the message box is to appear)
    -   Text that is to appear in the message box
    -   Text that is to appear in the title bar of the message box
    -   Style of message box. There are 15 such styles available, two of which are *MB_OK* and *MB_ICONSTOP*

2.3   A device context is an abstraction of an output device such as a video display or a printer. When programming in C or with the OWL we use a handle to a device context, while we use an object of class *CDC* (or of a class that is derived from *CDC*) when we are using the MFC. For example, we can write

> *TextOut(hDC*, 10, 10, "ABC", 3);   in C and with OWL, and
> *dc.TextOut*(10, 10, "ABC");   with MFC (string length 3 not required)

2.4   To obtain and release a device context, we use *BeginPaint* and *EndPaint* in response to the *WM_PAINT* message. By contrast, the functions *GetDC* and *ReleaseDC* are used in response to messages other than *WM_PAINT*.

2.5   Function *InvalidateRect* 'invalidates' a rectangle, that is, it marks that rectangle as 'invalid', which causes a *WM_PAINT* message to be sent to the window. In many cases this rectangle is the entire client rectangle. However, it may also be smaller than the client rectangle, as we will see in Chapter 7.

2.6   With MFC we use a *CPaintDC* object in an *OnPaint* function (called in response to a *WM_PAINT* message, see Answer 2.4). A *CClientDC* object can be used in other message-response functions.

2.7   The *static* keyword, used for local variables, means that these variables retain their values between two successive calls to the function to which they belong. For example, variable *xWindow* is given a value when function *WndProc* is called in response to a *WM_SIZE* message. This variable is used in a later call to this function in response to a *WM_PAINT* message. Then it still has the value assigned to it in a previous call because of the *static* keyword.

2.8   Instead of one function *WndProc* for all messages, we use a separate function for a given message when programming with MFC or OWL. We can make these functions use the same variables (such as *xWindow*) without having to resort to global variables. Since the message-response functions are members of our window object, we simply make *xWindow,* etc., also members of this object. When they are used *only* in member functions, we preferably make them private.

2.9   The correspondence between Windows messages and message-response functions is specified as follows:
- with MFC: by means of a message map, which is a set of macros
- with OWL: by means of a language extension of the form = [...], used in class declarations (OWL does not conform to the C++ language in this respect)

3.1   An OK button and an edit control (a rectangle in which the user can enter data) are examples of controls.

3.2   Unit for *x*: 1/4 of average width of character.
Unit for *y*: 1/8 of character height.
(See also Section 3.2.)

3.3   The *EDITTEXT* and *DEFPUSHBUTTON* statements in resource script files specify details such as the position and the size of these controls. They also contain identifiers (*ID_INPUT* and *ID_OK* or *IDOK* in our example) that we use in our program files (except for *IDOK*, which is a predefined name with MFC; see also Answer 3.5).

3.4   The *MakeProcInstance* function is required to obtain a pointer (called *lpProcInput* in our program) that we need as the final argument of the *DialogBox* function. This pointer points to our *InputProc* function, or rather, to the prolog code for that function. After calling *MakeProcInstance*, we must not forget to call *FreeProcInstance* as soon as we do not need the pointer in question (*lpProcInput*) any longer.

3.5   In our C program we refer to the OK button by means of the identifier *ID_OK*. When the user clicks this button, Windows sends a *WM_COMMAND* message, with *wParam* equal to *ID_OK*.

With MFC, we use the predefined name *IDOK* in the resource script file. This would cause the MFC function *CDialog::OnOK* to be called when the user clicks the OK button. In our own class *CInput*, derived from *CDialog*, we override the default *OnOK* function with one of our own, so we can react in this function to the user's clicking the OK button.

With OWL, we can use a very small resource script file, in which the OK button is not directly referred to. We also use the predefined name *IDOK* as the following program line shows:

```
if (GetApplication()->ExecDialog(p) == IDOK)
```

3.6   The name *X_INPUT*, occurring in the *DIALOG* statement of the resource script files of our C and MFC solutions, is used as follows:
-    in program file INP.C: in response to a *WM_LBUTTONDOWN* message in the *WndProc* function
-    in the header file INPMFC.H: as an argument for the constructor of class *CDialog*, the base class of *CInput*

4.1   We use the identifier *IDM_BIRDS* in our programs as follows:
-    MENUS.C: In function *WndProc*, when *message* is equal to *WM_COMMAND* we test if *wParam* is equal to *IDM_BIRDS*.
-    MENUSMFC.CPP: In the message map, to associate this identifier with the function *OnBirds*.
-    MENUSOWL.H: In the following line, which deviates from the C++ language rules:

```
void OnBirds(RTMessage Msg) = [CM_FIRST + IDM_BIRDS];
```

4.2   The name *SampleMenu*, occurring in the resource script files and denoting the whole menu, is referred to in the programs as follows:
-    MENUS.C: By assigning "SampleMenu" to wndclass.lpszMenuName.
-    MENUSMFC.CPP: By using "*SampleMenu*" as the final argument in the call to *Create* in the constructor of *CMyWindow*.

- MENUSOWL.CPP: By using *"SampleMenu"* as the argument of function *AssignMenu* in the *TMyWindow* constructor.

4.3 With OWL, we use *CM_FIRST* for menu items (the letter *C* in this name being related to that in the message *WM_COMMAND*). An example is shown in Answer 4.1. The name *WM_FIRST* is used for functions that respond to Windows messages other than *WM_COMMAND* (see Section 3.5).

5.1 A viewport is a rectangle in which points are denoted by their device coordinates (that is, by numbers of pixels). A window is the same rectangle but with points specified by logical coordinates.

5.2 A mapping mode is the relationship between device coordinates and logical coordinates (see also Answer 10.3).

5.3 In the call *SetViewportOrg(hDC, x, y)* the arguments *x* and *y* are expressed in device coordinates; the point they denote is the origin of the logical coordinate system.

5.4 After creating a pen, we cannot use it until it is selected into the device context. This is because several pens can be created, but only one can be the 'current' one. This is the pen that is selected into the device context. The default pen, which is initially selected into the device context, is not replaced until another one is selected into the device context.

5.5 We use *CreatePen* to create a pen, and *CreateSolidBrush* to create a brush.

5.6 When responding to a *WM_PAINT* message, we obtain and dispose of a device context as follows:
- In C: We use the statements *hDC = BeginPaint(hWnd, &ps)*; and *EndPaint(hDC, &ps)*;
- With MFC: We write *CPaintDC dc(this)*;. The constructor of *CPaintDC* (provided by MFC) calls *BeginPaint*, while its destructor calls *EndPaint*.
- With OWL: We can simply use the device-context handle supplied as a parameter by function *Paint*, which is a member of the ObjectWindows class *TWindow* and therefore also of our class *TMyWindow*, derived from *TWindow*. We do not use *BeginPaint* and *EndPaint* ourselves.

5.7 - We must not delete a pen or a brush while it is still selected into the device context.
- We must forget to delete pens and brushes that we have created when we do not need them any longer, provided they are selected *out of* the device context (or provided we dispose of the device context first; see Answer 5.8).
- We must not delete stock pens and brushes (not created by ourselves).
- We must not delete a pen or a brush more than once.

5.8 Function *SelectObject*, when selecting a new pen or brush into the device context, returns the (old) pen or a brush that is currently selected. We often use such return values to restore the old pens and brushes, before deleting those generated ourselves. In program GR.C all this is done before the call to *EndPaint*. Instead, we can write this call immediately after drawing the rectangle. After this, we have disposed of the device context, which implies that our pens or brushes are no longer selected into it and that we can no longer use *SelectObject*. It is then allowed to delete our pens and brushes (not being stock objects) by applying *DeleteObject* to them.

6.1   Windows extends the number of available colors by a technique called *dithering*.

6.2   Black is obtained as *RGB*(0, 0, 0), white as *RGB*(255, 255, 255).

6.3   We can change the background color by assigning a new value, say, *RGB(cRed, cGreen, cBlue)*, to the *hbrBackground* member of the window class structure, in the following way:

```
SetClassWord(hWnd, GCW_HBRBACKGROUND,
CreateSolidBrush(RGB(cRed, cGreen, cBlue)));
```

When programming with MFC, we assign a value to the *CString* variable *ClassName* by calling *AfxRegisterWndClass* and use this variable as the first argument of *Create*, as discussed at the end of Section 6.4.

With OWL, we replace *hWnd* with *HWindow*, a public member of *TMyWindow*. See also Answer 6.5.

6.4   Typical functions related to memory allocation for Windows programming are *LocalAlloc*, *LocalFree*, *LocalLock*, *LocalUnlock*, *GlobalAlloc*, *GlobalFree*, *Global-Lock*, and *GlobalUnlock*.

6.5   When programming in C, we assign values to the *hbrBackground*, *hIcon*, *hCursor* and *style* members of *wndclass* in our *WinMain* function. The *SetClassWord* function enables us to change these values. A call to this function has the form

```
SetClassWord(hWnd, nIndex, wNewWord)
```

where we write *GCW_HBRBACKGROUND*, *GCW_HICON*, *GCW_HCURSOR* or *GCW_STYLE* for *nIndex*. These constants correspond to the four *wndclass* members mentioned above. We supply the new value for the *wndclass* member in question as the third argument, *wNewWord*. Function *SetClassWord* returns the previous value of this member.

6.6   The *i*th color of the currently selected palette is obtained as *PALETTEINDEX(i)*. Like *RGB*, *PALETTEINDEX* is a macro that returns a *COLORREF* value, which can be used, for example, as an argument of *CreateSolidBrush*.

7.1   See Answer 2.7.

7.2   In C and with OWL, we can write, for example,

```
hCursor = LoadCursor(hInst, "IDCURSOR");
hIcon = LoadIcon(hInst, "IDICON");
hBitmap = LoadBitmap(hInst, "IDBITMAP");
```

In these calls *hInst* is the instance handle, supplied by Windows as the first parameter of *WinMain*. Names such as *IDCURSOR* refer to corresponding lines in a resource script file.

With MFC, we can use the *LoadCursor* member function of *CWinApp*, which returns a handle to a cursor resource. A pointer to the *CWinApp* object for the application is returned by the function *AfxGetApp*. Icons can be dealt with similarly, so we can replace the first and second of the above statements with

```
hCursor = AfxGetApp()->LoadCursor("IDCURSOR");
hIcon = AfxGetApp()->LoadIcon("IDICON");
```

Still programming with MFC, a bitmap can be loaded by declaring a *CBitmap* object and using its *LoadBitmap* member function:

```
CBitmap bm;
bm.LoadBitmap("IDBITMAP");
```

7.3 We use a memory device context to select a bitmap into it. We can then copy part of it to the normal device context, using a bit-block transfer function, such as *StretchBlt*. Another way of using a memory device context is discussed in Chapter 9 (see also Question and Answer 9.4). We create a memory device context by calling the function *CreateCompatibleDC*.

7.4 We can display an icon in the client rectangle by using the function *DrawIcon*. When programming in C or with OWL, we use the following arguments: a device context handle, the *x*- and *y*-coordinates of the upper-left corner, and a handle *hIcon*, of type *HICON* (see Answer 7.2). With MFC, we write *dc* followed by a dot in front of the function name instead of using a device context handle as the first argument.

7.5 When the size of the window changes, the style *CS_HREDRAW | CS_VREDRAW* causes the entire client rectangle to be cleared before it is repainted. Replacing this style with *NULL* gives strange effects. For example, suppose that the situation is as shown in Figure 7.1. If we now reduce the window size, parts of some bitmaps may be cut off because they fall outside the reduced client rectangle. If we then make the window larger again, those bitmap portions will not come back. Consequently, only part of the face of a man or a woman will appear in the middle of the screen. Another strange effect is that there may appear several icons (resulting from the file PEOPLE.ICO) in the bottom-right corner. This is because changing the window size causes the client rectangle to be repainted; each time there is a call to *DrawIcon* with different values of *xScreen* and *yScreen*. In the current version of the program, with style *CS_HREDRAW | CS_VREDRAW*, the screen is cleared before a new icon is drawn, so that there will always be exactly one such icon in the client rectangle.

8.1   When programming in C, replacing the normal (arrow) cursor with a crosshair cursor is very simple. We only have to write *IDC_CROSS* instead of *IDC_ARROW* in the call to *LoadCursor*, used to assign a value to *wndclass.hCursor*.

With MFC, we replace the program text *Create(NULL* in the *CMyWindow* constructor with *Create(ClassName*, where *ClassName* is a *CString* object. The definition of *ClassName* has the form

```
CString ClassName = AfxRegisterWndClass(..., ..., ...);
```

where the second argument is

```
AfxGetApp()->LoadStandardCursor(IDC_CROSS)
```

Further details can be found in program file DRAGMFC.CPP.

With OWL, we write two member functions *GetWindowClass* and *GetClassName* of class *TMyWindow*, as shown in program file DRAGOWL.CPP. Frankly speaking, neither MFC nor OWL makes programming easier as far as this problem is concerned.

8.2   We draw new lines directly in response to *WM_MOUSEMOVE* messages because if we used *InvalidateRect*, we would have to specify a rectangle to be redrawn, and this could destroy lines drawn earlier.

8.3   We use the *R2_NOT* drawing mode as long as the line does not have its final position. In this way lines are removed in the same way as they are drawn. Since drawing a line twice in this mode restores the original situation, we have no problems with intersecting lines.

8.4   When the window is made smaller, all portions of lines that do not fit into the client rectangle disappear forever: they do not reappear if the window is made large again (see also Answer 7.5). In real draw programs, both end points (possibly together with other attributes) of each line are therefore stored in a data structure. Then when the window size changes, the *WM_PAINT* message can be used to redraw all lines on the basis of the data structure, as far as they fit into the client rectangle.

9.1   We use a timer by (1) calling *SetTimer*, at the beginning, (2) responding to the *WM_TIMER* message, and (3) calling *KillTimer*, at the end (see Section 9.2).

9.2   The Boolean function *DSo* (in Reverse Polish) for the ternary raster operation *SRCPAINT* gives *EE* as its hexadecimal code. Observing that *DSo* stands for $D \mid S$, we can derive this hexadecimal code as follows. First, we write all possibilities for *P*, *S* and *D* in a table, as shown on the next page. Its lines are in increasing order of zeros and ones, and include the result *R*, which is equal to $D \mid S$, that is, *R* is equal to 1 if at least one of the operands *D* and *S* is also equal to 1 (the value of *P* being irrelevant). Turning column *R* of this table through 90° clockwise, we obtain

```
1 1 1 0   1 1 1 0
   E         E
```

P	S	D	R
0	0	0	0
0	0	1	1
0	1	0	1
0	1	1	1
1	0	0	0
1	0	1	1
1	1	0	1
1	1	1	1

9.3   Only in response to *WM_SIZE* messages do we compute the vertices of a star and build a bitmap for it. The memory device context created for this purpose is then deleted, but the bitmap remains; note that, when programming in C, we use a *static* variable *hBitmap* for its handle. The fast operation of transferring a bit block to the normal device context is done very frequently, in response to *WM_TIMER* messages.

9.4   Although we are not drawing anything on the normal device context in response to a *WM_SIZE* message, we still need one in this case because it must occur as an argument for the functions *CreateCompatibleDC* and *CreateCompatibleBitMap*. As their names indicate, the memory device context and the bitmap that are to be created must be made compatible with our normal device context.

10.1   In program FDLG the variables *szFileName*, *szFileTitle*, and *MenuUsed* are *static* local variables of function *WndProc* because they are assigned values in one call (with *message* equal to *WM_COMMAND*) of this function, while these values are used in another call (with *message* equal to *WM_PAINT*).

10.2   In all three programs, the variable *MenuUsed* is initially equal to 0 and given the value 1 as soon as the user has selected a menu item. This variable is used to prevent displaying text output about a selected path name before the user has the opportunity to select a path name (by using the menu).

10.3   By displaying the path and file names in response to *WM_PAINT* messages, we start with a fresh client rectangle each time. If we instead displayed these names immediately when they become available, a short name might only partially replace a longer name that is already on the screen. (Of course, this could be prevented by first filling a large rectangle, into which the longest possible name fits, with the background color.) Responding to *WM_PAINT* messages is also a better solution in view of the window size being changed by the user. The client rectangle is then simply redrawn, while otherwise text could be distorted if the window is first made smaller and then larger again (see also Answers 7.5, 8.4, and 10.4).

10.4   Since 180 is used as the *y*-coordinate for the third line of text, not all text will be visible if the height of the client rectangle is made less than 180 pixels. As follows from our discussion in Answer 10.3, the full text will appear again if the original height is then restored.

11.1   Strictly speaking, the words *font* and *typeface* have different meanings. For example, New Century Schoolbook is a typeface, while New Century Schoolbook 10 pt is a font. However, many people use the term *font* rather loosely, when they actually mean a *typeface*. Another term frequently used for typeface is *font family*.

11.2   A *LOGFONT* object is a logical-font descriptor, which defines the attributes of a font. Type *CHOOSEFONT* is related to the common dialog box for fonts. It is possible to manipulate fonts without using a dialog box; in that case we would use only type *LOGFONT*, not *CHOOSEFONT*.

11.3   The following functions are used to generate a font dialog box:
-    in FONT.C and in FONTOWL.CPP: *ChooseFont*
-    in FONTMFC.CPP: *CFontDialog::DoModal*

11.4   A color is not a font attribute. It can be specified in the *rgbColors* member of a *CHOOSEFONT* object. We do this in the bottom-left corner of the font dialog box.

11.5   If our *CHOOSEFONT* object is *cf*, the user can set the value of *cf.rgbColors* by using a font dialog box (see Answer 11.4). We use this value in a call to *SetText-Color*, writing, for example,

```
SetTextColor(hDC, cf.rgbColors);
```

Note, however, that the second argument in this call need not be obtained by means of a font dialog box. For example, if we want text in red, we could simply write

```
SetTextColor(hDC, RGB(255, 0, 0));
```

The color specified by *SetTextColor* will be used for subsequent text output.

12.1   It is possible to print in a Windows program without using a dialog box. We then have to create a device context for the printer by using *CreateDC*.

12.2   We use the address of *PRINTDLG* structure *pd* as an argument in a call to *PrintDlg*. If we assign *PD_RETURNDC* to *pd.Flags* before this call, this function places a device context handle for the printer in *pd.hDC*. When programming with MFC, we use a *CPrintDialog* object instead of a *PRINTDLG* structure, and we call the *Do-Modal* member function of this object instead of *PrintDlg*. Except for these differences, the same principle applies.

12.3   We use the address of a *DOCINFO* structure *DocInfo* in a call to *StartDoc*. Prior to this call, we place the start address of the text to be printed in *DocInfo.lpszOutput*.

12.4   The following functions are related to a document. We use them in our program in this order: *StartDoc*, *StartPage*, *EndPage*, *EndDoc*.

12.5   The functions listed in Answer 12.4 have a handle to a printer device context as their first argument. Only *StartDoc* has a second argument, which is *&DocInfo*, as discussed in Answer 12.3.

13.1   In the non-Windows C++ program of Section 13.1, function *Hanoi* is called only once in the *main* function. Its task is to move an entire tower from a given source to a given destination peg. This tower consists of as many disks as the final parameter of this function indicates. By contrast, the three other functions *Hanoi* in this chapter only find the source and destination pegs for the next move and return the value 1, that is, if there is still another move to be done. Otherwise, when all work has been completed, *Hanoi* returns 0.

13.2   We apply function *GetTextExtend* to the longest line to be displayed, to obtain the width to be reserved for the text. We then compute the size of the left margin by subtracting this width from the available width and dividing the difference by 2.

13.3   We draw and fill a rounded rectangle by calling the function *RoundRect*.

13.4   There are three stacks that we can associate with the three pegs A, B and C. For any disk on a given peg, the number of that disk is stored in the corresponding stack. The three stacks are collectively implemented as a two-dimensional array *Stack*, together with a stack-pointer array *StPtr*. These arrays are declared as

```
int Stack[3][NMAX], StPtr[3], ...
```

where *StPtr*[*j*] indicates how many disk numbers are currently stored in *Stack*[*j*] (*j* = 0, 1, 2 denoting the pegs A, B and C, in that order). There are *NMAX* positions on each of the three stacks.

There is also a 'linked stack', used to store deferred tower-moving tasks. Instead of performing a recursive function call in Section 13.1, representing the move of a tower, we place the data for such a call onto the linked stack.

13.5   In response to a *WM_PAINT* message we begin by setting the *anisotropic* mapping mode, because we want to use most of the client rectangle, regardless of its shape. For example, if the height of the window is made very small compared with its width, the height of the disks will also be small compared with their diameters. By contrast, we used the *isotropic* mapping mode in Chapter 5 because we wanted to draw isosceles triangles, regardless of the shape of the window.

B

MFC Hierarchy

This appendix shows the Microsoft Foundation class hierarchy in diagrams with regard to classes that occur in this book or are closely related to those classes. It is therefore not complete. Most Microsoft Foundation classes that are used for Windows Programming are derived (either directly or indirectly) from *CObject*. Figure B1 shows which classes are derived directly from this base class.

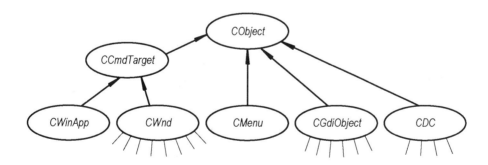

Figure B1. Classes derived directly from CObject

The classes *CSize*, *CPoint* and *CRect*, also used in this book, are not derived from *CObject*. The classes *CWnd*, *CGdiObject* and *CDC*, shown in Figure B1, are themselves base classes for other derived classes, as Figures B2, B3 and B4 illustrate:

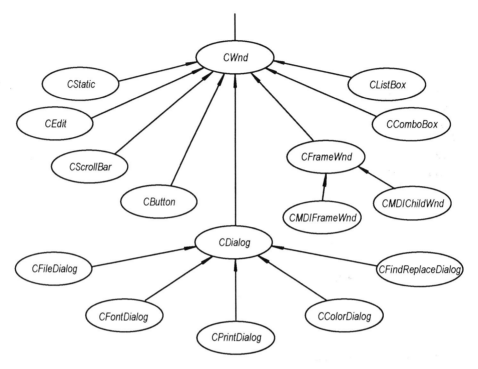

Figure B2. *Classes derived from* **CWnd**

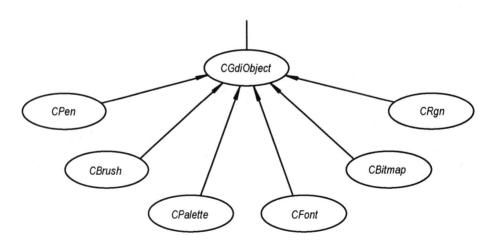

Figure B3. *Classes derived from* **CGdiObject**

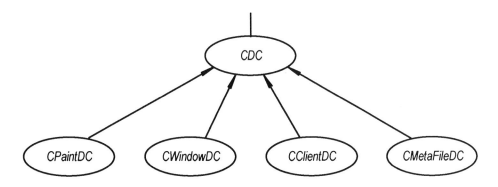

Figure B4. *Classes derived from* **CDC**

OWL Class Hierarchy

As Figure C1 shows, the important ObjectWindows class *TWindowsObject* is derived from two base classes, *Object* and *TStreamable*. (This is one of the few practical examples of *multiple inheritance*.) Note also the class *TApplication*, the name of which occurs in every OWL program.

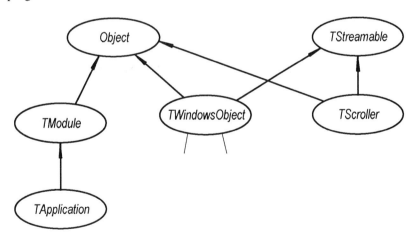

Figure C1. TApplication, TObjectWindows and some other classes

Class *TWindowsObject* is important because all classes related to windows are derived from it, as Figure C2 shows.

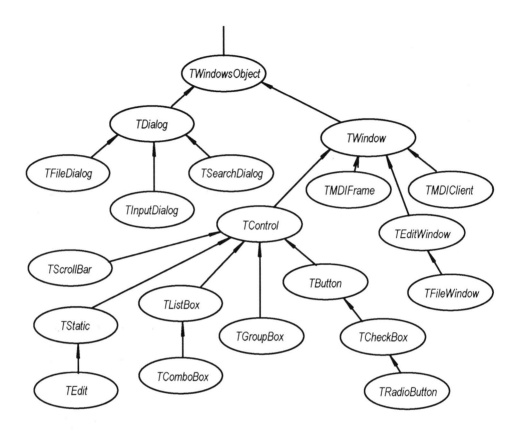

Figure C2. *Classes derived from* **TWindowsObject**

Bibliography

Ammeraal, L. (1991) *C for Programmers, 2nd Edition*, Chichester: John Wiley.

Ammeraal, L. (1991) *C++ for Programmers*, Chichester: John Wiley.

Ammeraal, L. (1992) *Programs and Data Structures in C, 2nd Edition*, Chichester: John Wiley.

Ammeraal, L. (1992) *Programming Principles in Computer Graphics, 2nd Edition*, Chichester: John Wiley.

Christian, K. (1992) *C++ Programming*, Redmond: Microsoft Press.

Heiny, L. (1992) *Windows Graphics Programming with Borland C++*, New York: John Wiley.

Heller, M. (1992) *Advanced Windows Programming*, New York: John Wiley.

Kernighan, B. W. and D. M. Ritchie (1988) *The C Programming Language, 2nd Edition*, Englewood Cliffs, NJ: Prentice Hall.

Petzold, C. (1992) *Programming Windows, 3rd Edition*, Redmond: Microsoft Press.

Stroustrup, B. (1991) *The C++ Programming Language, 2nd Edition*, Reading, MA: Addison-Wesley.

Index